Song and Story in
Biblical Narrative

Indiana Studies in Biblical Literature

Herbert Marks and Robert Polzin, general editors

Mieke Bal. *Lethal Love: Feminist Literary Readings of Biblical Love Stories*

Mieke Bal. *Murder and Difference: Gender, Genre, and Scholarship on Sisera's Death*

Adele Berlin. *Biblical Poetry Through Medieval Jewish Eyes*

Daniel Boyarin. *Intertextuality and the Reading of Midrash*

Robert L. Brawley. *Text to Text Pours Forth Speech: Voices of Scripture in Luke-Acts*

Leslie Brisman. *The Voice of Jacob: On the Composition of Genesis*

Martin Buber. Tanslated by Lawrence Rosenwald with Everett Fox. *Scripture and Translation*

Max H. Fisch. *Poetry with a Purpose: Biblical Poetics and Interpretation*

Michael Fishbane. *The Garments of Torah: Essays in Biblical Hermeneutics*

Herbert Levine. *Sing Unto God a New Song: A Contemporary Reading of the Psalms*

Peter D. Miscall. *1 Samuel: A Literary Reading*

James Nohrnberg. *Like Unto Moses: The Constituting of an Interruption*

Robert Polzin. *David and the Deuteronomist: A Literary Study of the Deuteronomic History, Part Three: 2 Samuel*

Robert Polzin. *Moses and the Deuteronomist: A Literary Study of the Deuteronomic History, Part One: Deuteronomy, Joshua, Judges*

Robert Polzin. *Samuel and the Deuteronomist: A Literary Study of the Deuteronomic History, Part Two: 1 Samuel*

Joel Rosenberg. *King and Kin: Political Allegory in the Hebrew Bible*

Jason P. Rosenblatt and Joseph C. Sitterson, Jr., editors. *"Not in Heaven": Coherence and Complexity in Biblical Narrative*

George Savran. *Telling and Retelling: Quotation in Biblical Narrative*

Uriel Simon. *Reading Prophetic Narratives*

Meir Sternberg. *The Poetics of Biblical Narrative: Ideological Literature and the Drama of Reading*

Song and Story in Biblical Narrative

The History of a Literary Convention in Ancient Israel

Steven

Weitzman

INDIANA UNIVERSITY PRESS

BLOOMINGTON AND INDIANAPOLIS

The paper used in this publication meets the minimum requirements
of American National Standard for Information Sciences—
Permanence of Paper for Printed Library Materials, ANSI Z39.48-1984.

Manufactured in the United States of America

Library of Congress Cataloging-in-Publication Data

Weitzman, Steven, date
Song and story in biblical narrative : the history of a literary
convention in ancient Israel / Steven Weitzman.
p.   cm. — (Indiana studies in biblical literature)
Includes bibliographical references and index.
ISBN 0-253-33236-2 (alk. paper)
1. Bible. O.T.—Language, style. 2. Hebrew poetry, Biblical—History
and criticism. 3. Narration in the Bible. 4. Bible. O.T.—Criticism,
interpretation, etc. I. Title. II. Series.
BS1171.2.W45 1997
221.6′6—dc21   96-29526

1 2 3 4 5 02 01 00 99 98 97

For my parents

"Do you know, I've had such a quantity of
poetry repeated to me to-day," Alice began, a
little frightened at finding that, the moment
she opened her lips, there was dead silence,
and all eyes were fixed upon her; "and it's a
very curious thing, I think—every poem was
about fishes in some way."

—Lewis Carroll, *Through the Looking Glass*

CONTENTS

PREFACE

This study did not turn out as I expected. It began as an attempt to answer a specific question about the Bible that had somehow managed to slip through the cracks of modern scholarship: why did the authors of biblical narrative so often combine prose and poetry in telling their stories? What surprised me about the answer I found is that it did much more than account for a curious literary practice; it shed light on literary behavior in general in ancient Israel. What was the relation of literary practice in ancient Israel to that of other cultures in the ancient Near East? What impact did the elevation of the Bible to scriptural status have on literary practice in early Judaism? And how did the "scripturalization" of biblical narrative affect the course of its literary development? To understand why the Bible fuses song and story is to gain insight into all these questions and their various relationships to one another.

Most of the ideas reflected in this study were first laid out, in much cruder form, in a doctoral dissertation under the direction of James Kugel. I thank Jim for reading my work with acumen, for sharing with me his insights about our craft, and for encouraging me to think carefully about how readers relate to texts. I have tried in the present form of this study to live up to his high expectations, and successful or not, I thank him for having them.

Neither the research for this study nor its publication would have been possible without financial support from several institutions, public and private. A Fulbright grant gave me a year in 1991–92 to undertake research at the Hebrew University in Jerusalem. A dissertation fellowship from the Memorial Foundation for Jewish Culture helped to support completion of my dissertation in 1992–93. A Summer Faculty Fellowship from Indiana University supported me through one more precious summer as I undertook much-needed revisions. Finally, a subvention grant from Indiana University's Jewish Studies Program, Research and the University Graduate School, and the Religious Studies Department facilitated the book's publication. I am much indebted to four colleagues for their support and advice: Alvin Rosenfeld, Herbert Marks, James Ackerman, and Steve Stein. At a time when many of our public institutions are having difficulty finding value in the humanities, these scholars represent fine examples of what the humanities can produce: generous and insightful human beings who recognize that interpretation makes a difference. I am also grateful to Vice President George Walker and Associate Dean Jeff Alberts of the Research and the University Graduate School at Indiana University, Robert Polzin, general editor along with Herbert Marks of the Indiana Studies in Biblical Literature series, and Robert Sloan, sponsoring editor for Indiana University Press, for their invaluable support of my research as it made its way to publication.

Many individuals have left their imprint on my writing and on me during the time that I worked on this project. My teachers Jo Ann Hackett, John Huhnergard, Peter Mechinist, Bernard Septimus, Jon Levinson, Sara Japhet, Michael Stone, and Avi Hurvitz gave generously of their time and wisdom. Any mistakes that I have made in this work are signs that I have more to learn from them still, and I intend to do so. The following friends and colleagues read my work, or discussed it with me, or endured me while I rambled on about it: Kevin Gerson, Judy Newman, the Teshima family, Kathryn Slanski, Bernie Levinson, David Brakke, Jeff and Wendy Cohen, and Rachel Rockenmacher. When on occasion I tried to visualize my audience, these were the people sitting in the front row, smiling.

There is hardly a page of this work that does not reflect the intelligence and love of my wife, Mira Wasserman. She has critiqued the entire work, helped me clarify my ideas, and at times seen the point even when I did not. How do I express my gratitude to the person through whom my life has become a fusion of song and story?

I have dedicated the book to my parents, who first pointed me toward the horizon and made me believe that I could see beyond it.

Chapter 3 draws on material from my article "Lessons from the Dying: The Narrative Role of Deuteronomy 32," *Harvard Theological Review* 87.4 (1994); chapter 4 makes use of material previously published in my article "Allusion, Artifice and Exile in the Hymn of Tobit," *Journal of Biblical Literature* 115 (1996); and appendix A represents a revision of an article that first appeared as "David's Lament and the Poetics of Grief," *Jewish Quarterly Review* 115 (1996). I am grateful to all three journals for permission to draw on this material in the present study.

A note on citations. The Hebrew Bible, the Apocrypha, and the New Testament are quoted in English translation from the New Revised Standard Version. On occasion I have introduced minor changes into the translation but only when the evidence justifies it and my argument requires it.

ABBREVIATIONS

Frequently cited texts from the Hebrew Bible, Apocrypha, Pseudepigrapha, Dead Sea Scrolls, New Testament, and Rabbinic sources

4Q	Manuscripts found in cave 4 at Qumran
11Q	Manuscripts found in cave 11 at Qumran
Abod. Zar.	*Abodah Zara*
Ag. Shir hashirim	*Agadat Shir Hashirim* (Ed. S. Schechter, London: Deighton Bell, 1896)
Arak.	*Arakin*
b.	Babylonian Talmud
B. Tanh.	S. Buber's edition of *Midrash Tanhuma* (Wilna: Witwe & Gebrüder Romm, 1885)
Bab. Bat.	*Baba Batra*
Bib. Ant.	Pseudo-Philo's *Biblical Antiquities*
Cant	Canticles/Song of Songs
Chr	Chronicles
Dan	Daniel
Deut	Deuteronomy
Eccl	Ecclesiastes
Esth	Esther
Exod	Exodus
Ezek	Ezekiel
Gen	Genesis
Gen. Rab.	*Genesis Rabbah* (*Midrash Bereshit Rabbah: Critical Edition with Notes and Commentary*, J. Theodor and C. Albeck, Jerusalem: Wahrman, 1965)
Git.	*Gittin*
Hab	Habakkuk
Hag	Haggai
Hag.	*Hagiga*
Hos	Hosea
Hul.	*Hullin*

Isa	Isaiah
Jdt	*Judith*
Jer	Jeremiah
Josh	Joshua
Judg	Judges
Kgs	Kings
Lam	Lamentations
Lev	Leviticus
LXX	Septuagint
m.	Mishnah
MS	manuscript
MT	Masoretic Text
1-2-3-4 *Macc*	1-2-3-4 *Maccabees*
Mal	Malachi
Meg.	*Megilla*
Mek. Ishmael	*Mekilta de Rabbi Ishmael* (Ed. J. Lauterbach, Philadelphia: Jewish Publication Society of America, 1933-35)
Mic	Micah
Midr. Tehillim	*Midrash Tehillim* (Wilna: Witwe & Gebrüder Romm, 1891)
NRSV	New Revised Standard Version
Nah	Nahum
Neh	Nehemiah
Obad	Obadiah
Pesah	*Pesahim*
Prov	Proverbs
Ps	Psalm (plural Pss)
Rab.	*Rabbah* (following abbreviation for biblical book: *Gen.* Rab. = *Genesis Rabbah*)
Rev	Revelations
Rosh. Hash.	*Rosh Hashanah*
Sam	Samuel
Sanh.	*Sanhedrin*
T.	Testament (as in the *Testament of Job*)
Tg.	Targum (as in *Targum Onkelos*)
Tanh.	*Midrash Tanhuma* (Jerusalem, 1960)
Tob	*Tobit*
y.	Jerusalem Talmud
Zech	Zechariah
Zeph	Zephaniah

Periodicals, reference works, and serials

AB	*Anchor Bible*
AJSL	*American Journal of Semitic Languages and Literatures*
AOAT	*Alter Orient und Altes Testament*
ASTI	*Annual of the Swedish Theological Institute*
BASOR	*Bulletin of the American Schools of Oriental Research*
Bib	*Biblica*
BibRev	*Bible Review*
BJRL	*Bulletin of the John Rylands Library,* University of Manchester
BKAT	*Biblischer Kommentar: Altes Testament*
BM	*Bet Mikra*
BZ	*Biblische Zeitschrift*
BZAW	Beihefte zur ZAW
CBQ	*Catholic Biblical Quarterly*
DJD	*Discoveries in the Judaean Desert*
DSD	*Dead Sea Discoveries*
EstBíb	*Estudios Bíblicos*
ETL	*Ephemerides theologicae Iovanienses*
Greg	*Gregorianum*
HKAT	*Handkommentar zum Alten Testament*
HTR	*Harvard Theological Review*
HUCA	*Hebrew Union College Annual*
ICC	*International Critical Commentary*
Int	*Interpretation*
JANES	*Journal of the Ancient Near Eastern Society of Columbia University*
JAOS	*Journal of the American Oriental Society*
JBL	*Journal of Biblical Literature*
JCS	*Journal of Cuneiform Studies*
JEA	*Journal of Egyptian Archaeology*
JJS	*Journal of Jewish Studies*
JNSL	*Journal of Northwest Semitic Languages*
JNES	*Journal of Near Eastern Studies*
JQR	*Jewish Quarterly Review*
JRAS	*Journal of the Royal Asiatic Society*
JSJ	*Journal for the Study of Judaism in the Persian, Hellenistic and Roman Periods*
JSOT	*Journal for the Study of the Old Testament*
JSP	*Journal for the Study of the Pseudepigrapha*
JSS	*Journal of Semitic Studies*

JTC	*Journal for Theology and the Church*
JTS	*Journal of Theological Studies*
KTU	M. Dietrich, O. Loretz, and J. Sammartin, eds., *Die keilalphabetischen Texte aus Ugarit einschliesslich der keilalphabetischen Texte ausserhalb Ugarits*
LB	*Linguistica Biblica*
NCB	*New Century Bible*
Or	*Orientalia*
OTS	*Oudtestamentische Studiën*
PSBA	*Proceedings of the Society of Biblical Archaeology*
RB	*Revue biblique*
RQ	*Römische Quartalschrift für christliche Altertumskunde und Kirchengeschichte*
RevQ	*Revue de Qumran*
SAK	*Studien zur Altägyptischen Kultur*
ST	*Studia theologica*
UF	*Ugarit-Forschungen*
VT	*Vetus Testamentum*
VTSup	*Vetus Testamentum, Supplements*
ZAW	*Zeitschrift für die alttestamentliche Wissenschaft*
ZDMG	*Zeitschrift der deutschen morgenländischen Gesellschaft*

· 1 ·

MOVING BETWEEN
PROSE AND POETRY

Let me begin by confiding a trade secret of biblical scholarship. When modern scholars treat the Hebrew Bible as a work of literature, they inevitably project upon it literary categories foreign to the biblical world. Applied to biblical literature, even concepts as elemental as "prose," "poetry," "history," and "fiction" are but a kind of translation, rendering biblical form into terms understandable to readers far removed from ancient Israel. This is not to say that these categories do not more or less correspond to what is actually there in the biblical text, but the "more or less" is a significant qualification. For however much the Bible may seem to accord with—even exemplify—the literary norms and standards of our day, its contents were produced in an ancient culture that had its own sense of what literature is and does. Professional readers of the Bible often operate, unconsciously or consciously, as if this were not the case—a modus operandi that is not without its rewards—but by doing so, they sometimes lose sight of precisely those aspects of biblical literature which do not accord with what modern readers expect of literature.

Consider what is obscured when we impose upon the Bible the familiar categories of prose and poetry. These categories have deep roots in the history of biblical interpretation; they were in place by the late Hellenistic-Roman era, when readers such as Flavius Josephus first claimed (incorrectly, by the way) that certain biblical compositions, the songs in Exodus 15 and Deuteronomy 32 and the Psalms of David, were written in Greek-style meters.[1] Since then, the prose-poetry distinction has become deeply ingrained in our understanding of the Bible, affecting the way we think about it and translate it, even the way we print it.[2] And yet several recent studies have shown that prose and poetry are at best only approximations of what we actually find in the biblical corpus, where there is scarcely a book which does not at some point modulate into a mode of discourse that resists classification as either prose or poetry.[3] Scholars have proposed various hypotheses to account for this slippage between their analytical categories and the biblical evidence. Some assert that the poetry within

biblical prose has been distorted in the process of oral or scribal transmission;[4] others, that there was available to the biblical authors a third
mode of discourse—a metrical prose or a prosaic verse—which exhibits
traits of both prose and poetry.[5] Whatever the merits of these explanations
when applied to individual books or passages, the fact that biblical scholars
so frequently resort to them suggests how much in biblical literature is
left out by our attempt to read it as either prose or poetry.

I begin with this disclosure because it offers something of an explanation
for why the present book is one of the first to explore a biblical literary
form which, by its very nature, cannot easily be confined within the literary
categories of prose and poetry: the insertion of songs within biblical narrative. The Bible's mixing of song and story is probably familar to the
reader from such well-known examples as the Song of the Sea (Exodus
15) sung by Israel after it escapes across the Red Sea, the Song of Moses
(Deuteronomy 32) recited by the prophet shortly before his death, and
the Song of Deborah (Judges 5) sung just after Israel defeats the army
of Sisera.[6] The songs embedded within these passages are among the most
carefully analyzed passages in the Hebrew Bible. Their contents, their structure, even their orthography have been subjected to the most painstaking
analysis. Their roles within their present narrative settings have received
little attention, however. In a field which has accumulated an arsenal of
methods to analyze the forms and functions of prose and poetry, there is
scarcely even a vocabulary to describe the forms and functions of their
interaction. The reason for this neglect, I suspect, is that from the vantage
point of scholars trained to think of prose and poetry as distinct, even
opposing modes of discourse, the Bible's fusion of song and story represents
an act of miscegenation, a bizarre mixing of different species of discourse
kept separate in more civilized literary cultures. The genetics imagery is
not my invention, by the way, for some scholars, unable to provide an
aesthetic reason for this and other mixtures of prose and poetry in Semitic
literature, resorted to racial theory for an explanation attributing such
behavior to the inherent indecorousness and unruliness of the "Asiatic
mind."[7]

None of this is to deny that, here and there, individual scholars have
ventured literary explanations for why songs appear in biblical narrative,
describing them as a vehicle for the author to express his sentiments, as
a way of winning the audience's sympathy, or as a structuring device for
breaking up the narrative into logical units.[8] Almost always, however, such
explanations reflect an attempt to reconcile this puzzling practice with the
commentator's own intuitive sense of how prose and poetry operate. Indeed, these studies are often quite explicit about how they see the functions
of prose and poetry: the former is the medium best suited for the con-
veyance of fact and objectivity, the latter for expressing emotion and sub-

jectivity.[9] Once one accepts this distinction, the explanation for the incorporation of songs within biblical narrative is almost predictable: it represents a deliberate merging of prose and poetry in order to convey both fact and passion, objectivity and subjectivity. Some have suggested, for instance, that the songs were inserted in order to relieve the tedium generated by the prose's dry and relentless recitation of data.[10] Others claim that song heightens the emotional intensity of the narrative, interjecting itself into the passionless prose like a Greek chorus so as to express the author's sentiments and stir up the audience's emotions.[11] Such explanations differ in how precisely they explain the songs' narrative role, but they agree on one fundamental point: the biblical authors incorporated poetry within biblical narrative in an effort to convey what the medium of prose could not communicate by itself.

The problem with this kind of explanation is that it makes certain presuppositions about prose, poetry, and the differences between them that are not necessarily valid when applied to biblical literature. As we have seen, the prose-poetry distinction does not fully accommodate the various forms of discourse found in the Bible. We are not even entirely safe in assuming that the songs themselves are written in poetry, since premodern biblical commentators working from a different set of literary assumptions—the medieval Jewish poet and literary theorist Moses Ibn Ezra (1055-1140), for example—found reason to classifiy many of them as prose.[12] Even if we assume that the songs do represent poetry, however, it does not follow that they functioned as we expect poetry to function. The idea, for example, that poetry connotes spontaneity and emotion may have some validity for works of verse composed in our culture—influenced as it is by the Romantic conception of poetry as the language of passion—but it was not necessarily true of poetry composed in ancient Israel. In biblical wisdom literature, for instance, poetry—or what we would identify as poetry—evidently connoted insight, instruction, and self-control, not spontaneous emotion (see, for example, Proverbs 1:1-6, which associates proverbs and riddles, supposedly poetic genres in biblical literature, with the acquisition of wisdom, understanding, and discernment). My point is that while the Bible contains modes of discourse similar to what we call prose and poetry, that does not mean that these media signified in the way they do for us; rather, as is true of signifiers generally, their connotations have been conditioned by their literary and cultural contexts. If I do not accept the psychologizing explanations cited earlier as the last word on why songs appear in biblical prose narrative, it is because they project their own understanding of prose and poetry onto the Bible without considering the possibility that its authors, living in another culture, may have had a different conception of these literary modes and their expressive registers.

I have learned from Hans-Georg Gadamer not to presume that I can

shed my own literary assumptions and expectations when trying to understand a literature from another time and place.[13] Granting this point, however, is not the same as surrendering to the conclusion that one cannot—or
should not—try to construct the literary assumptions and expectations of
another culture. One of the fundamental presuppositions of this study is
that while I cannot escape the prejudices I have inherited from tradition
when interpreting the biblical text, I can nevertheless recognize the "oth-
erness" of the biblical text, its resistance to my presuppositions. In the
course of this book I will be presenting an alternative explanation—or
rather series of explanations—for why there are songs in biblical narrative.
I believe these explanations are preferable to those described earlier, not
simply because they are more nuanced nor simply because they fit better
with what is known of literary behavior in the ancient Near East but also
because, to the extent that I was able, I have sought to take stock of how
my literary presuppositions have shaped my interpretation of the evidence.

What I have found as a result is that far from standing as an obstacle
in our way, the role that readers' standards and expectations play in shaping
their understanding of texts is the key to understanding why songs appear
in biblical narrative. For my argument is that those who inserted the songs
into biblical narrative were themselves readers who imposed their own
literary standards and expectations onto the songs through the act of inserting them within a narrative setting. For this claim to make sense, one
needs first to digest the evidence indicating that the songs were not composed by the authors of biblical narrative but had some sort of prehistory
as independent documents before they were incorporated within narrative
settings. Consider the case of the Song of the Sea in Exodus 15, attributed
by its narrative setting to Moses and the Israelites after they cross the Red
Sea. Modern biblical scholarship has long suspected that this song predates
its narrative frame (as indeed the narrative itself claims), perhaps having
originated as a cultic hymn recited within a ritual celebration of God's
triumph over the Egyptians.[14] Though these scholars perhaps are over-
confident in their attempts to pinpoint the song's original cultic setting,
they have uncovered several striking pieces of evidence that the song was
composed independently of the narrative. First, the song's language seems
much older than that of the surrounding prose, exhibiting forms and
idioms characteristic of Late Bronze Age sources such as Ugaritic literature
and the Amarna letters, whereas the prose of Exodus belongs to a later
period in the history of Hebrew. If sound, this linguistic contrast indicates
that song and story were composed at two different times.[15] Second, the
song is perfectly coherent as an independent document; but as part of
the narrative, its contents violate the narrative's temporal frame, anach-
ronistically assigning to Moses and the Israelites knowledge of events not
yet recounted by the incorporating narrative (e.g., Israel's entrance into

the land of Canaan alluded to in verses 16-17).[16] This kind of prolepsis is rare in biblical narrative (when it occurs, it is usually introduced explicitly as prophecy or divine revelation, or appears in a narratorial aside), and no explanation is offered for it by the song's narrative's setting; but it is understandable if the song was not composed for its present narrative role but represents an adaptation of a preexisting hymn designed to commemorate both the sea event and Israel's entrance into the land (in chapter 3 we will see another example where biblical narrative seems to reflect a misunderstanding of a song embedded within it).

Other kinds of evidence lead to a similar conclusion for songs such as the Song of Deborah and Barak in Judges 5, the Song of David in 2 Samuel 22, and the song of Daniel's three friends in the Greek versions of Daniel 3. The Song of Deborah and Barak describes the Israelites' battle against the Canaanites in a way that seems to contradict the account in the preceding narrative in Judges 4, an incongruity that would be very difficult to understand if both song and story were written by the same author but could be plausibly explained if the song originated independently of the narrative.[17] The fact that the Song of David appears in two literary contexts within the biblical corpus—once in a narrative setting (2 Samuel 22), once as a freestanding poem (Psalm 18)—shows that the song was at some point circulated independently of its narrative frame.[18] Even more compelling is the fact that the song of Daniel's friends is not found in all versions of Daniel 3 (the song is present in the Greek versions but absent from the Masoretic text), incontrovertible evidence that Daniel 3 was once circulated without the song.[19] Finally, one should note that biblical narrative itself alleges that a few of the poems within it—notably, David's lament in 2 Samuel 1 and Joshua's command to the sun and moon in Josh 10:12-13—had already been published in the mysterious *Book of Yashar*, a poetic composition or anthology of some sort which has been lost.[20] It may not always be the case that the song predates its narrative setting; some songs, such as that of Daniel's friends, were evidently added to already existent episodes, and perhaps others not mentioned here were composed by the author of the surrounding story. Nevertheless, it is hard not to conclude from the evidence cited that the insertion of at least some of the songs in biblical narrative amounts to a reuse of existing literary material that imposed upon it a role different from that which it was composed to play. This conclusion has significant implications for how we proceed in our investigation, for it suggests that to explain the appearance of songs in biblical narrative, we must do what we can to reconstruct how they were read—or misread—by those who placed them there.

What prompted the authors of biblical narrative to recontextualize existing songs within their compositions is difficult to say. Some scholars have surmised that the centralization of Israel's cult in the reigns of

Hezekiah and Josiah and the conquest of Israelite territory by the Assyrians and the Babylonians in the eighth to sixth centuries B.C.E. eliminated the cultic contexts within which many of Israel's sacred songs were recited, forcing Israel to find new uses and new contexts for its sacred poetry.[21] If later generations continued to transmit these songs and find meaning in them long after their displacement, it was because they had found uses for them outside the context of the cult. This is a cogent—albeit un-verifiable—answer to our question, but even if one accepts it, it leaves many other questions unanswered: how exactly were the cultic songs of ancient Israel reinterpreted; why were some of them recontextualized within narrative settings; and what literary and cultural functions were served by their recontextualization?

The approach of this study has been shaped by these questions. It is precisely because many of the songs were not created for use in their present literary settings that we will rely primarily on what the surrounding prose says—or implies—about the songs as our main source of information about their narrative roles. As I suggested, this evidence may tell us little about when or why the songs were originally composed, but it does tell us something of how they were understood or meant to be understood by those who incorporated them within the narrative. The goal of this study is to determine how the authors of biblical narrative reinterpreted the songs' form and content to serve their own literary purposes. The only direct evidence we have of this reinterpretation lies in the narrative itself—how it introduces the songs, where it places them in the plot, and what it says about their origins—and so it is the narrative upon which we will focus. I do not mean by this that the songs themselves—their form, their structure, their content—are not important for our study, but they are important only to the extent that they serve the literary roles imposed upon them by the surrounding story. What we are investigating, after all, is not what the songs meant when they were created but what they came to mean when they were incorporated within narrative contexts.

The main problem with relying on the narratives' testimony for deter-mining the songs' narrative roles is that it is in very short supply. Even the most extensive prose introduction to a song, that which introduces the Song of Moses, amounts to only a few problematic verses (Deut 31:14–30). If we are to make the most of what little evidence there is, therefore, we will need to supplement the testimony of biblical narrative using an interpretive procedure that has long played a central role in the study of the Bible: the use of analogies drawn from other, more fully documented literatures.

The comparative method, as this approach is sometimes called, is really not a method at all but a loosely defined set of heuristic maneuvers. Those who have given this subject some thought have observed that there are actually two kinds of comparison used by scholars, at least in the human-ities.[22] The first, labeled by the historian Marc Bloch as "the comparative method on the grand scale," involves the comparison of phenomena—texts, behaviors, social forms, etc.—which share a formal or functional similarity but where the similarity cannot be attributed to shared inheritance from a common ancestor or historical contact. Biology provides a textbook ex-ample: the wing of a bat seems similar to the wing of a bird not because bats and birds inherited this trait from a common ancestor but because each has evolved along parallel lines in response to similar environmental conditions.[23] So too it happens in the history of literature that cultures unrelated to one another sometimes develop similar literary practices. Be-cause such similarities do not appear to reflect a shared ancestry or his-torical contact, scholars once prized them as evidence that certain behaviors are ingrained in human nature, arising from what Bloch called "the fun-damental unity of the human spirit." Nowadays scholars are much less inclined to use this sort of comparison in so grandiose a way, but they still often resort to it to fill in gaps in whatever direct evidence they have at their disposal. In order to explain why songs appear in biblical narrative, for example, biblical scholars sometimes compare this phenomenon with mixtures of prose and poetry in other, unrelated literatures—the embed-ding of verse passages within Icelandic prose saga, for example, or the shifting from prose speech to song in Broadway musicals.[24] The use of these analogies assumes that if the Bible's mixing of song and story is formally similar in certain respects to the mixing of song and story found in other literatures, there must be other points of correspondence as well.

As intriguing as these analogies are, I will not be evoking them in this book for two reasons. First, it is all too easy to overstate or simplify the Bible's resemblance to other literatures. At an early stage in my research, for example, I was impressed by the similarities between the songs in biblical narrative and the insertion of lyrics within medieval French nar-rative, a literary practice which has received much attention in recent years.[25] Like the songs in biblical narrative, the lyrics in medieval French narrative appear repeatedly in the story at key moments in the plot; they are often attributed to figures within the story; and sometimes they appear to have been drawn from preexisting lyric collections. The more I thought about the comparison, however, the more I realized that the insertion of lyrics in medieval French narrative is as different from the use of songs in biblical narrative as it is similar. In fact, several studies have shown that it was actually quite a variegated phenomenon in its own right. In some texts the poetry is imputed to characters within the story; in others it is woven into the fabric of the narration. In some texts the poetry is drawn from preexisting sources; in others it is invented anew. Equating these various examples with the songs in biblical narrative not only exaggerates their resemblance, it also ignores the diversity of ways in which prose and poetry interact within medieval French narrative itself.

Jonathan Z. Smith has observed that "comparison requires the acceptance of difference as the grounds of its being interesting, and a methodological manipulation of that difference to achieve some stated cognitive difference."[26] While I recognize the truth of Smith's claim, there is nevertheless one difference that is not so easily manipulated in the present instance: the completely different cultural and aesthetic contexts in which biblical narrative and French medieval narrative were composed. It has been claimed that the mixing of prose and poetry within the latter reflects an "aesthetic of contrasts" characteristic of literary practice in the twelfth and thirteenth centuries. Manifest not only in the alternation of prose and poetry but also in the use of different colored inks, varying page arrangements, and other scribal behaviors that heighten contrast, this aesthetic delighted in juxtaposing different literary forms and in sharpening their differences.[27] We will soon see that when considered in the context of ancient Israelite and Near Eastern literary practice, the insertion of songs in biblical narrative reflects a different set of aesthetic priorities. To identify the two forms is to rend both from the cultural systems within which they signified—precisely what this study is doing its best to avoid.

This brings us to the second kind of comparison, which correlates objects from the same culture or from cultures in contact with one another. If these objects share a similarity it is because at some point in their respective backgrounds there is a moment of convergence: perhaps they shared a common ancestor, encountered a mutual intermediary, or influenced one another directly. Indeed, one of the functions served by this kind of comparison is to reconstruct the moment of convergence itself, which often lies concealed in the mists of prehistory. Comparative linguists, for example, rely on similarities between related languages to reconstruct the parent language from which they inherited their shared traits. More relevant for this study is the use of such comparisons for heuristic purposes—that is, what is known about one object of the comparison can be used to illuminate the other. What distinguishes this kind of comparison from the "comparison on the grand scale" is that the connections it draws are less likely to lead to decontextualization, since the objects being compared not only share formal similarities but also come from the same or closely related cultural contexts.

This mode of comparison has long played a central, if often controversial, role in the study of biblical literature, where scholars routinely draw inferences about the Bible's origins, form, and function from similarities which it shares with other ancient Near Eastern literatures. The book of Deuteronomy offers a classic example. The discovery that Deuteronomy is formally similar to Hittite treaties from the Late Bronze Age has led scholars to conclude that they reflect variations of the same literary form, perhaps borrowed by Israel from its neighbors or inherited by all from a common source.[28] This conclusion has shed new light on a number of questions surrounding the origins and purpose of Deuteronomy that could not be answered using biblical evidence alone, questions ranging from the circumstances of its composition to the logic of its organization. Of course, as is inevitable in the history of research, some scholars have come to question the historical validity of the comparison and the literary inferences drawn from it.[29] Their criticisms are sufficiently trenchant to suggest that one should not rush into accepting the analogy wholesale, but they do not diminish the service rendered by this comparison as a heuristic device, which has focused attention on details ignored in the past, suggested new answers for exegetical problems which formerly eluded solution, and opened up once-inconceivable perspectives on Deuteronomy's nature and purpose.

Seduced by the interpretive power of this method, scholars often over-extend or misuse it, arguing for affinities which subsequently prove to be illusory and disregarding differences which are later shown to be significant. An apt illustration is provided by the only other book-length study of the songs in biblical narrative, James Watts's *Psalm and Story*. In an appendix to his study, Watts points to a number of ancient Near Eastern texts which combine prose and poetry in some way.[30] He concludes from these alleged parallels that the insertion of songs within biblical narrative is but one example of a larger literary trend in the ancient world to combine prose and poetry. What undermines this conclusion is that it depends upon a rather imprecise use of comparative evidence. Most of the parallels adduced by Watts—the use of hymnic material in the prologues of Mesopotamian and Homeric epics, the seemingly random alternation of verse and prose in Egyptian narratives—bear only a superficial resemblance to the use of songs within biblical narrative.[31] Few of these texts attribute the poetry to figures within the story, for example, as biblical narrative does consistently. Moreover, Watts culls his parallels from a wide variety of times and places within the ancient world, as if antiquity were one great cultural common market in which Mesopotamian poets, Egyptian scribes, Homeric bards, and Israelite authors freely exchanged literary practices across vast distances of time and space. By thus minimizing significant differences in form, function, and context, Watts reduces a wide array of distinct literary practices into a single shapeless phenomenon encompassing almost every conceivable combination of narrative and poetry and explaining little about any particular combination. This is not to deny that ancient Near Eastern comparisons can help us to understand why songs appear in biblical narrative—my own argument depends on them at several points—but not all comparisons are of equal validity or value.

Before we compare the Bible with other ancient Near Eastern texts, therefore, we would do well to establish some criteria for assessing the merits and weaknesses of such comparisons. Unfortunately, there is at present no consensus on what these criteria should be. The best we can do—perhaps the best one can ever do—is to turn for guidance to previous studies of the Bible which have used comparative data in a way that has proved convincing to a majority of scholars. These studies tend to follow certain criteria which, while not amounting to a foolproof methodology, minimize the risk of misconstruing or overinterpreting alleged similarities.

First, in arguing for an affinity between the Bible and an ancient Near Eastern counterpart, such studies almost always depend not upon one isolated similarity but upon a configuration of many similarities. One reason that the comparison of Deuteronomy with vassal treaties has been so well received is that it is based on a complex pattern of similarities in content and structure. As the number of correspondences mounts, it becomes less likely that the resemblance between Deuteronomy and vassal treaties is simply a coincidence without any interpretive or contextualizing value.

Second, the significance of the comparison increases still further when the evidence allows one to account for it either by showing that one text was in a position to influence the other or by establishing the possibility of a shared literary ancestry. A chief objection to the Deuteronomy/vassal treaty comparison was that there was a sizable chronological gap between the time of Deuteronomy's composition (seventh century B.C.E.) and that of Hittite treaties, composed long before in the second millennium B.C.E. It simply was not clear how or why a literary form used in the Late Bronze Age would have had such a profound influence on the form of a text composed centuries later in the Iron Age. This problem was resolved when scholars realized that many of the formal characteristics of Late Bronze treaties also surface in Neo-Assyrian fealty oaths in use in precisely the period when Deuteronomy was believed to have been composed.[32] Given the historical and cultural interaction between Israel and Assyria in the seventh century B.C.E., this find suggests how it is that Deuteronomy resembles a literary genre from the Late Bronze Age: there were evidently intermediary literary forms that preserved the characteristics of the vassal treaty well into the Iron Age when they could exert an influence on Israelite literary practice.

A third trait shared by successful comparisons is that they do not disregard or minimize differences between the objects of comparison. To cite Jonathan Z. Smith again, "The questions of comparison are questions of judgment with respect to difference: What differences are to be maintained in the interests of comparative inquiry? What differences can be defensively relaxed and relativized in light of the intellectual tasks at hand?"[33] The answers to these questions can reveal weaknesses in the comparison, but they can also lead to its refinement. There is no denying that there are many differences between Deuteronomy and Neo-Assyrian fealty oaths, for instance, but these differences have not led scholars to abandon the comparison; rather, they have helped scholars recognize that the relation between these texts is complex, reflecting not only a connection between the cultures of Israel and Assyria but also the unique traits of each culture. Indeed, the identification of these unique traits has led to a more nuanced understanding of how the biblical authors adapted the form of the fealty oath to serve their own literary and ideological objectives.

Finally, successful comparisons not only reveal affinites between the Bible and extrabiblical texts; they also shed light on exegetical problems within the Bible that could not be resolved using biblical evidence alone. In light of ancient Assyrian loyalty oaths, scholars have been able to illumine Deuteronomy's use of the word *love* to command loyalty to the Lord (*love* is a technical term in Assyrian oaths used in reference to political loyalty),[34] the book's abrupt shifts from the singular to the plural when addressing its audience (often found in ancient Near Eastern treaties),[35] the order of the curses in Deuteronomy 28 (which follow a conventional order of curses attested in the corresponding section of Assyrian fealty oaths),[36] and a variety of other literary and philological details that would otherwise remain obscure. The successful comparison, in other words, is one with interpretive rewards, generating not only new solutions to old questions but also new questions that can revolutionize one's understanding of the phenomenon under investigation.

In chapters 2 and 3 I turn to this kind of analogy in an effort to shed light on the narrative roles of Exodus 15, Deuteronomy 32, and Judges 5. I posit that the meanings imposed upon these songs by their narrative settings have been conditioned by literary practices and expectations reflected elsewhere in ancient Near Eastern narratives of the first half of the first millennium B.C.E., the general time in which Exodus, Deuteronomy, and Judges were composed. None of the comparisons proposed in chapters 2 and 3 is without its complications, but as we measure them against the criteria just described, we will indeed find that they help us understand how and why the songs in Exodus 15, Deuteronomy 32, and Judges 5 were reinterpreted—and repurposed—by those who placed them in their narrative settings.

As important as comparative evidence is to this investigation, however, there are many questions it does not answer. For example, no ancient Near Eastern analogue can account for why the practice of inserting songs within biblical narrative enjoyed such a long life in Israelite literary history. In the eight or nine centuries it took for biblical narrative to assume its final, canonical form, literary behavior in ancient Israel changed dramatically, as new genres, styles, and conventions emerged to replace expiring literary forms. And yet, throughout all this time, the use of songs within narrative settings remained a literary constant, surfacing both in biblical narratives of every conceivable date and in postbiblical narratives from the Apocrypha, Pseudepigrapha, and New Testament. To understand this phenomenon fully is to understand its persistence, and here ancient Near Eastern literature offers little help. Our challenge, therefore, is to find an explanation for why in some respects the use of songs in biblical narrative represents a point of convergence between Israelite literature and ancient Near Eastern literary practice while in other ways it stands out against this backdrop as one of the most distinctly "biblical" of literary forms.

To find an explanation we must travel to the very heart of what makes the Bible a unique literature, different from any other surviving text from the ancient Near East. At some point in the history of ancient Israel, the contents of the biblical corpus—first the Pentateuch, then the Prophets, then the Writings—came to be perceived as sacred scripture, an eternally binding authority for behavior and belief. This development is often associated with the canonization of the Bible, the fixing of a finite collection of texts as sacred scripture, but it actually originates long before the first references to a biblical canon. As we will see in chapter 4, some scholars trace the origins of the idea of scripture to the religious trauma of the Babylonian exile, which, they say, forced Jews to find a more portable basis for their faith after losing the Temple and the monarchy.[37] Others place its beginnings in the days of King Josiah, who allegedly commissioned the Book of Deuteronomy, the first sacred book, to legitimize his cultic and politicial reforms.[38] A third approach suggests that the idea of scripture actually predates biblical Israel, having arisen from the common ancient Near Eastern idea that the gods sometimes recorded their decrees in books or tablets kept in heaven.[39] Whichever theory is correct—and it seems likely they all capture part of the truth—the point of interest to us is that the idea of scripture appears to have arisen early enough in Israel's history to have affected not only the reception of biblical literature but its compositional development as well. As some recent scholars have shown, in fact, significant portions of the Bible were recast in light of their scriptural status.[40] To cite an example discussed by Brevard Childs, perhaps the most influential scholar to explore this subject, the work now known as Deutero-Isaiah (Isaiah 40–55) was not originally composed by the prophet Isaiah in the eighth century B.C.E.; rather, it was created in the context of Judea's return from exile in the sixth century B.C.E.[41] It was only after this text was perceived as part of Israel's scripture, having significance not for a specific community in a specific historical situation but for all communities at all times, that it was recontextualized—or rather decontexualized—within the Book of Isaiah. What happened to Second Isaiah, Childs argues, is but one manifestation of a much larger process which transformed a miscellany of disparate Israelite stories, oracles, and poems into a unified scripture of perpetual relevance.

This transformation is the key to the explanation that we are seeking. We will see in chapters 4 and 5 that many of the songs within biblical narrative—the Psalm of Hezekiah in Isaiah 38, the Psalm of David in 1 Chronicles 16, the song of Daniel's three companions in the Greek versions of Daniel 3, and perhaps other songs as well—were placed in their present literary settings at a late stage in the Bible's compositional development. Some of these songs were interpolated at a late date (in the case of the song of Daniel's three friends, as late as the second or first century B.C.E.) into already existing narratives; others were incorporated into narratives which were themselves composed at a late date. There is nothing particularly original about this conclusion, which is based on literary and textual evidence long familar to biblical scholars. What is new here is my proposal that the addition of these songs represents a kind of scripturalizing revision, a reshaping of biblical narrative triggered by its emergence as part of Israel's sacred scripture.

To demonstrate this claim, I will show in chapter 4 that the scripturalization of biblical literature had immense consequences for literary practice and expectation, prompting imitations, paraphrases, and other literary behaviors which attest to the Bible's grip on the religious and artistic imagination of early Judaism. At the core of this imagination lay the belief that alongside its status as an authoritative guide for conduct and belief, the Bible was also an artistic model which exemplified the norms of literary expression. This belief licensed the creation of new kinds of literary expression which sought in different ways to capture the style and texture of the Bible. It also prompted the revision of existing biblical texts, which failed to satisfy the aesthetic and religious expectations engendered by their newly acquired status as scripture. Songs like the Psalm of Hezekiah and the song of Daniel's three companions are the products of such revisions. Their insertion represents nothing less than an attempt by early Jewish readers, dissatisfied with what they found—or rather did not find—in certain biblical episodes, to reshape them to suit their expectations of sacred scripture. My goal in chapter 5 is to locate the source of their dissatisfaction and to explore how it affected the literary development of the biblical text.

In our attempt to understand why songs appear in biblical narrative, therefore, we will need to traverse the entire length of Israelite literary history. This practice began as biblical literature itself began, emerging as an Israelite adaptation of literary practices shared with other cultures in the ancient Near East. It was only when the Bible was elevated to the status of scripture, only when it came to be perceived as a model for a sacred discourse belonging to Israel alone, that the insertion of songs was transformed into a uniquely biblical literary form employed in both the creation of new narratives and the revision of old. The scripturalization of biblical literature thus forged from an assortment of disparate compositional practices a full-fledged literary convention, one that early Jews believed they had inherited from their sacred past but that in fact they had created through the power of their belief.

With this proposition we return to the disclosure made at the beginning of the chapter. There I observed that we, as modern readers of the Bible, inevitably impose upon it literary categories which emerged long after ancient Israel was only a memory. What I am now suggesting is that earlier readers of the Bible who lived at a time when it had not yet developed into its final canonical form behaved in a similar way, imposing upon the Bible the literary norms and categories of their world. The biblical text as we now have it bears the mark of their efforts to rewrite the Bible in the image of their own literary presuppositions. Ultimately, that is why I believe that the songs in biblical narrative deserve the attention of anyone interested in the Bible's form and compositional history, for they help us recognize within our own response to the text some of the forces which have given biblical narrative its present literary shape.

·2·

A CHORUS OF
APPROVING VOICES

We saw in the last chapter that the Song of the Sea in Exodus 15 originated not as a spontaneous recital by Moses and the Israelites but as a cultic hymn drawn from some ancient ritual. This hypothesis was initially developed to solve certain exegetical problems posed by Exodus 15, especially the song's anachronistic reference to a "sanctuary" in the land of Canaan. In proposing this hypothesis, however, scholars raised a new set of problems which have not yet been resolved: if the song was not written for its present narrative setting, how did it end up in this setting, and what is it doing there? Such questions would never have occurred to a premodern reader who began from the assumption that the Pentateuch was completely—if not always obviously—coherent. For modern biblical scholars, however, the coherence of pentateuchal narrative was not something that could be taken for granted. They interpreted the Pentateuch's habit of telling the same story two or three times, its conflicting accounts of the same event, and its seemingly random alternation of different literary styles as signs that pentateuchal narrative was composed from distinct documents stemming from different historical circumstances and reflecting different religious-social perspectives. When it was first formulated, this conclusion had a wonderfully invigorating effect on biblical scholarship, opening up new vistas on biblical literature and ancient Israelite history. It also made it more difficult, however, to think about how the Pentateuch's parts relate to each other and to the whole. Even after decades of redactional criticism, rhetorical criticism, and other approaches that seek to reassemble what source criticism left disassembled, it is still unclear how the Pentateuch's components, even adjacent components, relate to one another. It is, I think, for this reason that while modern biblical scholars have never lacked for things to say about the Song of the Sea as an independent poem, they have had little to say about the meaning of the song as recontextualized in biblical narrative.

The purpose of this chapter is to explore how and why the Song of the Sea was integrated into its present literary setting. I will argue that the insertion of the song solved a basic rhetorical problem posed by the preceding narrative in Exod 14:1-31. Exodus 14 is perhaps best known for its description of the most sensational miracle in all biblical history, the parting of the Red Sea. The prominence of this miracle in recent cinematic retellings of the story obscures the fact that in the original form of Exodus 14, it is only one part of a larger account of how God fought on behalf of Israel against the pursuing Egyptian army. The rhetorical problem facing the author of this account was how to convince his audience that a supernatural being like God singlehandedly defeated the mighty Egyptian army without the help of a human army of his own. My argument is that the Song of the Sea plays a central role in the biblical author's solution to this representational problem, interacting with elements within the narrative of Exodus 14 to inscribe God into the action of the battle.

One of the obstacles I face in making such a proposal is the complex literary history of the narrative in Exodus 14. Most modern biblical scholars believe that Exodus 14, like the Pentateuch as a whole, is a composite of distinct literary sources which present alternative accounts of Israel's history. Scholars differ sharply in their reconstructions of these sources, but most would agree that at least two are detectable within Exodus 14: a Yahwist account (J) which describes the Red Sea incident as a battle between God and the Egyptians; and a Priestly account (P) — or, according to some, a Priestly redaction — which focuses on the figure of Moses and emphasizes the miraculous character of the event.[1] Some also detect the Elohist (E) source and a deuteronomistic editor within the narrative, but these two have left too few traces to be clearly reconstructed as coherent accounts.[2] So far, no one has been able to establish decisively whether the Song of the Sea was present in one of these sources prior to its combination with the other or whether it was added only after they were integrated into a single account. Some believe that only the Song of Miriam, the one-line song attributed to Miriam and the women of Israel in Exod 15:20-21, is an original part of the narrative, while the Song of the Sea in verses 1-18 represents a later expansion.[3] From this point of view, the Song of the Sea does not play an integral role in the preceding story but rather represents a secondary interpolation that obscured the original form of the narrative. Other scholars have claimed that the two songs represent variants of the same song transmitted independently in two distinct narrative sources, J and E.[4] According to this hypothesis, when these sources were combined into a single account, the two versions of the song were combined as well, creating the impression that the Song of Miriam was sung in antiphonic response to the Song of the Sea.[5] Each hypothesis proposes a different picture of the narrative's literary development and character, a divergence of opinion that raises a serious challenge for the present study: how can one explore the relation of the songs in Exodus 15 to their narrative setting when there are so many different conceptions of what this setting is?

Since I have found no way through this tangle of hypotheses and reconstructions, I propose to go around it by looking at Exodus 14-15 from a different angle, a comparative perspective that seeks to relate Exodus 14-15 as a whole to ancient Near Eastern literary practice. This approach takes us across enemy lines, as it were, leading us to the literary practices of God's foe in Exodus 14, the ancient Egyptians. In 1862, an inscription was discovered in the Temple of Gebel Barkal in southern Egypt which shares several striking similarities with the narrative in Exodus 14-15 as it presently appears in the Hebrew Bible. So far as I know, this text, known as the Piye Stela, is the only example of ancient Near Eastern prose historiography—outside of the Hebrew Bible and its imitations—that presents the contents of songs imputed to figures within its narrative. By looking carefully at this text, we can learn something of why an ancient Near Eastern scribe, writing in a literary culture in contact with that of ancient Israel, would incorporate songs in his narrative. Indeed, as I hope to show, some of what we learn from the use of songs in the Piye Stela can be applied directly to the Bible, helping us define more clearly how the songs in Exodus 15 relate to the story that precedes them.

Composed around 727 B.C.E., the Piye Stela represents one of the lengthiest and most complex prose compositions from the so-called Late Period in Egyptian history, recounting in 159 lines the conquests of the Nubian-born King Piye (also known as Piankhi) of the Twenty-Fifth Dynasty.[6] Few biblical scholars have thought to compare biblical narrative with the Piye Stela—something of a surprise, since the two texts share some rather intriguing similarities: both combine prose narrative, lists, lengthy speeches, and poetic passages in their accounts of national history; they appear to have drawn on and even to have incorporated wholesale preexisting sources;[7] and they were composed in contiguous cultures within roughly the same time frame (the Pentateuch draws on sources composed no earlier than the thirteenth or twelfth century B.C.E. and underwent its last major redaction probably no later than the fifth century B.C.E.—thus bridging the eighth century, when the Piye Stela was composed). One especially pertinent similarity was first observed by James Watts. He noticed that the Piye Stela, like biblical narrative, features several songs within the course of its narrative which it attributes to figures within the narrated world. The similarity, he explains, reflects a larger literary trend within ancient Near Eastern prose narrative to put poetic passages in the mouths of characters.[8] Watts has recognized an intriguing parallel, but in my view he has not interpreted it properly. As I mentioned briefly in chapter 1, many ancient Near Eastern texts mix prose and poetry, but beyond this, these texts share little in common, fusing prose and poetry in different

ways and for different reasons. As we will see, the inclusion of songs within
the Piye Stela is indeed comparable to the inclusion of songs within biblical
narrative, but a careful comparison reveals that it bears an especially striking
resemblance to the combination of story and song found in the Pentateuch's account of the Red Sea incident. Before we appeal to the Piye
Stela for an all-encompassing explanation for why songs appear in biblical
narrative, therefore, we would do well to examine the characteristics which
the incription shares with Exodus 14-15 in particular.

The Piye Stela actually features two songs. The first appears after Piye's
army defeats the city of Hermopolis; the second comes at the very end
of the text as Piye returns home from his campaign. Both are victory
songs sung by Piye's followers to celebrate the king's conquests. Here are
the two passages.

> His majesty arose in splendour [after the defeat of Hermopolis]
> and proceeded to the Temple of Thoth, Lord of Khmun. He sacri-
> ficed oxen, shorthorns, and fowl to his father Thoth, Lord of Khmun
> and the Ogdoad in the temple of the Ogdoad. And the troops of
> the Hare nome shouted and sang, saying: "How good is Horus at
> peace in his town, the Son of Re, Piye! You make for us a jubilee,
> as you protect the Hare nome!"[9]

> Then the ships were loaded with silver, gold, copper and clothing:
> everything of Lower Egypt, every product of Syria, and all plants
> of god's land. His majesty sailed south, his heart joyful, and all
> those near him shouting. West and East took up the announcement,
> shouting around his majesty. This was their song of jubilation: "O
> mighty ruler, O mighty ruler, Piye, mighty ruler! You return having
> taken Lower Egypt, You made bulls into women! Joyful is the mother
> who bore you, the man who begot you! The valley dwellers worship
> her, the cow that bore the bull! You are eternal, Your might abides,
> O ruler loved of Thebes!"[10]

The songs in Exodus 15 also celebrate a victory, God's defeat of the
Egyptian army. Here is part of Exod 14:30-15:21.

> Thus the Lord saved Israel that day from the Egyptians; and Israel
> saw the Egyptians dead on the seashore. Israel saw the great work
> that the Lord did against the Egyptians. So the people feared the
> Lord and believed in the Lord and in his servant Moses. Then
> Moses and Israel sang this song to the Lord: "I will sing to the
> Lord, for he has triumphed gloriously; the horse and rider he has
> thrown into the sea. The Lord is my strength and my song,[11] and

he has become my salvation; this is my God, and I will praise him, my father's God, and I will exalt him. The Lord is a man of war; the Lord is his name. Pharaoh's chariots and his host he has cast into the sea; and his picked officers were sunk in the Red Sea. The flood covers them; they went down into the depths like a stone. Your right hand, O Lord, glorious in power, your right hand, O Lord, shattered the enemy. In the greatness of your majesty you overthrew your adversaries; you sent out your fury, it consumed them like stubble. . . . The Lord will reign forever and ever." . . . Then the prophet Miriam, Aaron's sister, took a tambourine in her hand; and all the women went out after her with tambourines and with dancing. And Miriam sang to them:[12] "Sing to the Lord, for he has triumphed gloriously; horse and rider he has cast into the sea."[13]

Even a casual comparison reveals several similarities shared by the songs in Exodus 15 with the songs in the Piye Stela, especially the song that appears at the end of the inscription. Both sets of songs celebrate the might of a divine warrior[14] for an act of conquest. "O mighty ruler, Piye, mighty ruler. You have taken Lower Egypt, You made bulls into women" is similar to "The Lord is a man of war. . . . Your right hand, O Lord, glorious in power, your right hand, O Lord, shattered the enemy."[15] Both songs treat this divine warrior-leader as the sole participant in the combat, single-handedly reducing his foes from bulls into women or consuming them as a fire consumes stubble.[16] And most striking of all, both the Song of the Sea and the final song in the Piye Stela conclude with a triumphant shout that the divine warrior will rule forever: "You are eternal, Your might abides, O ruler loved of Thebes!" is similar to "The Lord will reign forever and ever." We will see that the last parallel is particularly important because it suggests that the purpose of both the Song of the Sea and the final song in the Piye Stela is not only to celebrate the victory of the divine warrior over his foes but also to acclaim him as an eternal, invincible ruler.

To appreciate the significance of these similarities, it is important to view them within the broader context of ancient Near Eastern royal propaganda. Many of the motifs shared by the songs in Exodus 15 and the Piye Stela surface elsewhere in other victory songs from the Bible and ancient Near Eastern literature. The final shout proclaiming the divine warrior's eternal rule, for example, is reminiscent of formulae found repeatedly in victory psalms within the Psalter, some of which actually may have been recited on festivals celebrating God's enthronement as king (See Pss 29:10, 47:7-8, 93:1, 95:3, 96:10, 97:1, 98:6, 99:1).[17] This and other motifs shared by the songs in Exodus 15 and the Piye Stela are so common throughout the region that they cannot be construed as evidence of a specific or direct literary relationship between the two compositions. Indeed, while the Song of the Sea resembles the songs in the Piye Stela in a general way, it shares much more specific similarities with Ugaritic poetry, especially the so-called Baal cycle, which describes how the deity Baal vanquished his enemies and then established his abode on a sacred mountain (compare the final verses of the Song of the Sea, where God, after his victory against the Egyptians, establishes a sanctuary on a mountain in Canaan).[18] Compared with this parallel—which, by the way, is one of the reasons scholars date the Song of the Sea to the Late Bronze Age when Ugaritic literature was composed—the parallels between Exodus 15 and the songs in the Piye Stela seem less impressive. Perhaps they establish that the songs belong to the same literary genre and convey similar messages, but not being exclusive to these two texts, they do not constitute evidence of a specific literary relation between them.

When we consider the literary contexts in which the two sets of songs appear, however, we find that they share one trait that ties them closely: the two sets of songs have been placed at analogous points in narratives which are themselves similar to one another in several respects. The two songs in the Piye Stela both follow battle accounts (the second song appearing at the end of Piye's entire campaign), and they function within the narrative as acts of acclamation from the king's subjects to Piye after his defeat of his foes. Similarly, the songs in Exodus 15 also appear at the end of the episode presented in Exodus 14, and they too function in the narrative as an act of acclamation from Israel to God after his defeat of the Egyptian army. Of course, we are not accustomed to thinking of the Red Sea story as a battle account. In fact, one recent scholar has described the episode in Exodus 14 as an antiwar account, since it describes a clash between God and the Egyptian army, not a clash between two armies.[19] That Exodus 14 could be described in this way, however, only confirms that there is something about its contents that suggests an affinity with battle literature. The fact is that Exodus 14—or at least one source woven into it—draws on terminology and motifs characteristic of Israelite battle literature.[20] Thus in Exod 14:24 the narrator reports that God "discomfited" the Egyptians (*wayyāhom*), a verb used elsewhere in biblical battle accounts to describe God's defeat of an enemy army (see Exod 23:27, Josh 10:10, Judg 4:15, 1 Sam 7:10).[21] The narrative's report in verses 19-20 and 24 that a "pillar of fire and cloud" intervened between Egypt and Israel resembles descriptions in ancient Near Eastern battle accounts of divine participation in battle. The Gebel Barkal inscription of Thutmose III of the Eighteenth Dynasty, for example, describes the sudden appearance of a fiery star sent by the god Amun against the enemy: "it shot straight at them and no one among them could stand. It slew as if they had never existed . . . they had no more teams of horses, these having bolted in terror to the mountain" (compare Exod 14:24, "the Lord in a pillar of fire and cloud looked down upon the Egyptian army, and threw the Egyptian army into panic").[22] Finally, as if to confirm one's impression of the narrative as a battle account, Moses informs a panic-stricken Israel not to fear because the Lord will "fight" for Israel against the Egyptians (Exod 14:14), an interpretation of events seconded by the Egyptians themselves, who flee when they recognize that the Lord "fights" against them (verse 25). If Exodus 14 still seems different from more conventional battle accounts such as the Piye Stela, it is because a deity—and not a human army—does all the fighting. In terms of its form, however, Exodus 14 exhibits motifs and plot elements characteristic of battle accounts. What is striking about Exodus 14-15 and the Piye Stela, therefore, is not simply that they both contain victory songs of similar content but that these songs appear at similar points within similar narrative settings.

By itself, this similarity does not tell us when the songs in Exodus 15 were placed in the Red Sea narrative—whether they were integrated into one of the sources prior to its combination with the other or were added only after the sources were combined into a single account. The analogy of the Piye Stela would lead one to suspect that if the songs in Exodus 15 were incorporated in one or the other of these sources prior to their combination, they originally belonged to the battle account in J, not the miracle account in P, but there is no way to confirm this suspicion.[23] At whatever point the songs in Exodus 15 entered biblical narrative, however, the fact remains that in the text's present form, the use of victory songs within the Red Sea narrative resembles the use of victory songs in the Piye Stela, a parallel so striking that it begs explanation. It seems highly unlikely that the similarity reflects the direct influence of one text upon the other. To establish a direct literary relationship, one would need to identify at least one or two precise verbal parallels between the two texts to serve as evidence that one writer was familar with the other text, but no such parallels are to be found. One would also have to find a way to overcome the linguistic barrier between biblical Hebrew and Egyptian. The latter problem is not insurmountable, since some Israelite scribes appear to have been familar with Egyptian literature either directly or in translation. According to many scholars, for example, Prov 22:17-24:22 represents a Hebrew adaptation of the Egyptian wisdom text *Instruction of Amenemope*.[24] Still, it would be stretching the evidence to conclude that a biblical author actually read an inscription erected in a remote corner of southern Egypt. In my view, a more likely possibility is that Exodus 15 and the Piye Stela preserve independent manifestations of a literary practice shared by Egyptian and Israelite scribes. A more generalized explanation of this sort is consistent with what we know of the cultural interaction between Canaan/Israel and Egypt. Palestine had extensive political, commercial, and cultural contacts with Egypt at the end of the second millennium B.C.E.; and in fact, New Kingdom military inscriptions sharing stylistic features with the Piye Stela have been found within Palestine itself.[25] Literary and archaeological evidence indicates that contacts continued throughout the first millennium, when both Exodus 14–15 and the Piye Stela were composed.[26] In the context of our present discussion it is interesting that a scarab containing a commemorative inscription from the reign of Shabako, brother and successor of Piye, has been found, evidently in Syria (it was later sold in Jerusalem).[27] Written to publicize Shabako's conquest over his enemies (including "sand-dwellers," possibly Asian semi-nomads), the text provides evidence that royal propaganda from the Twenty-Fifth Dynasty was dispersed in the region of Syria-Palestine—not particularly surprising given that Piye's successors sought to reassert Egypt's hegemony over this region.[28] With this kind of evidence in mind, the Egyptologist Donald Redford concluded that there must have existed in biblical Israel "a scribal elite still in touch with or mindful of Egypt from the 21st to the 26th Dynasties, that perpetuated the celebrated creations of the Egyptian New Kingdom and kept alive style and form."[29] Assuming Redford is right in his assessment of the evidence, the insertion of songs in battle accounts may have been one of the literary forms kept alive by Israelite scribes.

Of course, we should not mistake historical plausibility for concrete literary evidence.[30] If we are going to conclude that Exodus 14–15 and the Piye Stela reflect a shared literary convention, it will not be because we can trace the transmission of this convention from one culture to the other. Too few texts survive from Egypt and Israel in the first half of the first millennium B.C.E. to allow this kind of documentation. The strength of this hypothesis derives almost entirely from the cluster of the similarities shared by the two texts in combination with the explanatory power of the comparison. As we saw in the first chapter, the success of a comparison in biblical studies depends on its ability to shed light on interpretive problems that have not been resolved using biblical evidence alone. The Piye Stela provides exactly this kind of perspective, giving us a way to explain the insertion of the songs in the Red Sea narrative and to do so in a way that is consistent with what is currently known about scribal practice in the ancient Near East. Before we can fully appreciate the value of this analogy, however, we need to consider more carefully what led the author of the Piye Stela to incorporate songs within his narrative.

Thanks to recent advances in the understanding of ancient Egyptian military literature, we know that the songs in the Piye Stela do in fact reflect a scribal convention, one that was used in the composition of Egyptian battle accounts as far as back as the New Kingdom period. It was at this time that Egyptian scribes began a long period of experimentation in the art of military literature, developing several conventional forms and genres that would endure for centuries.[31] Among these were certain motifs and techniques used to bring the battle account to a close. Many inscriptions thus conclude with a scene or scenes of jubilation and acclaim in which the king's subjects celebrate the king's victory. These scenes can be recognized by their use of certain stock terms and phrases indicating praise, rejoicing, or shouts of approval (especially common is the word *nhm,* meaning "to exult" or "to be jubilant").[32] The end of the Assuan Philae inscription of Thutmoses II of the Eighteenth Dynasty can serve as an example:

> This land was made a subject of his majesty as formerly, the people rejoiced, the chiefs were joyful; they gave praise to the Lord of the Two Lands, they lauded this god, excellent in examples of divinity. It came to pass on account of the fame of his majesty, because his father Amon loved him so much more than any king who has been since the beginning. The King of Upper and Lower Egypt: Okhepernere, Son of Re: Thutmose, Beautiful in Diadems, given life, stability, satisfaction, like Re, forever.[33]

In this text the scene of public acclamation bleeds into the scribe's own praise of the king in which he explicitly credits him with the victory. Other texts integrate such explicit praise of the king into the action of the narrative by attributing it to participants in the events described by the text. An example is the partially preserved speech that appears in the second of two scenes of jubilation at the end of the great Karnak inscription of Merneptah (Nineteenth Dynasty):[34]

> They [the king's court] said: "How great are these things which have happened to Egypt!———Lybia is like a petitioner brought as a captive. Thou hast made them to be like grasshoppers, for every road is strewed with their [bodies]———[bestowing] thy provision in the mouth of the needy. We lie down with joy at any time; there being no———[the final two to four lines cannot be reconstructed].

Like the Assuan inscription, this text explicitly credits the king with the victory, but it transforms this praise into an historical event in its own right by representing it as a speech from the king's subjects.

The Egyptologist Anthony Spalinger has noted that this use of speech coda at the end of battle accounts occurs with increasing frequency and elaboration in Egyptian military documents.[35] Perhaps one reason for the success of this kind of conclusion is that it helps overcome a representational limitation often imposed upon the authors of Egyptian battle accounts. Many of the jubilatory scenes in Egyptian military literature appear in accounts in which the king does not personally lead the army into battle.[36] In these accounts the king typically plays a personal role in the narrative's action only at its beginning and end, reacting angrily to the threat posed by the enemy, dispatching the army, and reviewing the spoils of victory. The representational challenge before the authors of these accounts was how to establish the king as the hero of a battle in which he did not personally participate. Some scribes simply declared that the king's power extended far beyond his physical presence, inspiring terror even in far-flung corners of his kingdom. Thus, to return to the Assuan inscription of Thutmose II, after the narrator reports that the king was in his palace, he proclaims that

> the fear of him is in the land, [his] terror in the lands of Hauenbu; the two divisions of Horus and Set are under his charge; the Nine bows together are beneath his feet. The Asiatics come bearing to him tribute, and the Nubian troglodytes bearing baskets. His southern boundary is as far as the Horns of the earth, northern as far as the ends; the marshes of Asia are the dominion of his majesty, the arm of his messenger is not repulsed among the lands of the Fe[n]khu.

Other scribes used speech coda to extend the king's power beyond the confines of his physical presence. A clear example of this is provided by the Piye Stela itself, in which, before going off to battle, Piye's army gives a speech in which it declares itself a mere extension of the king's might.

> Then they placed themselves on their bellies before his majesty: "It is your name that makes our strength. Your counsel brings your army into port. Your bread is in our bellies on every way. Your beer quenches our thirst. It is your valor that gives us strength. There is dread when your name is recalled. No army wins with a cowardly leader. Who is your equal there? You are the mighty King who acts with his arms, the chief of the work of war!" They sailed north and arrived at Thebes; they did as his majesty had said. (Lines 14–16)

Through its own words Piye's army characterizes itself as a weapon wielded by the king in far-off Thebes. The army does the fighting, but the king gets all the credit for the victory. The two techniques serve the same rhetorical objective—to convince the account's audience that the king deserves all the glory for the victory even though he did not personally participate in the fighting.

The conventional scenes of jubilation at the end of battle accounts also reflect this rhetorical objective. Appearing just after the description of the battle, these scenes represent one final attempt to shape the reader's perceptions of the battle. The king may not have participated personally in the fighting, but it was his might that devastated the enemy, ensured the army's safe return, and guarantees the kingdom's continued prosperity and security. In inscriptions where these sentiments are voiced by figures within the narrative, the intended reader is presented with a model of how it should interpret the battle and assign credit for its victorious outcome. The response of the king's jubilatory subjects enacts the kind of response the scribe seeks to elicit from his audience.

Against the horizon of earlier Egyptian military literature we can better appreciate why songs appear in the Piye Stela. As I mentioned earlier, it is a composite text, combining within its narrative several distinct genres and sources. Egyptologists have detected within it language and motifs drawn not only from an earlier daybook account (a genre of military document recognizable by its use of the verbal infinitive form to communicate action) but also from Egyptian wisdom literature and the *iw.tw* report (a genre of battle account often used to describe campaigns in which the king did not personally participate).[37] Given the frequency with which the Piye Stela employs long-established genres and preexisting documents, it is not surprising to discover that its use of songs also represents an appropriation of an earlier literary form, the use of acclamatory speech coda to conclude the battle account.[38] Recall that both songs are represented by the narrative as praise offered to the king after a victory; both are introduced with conventional terminology used repeatedly in Egyptian battle accounts to introduce the jubilation of the king's subjects (the word *nhm* in the phrase "song of jubilation" is especially common in such scenes); and the second song appears as the last event in the text—a narrative slot typically reserved for jubilatory scenes. It turns out that the use of songs in the Piye Stela represents a conventional literary act, one with deep roots in the history of Egyptian scribal practice.

The appearance of this form in an inscription composed in the eighth century B.C.E. demonstrates that it remained viable for at least a few centuries into the first millennium, after Israelite literary history was well under way. By this time, in fact, it may have been used precisely because it was perceived to be characteristic of Egyptian battle accounts. Egyptologists have noted that the reigns of Piye and his Nubian successors are marked by an energetic effort to revive ancient Egyptian literary style and to restore old cultic sites (even the style of Piye's tomb was Egyptianizing, featuring a pyramidal superstructure probably modeled upon pyramids from the Old Kingdom or the New Kingom).[39] There may have been political forces fueling the Nubians' nostalgia and Egyptophilia. Piye, descended from a native Sudanese dynasty, expended considerable effort seeking entry into the northern part of Egypt, in part to fend off his most dangerous foe, Tefnakht, who sought to extend his power southward from the Delta region.[40] Piye eventually succeeded in gaining the submission of his northern rival—though he later withdrew from Egypt, leaving Tefnakht to reestablish himself. Still, he and his successors clearly had designs on Egypt, as demonstrated by his brother Shabako, who soon reasserted control over the Delta rulers. By seeking to revive archaic literary and cultic forms, Piye and his successors may have been seeking to represent themselves as the authentic continuation of long-established Egyptian cultural tradition. The Piye Stela can be read as part of this cultural campaign, serving not only to describe how Piye gained control over Egypt but also to suggest that his conquest returned Egypt to the way it had once been. That explains why the inscription draws upon archaic forms as it does in its final jubilatory scene, for the use of such forms would have reinforced the impression that Nubia's incursion represented not an invasion by foreigners but the resumption of Egypt's own glorious past.

The author of the battle account in Exodus 14-15 apparently faced representational challenges similar to those which faced the author of the Piye Stela and solved them in similar ways. At several points in the narrative in Exodus 14—or at least in the J strand woven into it—the author raises the issue of how God's action in the battle appeared to those observing it. Just before the destruction of the Egyptian army (Exod 14:14), Moses instructs Israel to "stand firm, and *see* the deliverance that the Lord will accomplish for you today, for the Egyptians whom you *see* today you shall never *see* again" (emphasis added). The same verb, "to see," resurfaces at the end of the narrative (verses 30-31): "Thus, the Lord saved Israel that day from the Egyptians; and Israel *saw* the Egyptians dead on the seashore. Israel *saw* the great work that the Lord did against the Egyptians." I submit that the narrative's concern with how the Israelites perceived the events at the Red Sea dramatizes authorial anxiety about how the reader perceives and interprets these events. The underlying rhetorical objective of the narrative in Exodus 14-15 (or J) is to convince the reader to acknowledge God's power even as Israel was convinced to "fear the Lord and believe in the Lord" after seeing the Egyptians strewn dead on the shores of the Red Sea (Exod 15:30). To win this affirmation, the narrative must first accomplish the much more basic task of convincing the reader that God did indeed defeat the Egyptian army. This challenge of representing God as the hero of the battle is not altogether different from that which faced the Egyptian scribes who had to persuade their readers that their kings won battles in which they did not physically participate. It is true that, according to Exodus 14, God is not removed from the action of the battle in the way Egyptian kings sometimes were as they sent orders from distant palaces; in fact, according to the biblical account, God fights the battle singlehandedly. Judging from the way he tells the story, however, the author of the battle account in Exodus 14 was not inclined to depict God wielding an axe or riding in a chariot like a human combatant—perhaps because he wished to avoid anthropomorphizing God—and so he too found other techniques to ensure that God was credited with the victory.

These techniques surface at several points within Exodus 14. I mentioned earlier, for example, that the author drew on motifs employed elsewhere in ancient Near Eastern military literature to represent divine intervention in battle. To recall one example, the pillar of fire and cloud mentioned in Exod 14:24 calls to mind reports in ancient Near Eastern and Greek battle accounts that the gods helped to defeat the enemy by sending against it shining clouds and consuming fire. For all their spectacle, however, these motifs do not play a large role in the overall battle account in Exodus 14, and the narrative passes quickly over God's actual participation in the combat (the battle is described in less than two verses). As if the biblical author were uncertain that he had completely convinced his audience of God's role, he turned to another strategy used with great frequency in Egyptian battle accounts: testimony from figures within the narrative to give the king credit for the victory. Like the Piye Stela, where declarations from Piye's army, vassals, and defeated foes repeatedly assert the king's might and heroism, Exodus 14 cites the words of Moses (14:14: "the Lord will fight for you") and the defeated Egyptians (14:25: "Let us flee before Israel for the Lord fights for them") to make doubly sure that God gets credit for the victory. Situated just before the narrative's depiction of the fight and then again after its conclusion, these citations help shape the reader's reaction to the battle by attributing the desired interpretation to figures within the narrative.

In light of what we have learned about the songs in the Piye Stela, the songs in Exodus 15 appear to reflect the narrative's strategy of using character testimony to make explicit God's role in the battle. Like the final song in the Piye Stela, the Song of the Sea and the Song of Miriam appear as the culminating acts of acclamation within the narrative, bestowing upon God all the glory for the battle just narrated. If the narrator in Exodus 14 was reluctant to represent God as bodily engaged in combat like a human warrior, the song more than compensates for this by vividly describing God in action against the Egyptians: "Pharaoh's chariots and his army he cast into the sea . . . your right hand, O Lord, smashes the enemy . . . you stretched out your hand, the earth swallowed them" (Exod 15:4, 6, 12). The author of the prose account has made much the same point in other less direct ways, but through the voices of the Israelites singing on the shores of the Red Sea he represents God's heroism explicitly, describing him as a warrior literally engaged in physical combat against his enemies. Moreover, the attribution of the songs to all the Israelites gives its message the authority of universal assent. What distinguishes the final song in the Piye Stela from earlier speeches of acclaim in the narrative is its attribution to the entire kingdom of Egypt: "West and East took up the announcement." In a sense, the narrative is an account of how Piye gradually persuaded all of Egypt to accept him as its ruler, and the final song sung by all the kingdom is meant to indicate that Piye succeeded in winning this acceptance. Similarly, what distinguishes the songs in Exodus 15 from earlier speeches of acclaim is its attribution to the entire Israelite people, Moses and the "sons of Israel" (Exod 15:1) along with Miriam and "all the women" (Exod 15:20). Prior to God's conquest of the Egyptians, the Israelites were quite suspicious of God as a ruler, preferring to serve the Egyptians instead: "Is this not the very thing we told you in Egypt, 'Let us alone and let us serve the Egyptians'? For it would have been better for us to serve the Egyptians than to die in the wilderness" (Exod 14:12).[41] The Israelites do not utter another word until they sing in Exodus 15, an act which signals a dramatic shift in their allegiance, for they are now willing to proclaim God as their savior/ruler: "I will sing to the Lord . . . he has become my salvation; this is my God . . . the Lord will reign forever and ever." Like the Piye Stela, Exodus 14 is more than a battle account; it is the story of how the divine warrior wrested the fealty of his subjects from the enemy. So too the songs in Exodus 15 are more than victory paeans; they offer Israel's pledge of allegiance to God.

Having reached this conclusion, we are now in a position to resolve an interpretive problem encountered at the beginning of the chapter. We saw that scholars have long wondered why there are two songs in Exodus, the Song of the Sea and the Song of Miriam, the second of which echoes the first. Some explain the apparent redundancy by arguing that the present form of the narrative conflates two parallel but distinct traditions, as the Pentateuch does elsewhere when it juxtaposes two creation stories or combines two flood stories into a single account. Others claim that only one song is original (probably the shorter Song of Miriam) and that the other was added secondarily (the Song of the Sea). Feminist biblical interpretation has revived the latter view with its proposal that the addition of the Song of the Sea represents a male author's attempt to drown out or co-opt the Song of Miriam, which if earlier than the Song of the Sea would suggest that women were the first to recognize the religious implications of the Exodus event.[42] Notwithstanding its recent vintage, this view resembles earlier explanations in that it is essentially diachronic, attributing the presence of two songs in Exodus 15 to different stages in the narrative's literary growth. It does not explain why, if the Song of Miriam was meant to be replaced by the Song of the Sea, it is preserved alongside it in the present form of the narrative, or how the two songs function in relation to each other. In light of the Piye Stela, we can answer these questions.

In the stela, the final song is the most inclusive act of speech within
the entire narrative, testifying that Piye has been accepted by all the people
as their ruler. Similarly, the songs in Exodus 15 work together to suggest
that God has been accepted by all of Israel. It was apparently the custom
in ancient Israel for the women to sing songs of victory to the men as
they returned from battle (see Judges 11:34 and 1 Samuel 18:6-7).[43] If in
Exodus 15 Moses and the sons of Israel join in the singing, it is because
in this extraordinary case God alone has done all the fighting and he
alone deserves all the praise. Normally assigned the role of returning warriors, the males of Israel must in this case play the role usually imposed
only upon females in the androcentric culture of ancient Israel, the role
of cheerleader. According to this reading, the attribution of a song to the
men is not meant to eclipse the role of women as the first to celebrate
God's role in Israel's life; it is meant to "feminize" the men in their relationship to God (in the sense that "feminine" behavior was perceived by
the presumably male authors of biblical narrative), that is, to represent
them as dependents upon and endorsers of God's military prowess. I do
not offer this interpretation to rebut the claim that the Song of Miriam
predates the Song of the Sea but only to suggest why both songs were
included in the story. In the Piye Stela the final act of acclamation is
presented as an all-encompassing act of speech so as to create the impression that there is only one possible response to the events described in
the preceding story—acceptance of the king's rule. This is also the effect
of the songs in Exodus 15 *when they are read as the narrative presents them,*
that is, as a unisomous act of praise.

Even as the comparison with the Piye Stela sheds light on a longstanding
interpretive problem within Exodus 14-15, however, it also raises one of
its own: why would an Israelite scribe appropriate an Egyptian literary
form to describe God's conquest of the Egyptian army? We may never
know for certain whether this scribe actually recognized the Egyptian origins
of this form—it may have passed to him indirectly through indigenous
Canaanite literary tradtition—but if he did, such knowledge may have
played a role in his decision to use this form. It will be recalled that just
before the battle, as Israel sees Pharaoh's army advancing against it, it is
ready to switch its allegiance back to Egypt: "it would have been better
for us to serve the Egyptians." God must not only deliver Israel from
Egypt; he must win their loyalty from Egypt as well. What better way to
mark God's success in this task than to conclude the account of the defeat
of Pharaoh with a form of closure normally used to celebrate Egyptian
victory. The reason Egyptian scribes closed their accounts with speeches
of acclamation in the first place was to publicize the king's invincible
strength and the permanence of his rule. In this light, it is tempting to
read the Bible's use of this form to celebrate Pharaoh's defeat as a

mischievous inversion of Egyptian political rhetoric aimed at subverting
the authority of Egypt.

Some scholars, in fact, have recognized a similar rhetorical strategy at
work within the Song of the Sea. They argue that the song actually contains
motifs used in Egyptian royal propaganda to represent the king's military
might.[44] The clearest example is the song's repeated references to the
power of God's arm in battle (Exod 15:6: "your right hand . . . shattered
the enemy"; 15:16: "terror and dread fell upon them by the might of your
arm"), a metonym which recalls an image used routinely in Egyptian battle
accounts, both verbal and iconic, to represent the king's might in combat.[45]
Those who have identified these Egyptian motifs see in them a deliberate
and highly sarcastic attempt to taunt the Egyptians by appropriating imagery used in Egyptian representations of the king's military victories.[46]
Our analysis suggests that the taunts within the Song of the Sea contribute
to the larger rhetorical strategy of Exodus 14-15, which mimics literary
forms employed within Egyptian military propaganda so as to undermine
the authority of the Egyptian king (this does not mean that Exodus 14-15
was literally aimed against Egyptian rule; Egypt may simply have been a
cipher for any force that rivals God's rule). Ironically, then, while the Piye
Stela and Exodus 14-15 end in similar ways, their conclusions serve very
different ideological agendas. The songs in the Piye Stela celebrate the
king's victory in a way that links them to the great triumphs of Egypt's
past. The songs in Exodus 15 evoke the trappings of Egyptian power only
to expose the limits of that power when it challenges God's rule over the
Israelites. The former seeks to insert an outsider into Egyptian military
tradition so as to solidify his position as Egypt's ruler; the latter represents
an outsider's attempt to subvert Egyptian military tradition so as to solidify
God's position as Israel's ruler.

If this interpretation of the evidence is correct, the songs in Exodus
15 are integrally related to the message and design of the surrounding
narrative, so much so that one is tempted to question the longstanding
hypothesis that the songs were composed long before their insertion within
the narrative. How can the evidence that the song predates its narrative
be reconciled with what appears to be an integral connection between
song and story? In actuality, there is no inherent conflict here, provided
we recognize that the insertion of the songs within the narrative represents
a literary act as deliberate as that which produced the songs in the first
place. Much of the art that produced biblical narrative is the art of com-
pilation and redaction, the integration of existing literary sources into
coherent and well-structured unities. Scholars have long sensed that the
narrative in Exodus 14 and the songs in Exodus 15 were combined for a
reason. The value of the Piye analogy is that it has helped us reconstruct
what this reason is by shedding light on the representational problems

addressed by the narrative's integration of song and story, the conventions that governed their interaction, and the skill with which the biblical author has reoriented these conventions to serve his or her own literary purposes.

Of course, like any hypothesis, the reading proposed here is to be judged not only by what it explains but by what it leaves unexplained. The songs in Exodus 15 are only the first of many songs embedded within biblical narrative, leading one to wonder whether we have discovered in Egyptian scribal practice a way to explain the insertion of other songs as well. What we have learned from the Piye Stela is indeed useful for understanding the narrative role of at least one other song, that sung by Deborah and Barak in Judges 5. Considered in isolation from its narrative context, the song in Judges 5 shares much less in common with the Song of the Sea than it does with the Blessing of Jacob in Genesis 49 and the Blessing of Moses in Deuteronomy 33, for like these, it centers on a lengthy catalogue of the tribes of Israel in which each is given a blessing or curse. The correspondence is at times so close that there is even a point within Judges 5 where its contents are almost identical to Genesis 49 (compare Judg 5:17 with Gen 49:13).[47] As striking as these correspondences are, however, they reveal little about the role of the Song of Deborah and Barak in its present narrative setting. The blessings of Jacob and Moses function in their narrative settings as the last words of dying biblical heroes, a common literary topos to be discussed at greater length in the next chapter. By contrast, the Song of Deborah and Barak functions in its narrative setting as a victory song sung after the defeat of the Canaanite forces of King Jabin. When considered in the context of its narrative setting, the song obviously bears a pronounced functional resemblance to the songs in Exodus 15; and indeed, a closer look at Judges 4-5 reveals that its combination of story and song reflects much of the same conventional behavior we have detected in Exodus 14-15.

We have seen that the narrative in Exodus 14 draws on several conventional strategies to pull God into the action of the battle against the Egyptians: it employs stock images and terms to indicate God's physical participation in the battle, and it relies heavily on the testimony of figures within the narrative to confirm God's role. The songs in Exodus 15 serve both strategies, explicitly depicting God as a warrior smashing his enemies and giving credence to this depiction by attributing it to all of Israel. The Song of Deborah functions in much the same way in relation to the preceding battle account in Judges 4. It is true that this time human heroes play a much more significant role in the fighting than they do in Exodus 14. Judges 4 is a battle account in the strictest sense of the word, starring the prophetess Deborah, who musters the Israelites for battle against the Canaanites; the Israelite general Barak, who leads the Israelites into battle; and the Kenite housewife Jael, who finishes off the general Sisera by smashing his skull with a tent peg while he sleeps in her tent. And yet, using many of the same techniques at work in Exodus 14, the narrative drives home the point that the true hero of the battle is the Lord. Hence, when describing the battle itself in Judg 4:15, the author represents the Lord as an actual participant in the fighting by using precisely the same language found in Exodus 14: "The Lord threw Sisera and all his chariots and all his army into a panic (*wayyāhom*)."[48] Moreover, just like Exodus 14, which cites the speech of Moses and the Egyptians to underscore God's role in the fighting, Judges 4 cites the speech of the prophetess Deborah, who repeatedly reminds Barak (and through Barak the reader) that God is leading Israel into battle: "Then Deborah said to Barak, 'Up! for this is the day on which the Lord has given Sisera into your hand. The Lord is indeed going out before you'" (Judg 4:14). And finally, like the songs in Exodus 15, the song in Judges 5 represents the culmination of the narrative's use of quoted speech to credit God with the victory, depicting God as a powerful warrior marching out of the south to save Israel:

> To the Lord I will sing, I will make melody to the Lord, the God of Israel. Lord, when you went out from Seir, when you marched from the region of Edom, the earth trembled, and the heavens poured water. The mountains quaked before the Lord, the One of Sinai, before the Lord, the God Israel.[49]

Placed at the end of the narrative, these words make explicit what the narrative intends as the definitive interpretation of the battle. Israel's victory, the song proclaims in its opening lines, is not simply the result of human valor. The tribes who fought in the battle were courageous, Jael was daring, but it is God who deserves Israel's praise first and foremost, because it was his intervention in the battle that made victory possible.

To be sure, this is not the song's only message. Like the prose account in Judges 4, the Song of Deborah and Barak acknowledges that human combatants played a significant role in the battle as well. The point of the tribal catalogue in Judg 5:14-23, mentioned earlier as the core of the song, is precisely to evaluate the contribution of each tribe to the victory, to praise those who fought (Ephraim, Benjamin, Machir, Zebulun, Issachar, and Naphtali) and to rebuke those who refused to fight (Reuben, Gilead, Dan, Asher, and Meroz).[50] The next four verses (24-27) play a similar role, blessing Jael for her role in killing Sisera. These two sections of the song, which constitute about two-thirds of its contents, have no analogue in the Song of the Sea, where God is celebrated as the sole hero of the battle.[51] Despite this difference, however, I would maintain that the ultimate purpose of the song in Judges 5 is to promote allegiance to God. In our discussion of the Piye Stela we saw that one way for the narrative to credit

Piye with the victory was to put in the mouths of those who did the actual fighting—Piye's army—the claim that they were merely extensions of the king's might, dependent on Piye for their strength and beholden to him for their success. The song of victory cited in Judges 5 serves a similar strategy. It celebrates the heroism of Israel and Jael, but it defines this heroism as loyal support for God in his battle. The song refers to those who fight as "the Lord's people" (5:11), as if they were his representatives.[52] This impression is strengthened by the phrase "may your friends be like the sun" in the song's final line in verse 31. The description of Israel and Jael as God's "friends" (literally "those who love him") implies that they functioned in the battle as God's vassals, since the verb "to love" was often used in the ancient Near East to describe the loyalty of a vassal to a stronger king.[53] In other words, the human heroes within the song are described as God's allies or supporters. On the other hand, those who refuse to fight are criticized not for cowardice but because "they did not come to the help of the Lord, to the help of the Lord against the mighty" (5:23). The chief attribute praised by the song is not valor per se but loyalty to God, a vassal's commitment to join the fight in support of his liege. The song's tribal list and its tribute to Jael are not meant to eclipse God's role in the battle; rather, they celebrate the fealty of those who fought as God's allies, "O Lord! May those who love you be like the sun."

A similar point is made by the prose account of Judges 4, which also acknowledges the participation of human combatants but seeks to represent this participation as a manifestation of God's power: "on that day God subdued King Jabin of Canaan before the Israelites" (verse 23). Particularly important in this regard is what the narrative does with the figure of Barak. As leader of the Israelite army, he stands to be given the glory for the victory, and it is precisely for this reason that the narrative goes to great lengths to minimize his contribution to the battle. This objective is clearly reflected in the battle account itself, which depicts Barak as a passive beneficiary of God's actions—"the Lord threw Sisera and all his chariots and all his army into a panic before Barak" (4:15).[54] It also helps explain the Jael episode at the end of the narrative (verses 17-22) in which a Kenite housewife slays Sisera, the leader of the Canaanite army, by luring him into her tent with an offer of hospitality. Just before the battle Deborah prophesies to Barak that the fighting will not lead to his glory, "for the Lord will sell Sisera into the hand of the woman" (4:9). Deborah's prediction makes explicit the intended rhetorical effect of the Jael episode—to ensure that Barak, leader of Israel's army, is not mistakenly credited for the victory. The author's effort to strip the general of his glory is not motivated by hostility to Barak nor by affection for Jael but by the drive to ensure that no human warrior rivals God as the story's hero.

The same rhetorical strategy may also explain why Barak sings, and is not sung to, after the battle. Before we can take up the issue of the song's attribution in Judg 5:1, we must recognize that like the songs in Exodus 15, the song in Judges 5 was probably not composed by the author of the surrounding narrative and may in fact predate it by centuries.[55] One implication of this insight is that what the narrative says about the song may have been derived—or at least constrained—by a reading of its contents. One can argue, for example, that the narrative's attribution of the song to Deborah and Barak was derived from verse 12 in the song: "Awake, awake, Deborah! Awake, awake, utter a song! Arise Barak and lead in your captives"—which seems to single out Deborah and Barak as participants in the victory celebration.[56] An apparent redundancy in verse 3 may also have suggested to early readers that the song combines at least two distinct voices: "to the Lord I will sing/I will make melody to the Lord." In a manner characteristic of parallelism in biblical literature, the second half of this line simply elaborates upon the point made in the first half.[57] It is possible, however, to (mis)read the line as if it recorded two separate statements uttered by two different individuals—first Deborah sang: "to the Lord I will sing"; then Barak responded: "I will make melody to the Lord." Later Jews often overinterpreted parallelism in this way even as they employed it correctly in their own writings, and it is conceivable that similar overreadings occurred in the biblical period as well.[58] A different but related explanation accounts for why the narrative's author did not include the rest of Israel in the song's performance. We have seen that the attribution of the songs in Exodus 15 to all of Israel was central to the role of these songs within the narrative, which seeks to demonstrate that God had won the unanimous support of a people once ready to serve the Egyptians. It is also important to note, however, that this claim is consistent with what the songs themselves say, or were thought to have said, about their performance: in verse 21 Miriam uses the masculine plural verb "sing" ("Sing to the Lord") as if she were addressing a group of males or males mixed with females, not a single individual. There is nothing in this or any other detail in the song that demands the conclusion that the entire Exodus generation sang it, but it does warrant such a conclusion. If the narrative role of Judges 5 is truly analogous to that of the songs in Exodus 15, one would expect it to be attributed to all the people as well. The song is not so attributed, I believe, because the scribe who incorporated it within the narrative was constrained by what he found in the song. Judges 5 makes clear that several tribes did not show up for the battle, which would suggest to someone looking for clues in the song about who sang it that the entire people was not present to celebrate the victory either. To claim that the people joined in the singing would be to contradict the testimony of the only surviving eyewitness to the song's performance, the song itself.[59]

All this suggests that the narrative's attribution of the song represents an act of interpretation based on what the song itself reveals about the circumstances of its performance. Even as I make this point, however, I would also argue that the author/redactor of Judges 4–5 was predisposed to this interpretation by the rhetorical requirements of the preceding story. Implicit in Deborah's prophecy in 4:9, where she explicitly proclaims that the Lord will deliver Sisera into the hand of a woman, is a rebuke of Barak *for not interpreting the battle properly*. In response to Deborah's request to lead the Israelites out into battle, Barak agrees on the condition that the prophetess herself will accompany him: "If you will go with me, I will go, but if you will not go with me, I will not go" (4:8). Barak's hesitancy costs him the glory of victory because it reveals his failure to recognize that it is God and not Deborah who ensures victory (Barak's doubts about God are made even more explicit in the Greek version of the narrative, where Barak adds, "for I never know what day the angel of the Lord will give me success"). For the author of the story, this is not simply a misunderstanding; it is *the* misunderstanding that threatens to undermine the central point of his narrative—that God is the hero of the story. It is for this reason that through the authoritative figure of Deborah the author immediately rules out Barak as a possible hero and reasserts God's role: "The road on which you are going will not lead to *your* glory, for the Lord will sell Sisera into the hand of a woman." The attribution of the song in Judg 5:1 to both Deborah and Barak furthers this strategy by indicating that in the end even the obtuse general came to recognize God's role as the hero of the battle. Like the Israelites at the Red Sea, who at first do not believe that God will save them from the Egyptians, Barak's attitude changes over the course of the narrative, evolving from incomprehension to affirmation of God. Barak's participation in the song signals that his view of the battle has finally converged with that of Deborah, who has all along recognized God's central role in the battle. In this light, the attribution of the song to both Deborah and Barak does not *simply* reflect a reading of the song's contents; it also helps to shape how the preceding narrative is read by making a figure within it, Barak, undergo the perspectival transformation the audience is meant to undergo as it follows the story.

We find then that the narrative role of the Song of Deborah and Barak is quite similar to the narrative role of the songs in Exodus 15. If we had only the biblical evidence at our disposal, we might explain this similarity by supposing that the mixing of song and story in one episode has been influenced by the other. The testimony of the Piye Stela offers another possible explanation, however: the insertions of the songs in Exodus 15 and Judges 5 within their respective narrative settings may simply represent independent manifestations of a single conventional form of closure taken over from Egyptian battle accounts. As it was originally developed, the form was intended to promote the king as invincible ruler and to render him the hero of battles in which he did not personally participate. As it was adapted by the authors of biblical narrative, it served to promote God as invincible ruler and to render him the hero of battles in which his participation was difficult to represent.

But what about all the other songs in biblical narrative? Do they also reflect the same conventional form of closure? This is where our hypothesis runs into a problem. My reading of the biblical and extrabiblical evidence clearly suggests that the songs in Exodus 15 and Judges 5 reflect a scribal convention connected specifically to the composition of battle accounts, but many of the other songs within biblical narrative do not appear in such a context. The so-called Song of Moses in Deuteronomy 32, for example, does not appear at the end of a battle account; nor do its contents celebrate a victory. As we will see in the next chapter, the song's narrative introduction in Deuteronomy 31 describes it as a document which Moses teaches to Israel shortly before his death. This example, along with other songs to be introduced later in our investigation, clearly resists the explanation we have developed for Exodus 15 and Judges 5. Does this mean that we have somehow gone astray in our effort to understand why biblical narrative so often combines song and story?

While we have indeed reached an impasse, I hope now to convince the reader that we have not been on the wrong road. Beginning in the next chapter I will present evidence that the insertion of songs within biblical narrative represents not repeated manifestations of the same literary practice but a congeries of disparate scribal behaviors tied to different genres of narrative. If I am right in this claim, what I have suggested for the songs in Exodus 15 and Judges 5 is inapplicable to other songs in biblical narrative not because it is wrong but because it represents only one piece of a larger puzzle, one reason among many that songs appear in biblical narrative. The purpose of chapter 3 is to provide a second piece of this puzzle by showing that the narrative role of the Song of Moses in Deuteronomy 32 was shaped by a scribal practice fundamentally different from that underlying the insertion of songs in Exodus 15 and Judges 5.

·3·

SWAN SONG

In the collective imagination of the ancient world the most significant words of a person's lifetime were those spoken just before death. This was the time when the wise traditionally epitomized their wisdom, when the powerful shared the secrets of their success, when the righteous revealed what they had learned about the good life. This fascination with the words of dying is reflected in dozens of texts from the ancient Near East and Mediterranean which purport to be the final speeches or testaments of kings, sages, and other figures of high social status. The majority of extant examples are from the Hellenistic period or later, including, for example, the *Testaments of the Twelve Patriarchs,* which preserves the deathbed speeches of Jacob's twelve sons, the parting words of Greek sages such as Apollonius of Tyana, the political testaments of Persian kings reflected in Iranian epic literature, and the last words of rabbinic sages to their disciples.[1] But there is substantial evidence that the words of the dying enjoyed a special status in pre-Hellenistic antiquity as well. Both Plato and Xenophon record the last words of Socrates before his death. Even earlier than this is the so-called *Instruction of Ptah-hotep,* the final teaching of an Egyptian official to his son, which suggests that in Egypt of the late third millennium B.C.E. the words of the dying were looked to for wisdom and practical advice about proper social behavior.[2] And the Bible contains several farewell speeches spoken by dying patriarchs and leaders in prophetic anticipation of their descendants' future in the land of Canaan. These examples show that the last-words topos was established and widely disseminated long before the Hellenistic age, surfacing in classical Greece, ancient Egypt, and biblical Israel.

In this chapter I posit that the narrative role of the Song of Moses in Deuteronomy 32 was shaped by conventions specific to the last-words literary topos. Scholars have long recognized that the entire book of Deuteronomy represents Moses' farewell speech to Israel, resembling in several respects the valedictory speeches punctuating "Deuteronomistic" compositions such as Joshua, Samuel, and Kings (e.g., the valedictory speech of Joshua in Joshua 23, Samuel in 1 Samuel 12, and David in 1 Kings 2).[3] What has not been noticed until now is that beyond the general affinity of Deuteronomy with testamentary literature, the Song of Moses and its narrative introduction bear a particularly close relationship to this kind of literature. By identifying these similarities, as I propose to do, we can gain a deeper understanding of both how the Song of Moses functions in its narrative setting and why this function is so different from those of the songs in Exodus 15 and Judges 5.

Particularly important for our investigation is the fact that ancient Near Eastern last words are often introduced by prologues which describe the speaker and setting of the last words, for it is here that the conventional characteristics of this literary tradition are most easily recognized. A survey of the various deathbed pronouncements, final testaments, and valedictory speeches found in the Bible and ancient Near Eastern literature reveals that there is no single characteristic shared by the last words themselves which can be used as an identifying marker. Some last words consist of sayings and proverbs loosely organized around central themes (the *Instructions of Ptah-hotep*); others have the form of an hortatory speech couched in prose (Cyrus's last words in Xenophon's *Education of Cyrus,* the *Testaments of the Twelve Patriarchs*); and still others appear as poetic blessings or prophecies (the Blessing of Jacob in Genesis 49, the Blessing of Moses in Deuteronomy 33, the last words of David in 2 Samuel 23). What connects these texts is not their content but how this content is contextualized: they all begin with some sort of preamble—sometimes a brief note, sometimes a lengthy narrative—that introduces the discourse as words uttered by the speaker in anticipation of his death. Deut 31:14-30, the narrative which introduces the Song of Moses, shares this defining feature of last-words literature, explicitly connecting the song to the fact that Moses is about to die: "The Lord said to Moses, 'Soon you will lie down with your ancestors. . . . Now therefore write this song. . . .'" (vss. 16-19). A conventional sign of the last-words topos, the narrative's reference to Moses' impending death suggests that we should begin by viewing what the narrative says about the song's purpose and meaning against the backdrop of other ancient Near Eastern prologues used to introduce the words of the dying.

But first a point of clarification is in order. In what follows we will not be investigating how the Song of Moses per se relates to last-words literature. Like the Song of the Sea and the Song of Deborah, the Song of Moses was probably not composed by the scribe who incorporated it into the narrative.[4] No one knows why or by whom the song was first composed, though it seems highly unlikely that it was composed by a dying Moses, since it refers to events (e.g., Israel's settlement in the land) that supposedly took place after his death. This much is clear, however. If one reads the song outside of its literary setting in Deuteronomy, one notices that its words contain no specific reference to the events of the preceding narrative.

Nowhere does it allude to Moses' impending death, describe itself as his last words, or even mention the prophet by name. In fact, as G. E. Wright and others have shown, the song's form and structure are quite conventional, exhibiting the generic traits of the so-called covenant-lawsuit genre, which was used repeatedly in prophetic literature to condemn Israel for violating its covenant (see Isaiah 1, Jeremiah 2, and Micah 6 for other examples).[5] We will see that the "lawsuit" elements within the song are in fact essential to its narrative role but that the significance of these elements within the narrative is different from what it is outside this context. To understand how the song's contents serve .its narrative role, therefore, we must seek to determine how the song was interpreted by the author who incorporated it within its present literary setting, and this brings us by another route to Deuteronomy 31. My goal is to show that this narrative's interpretation of the Song of Moses—how it represents the song, how it contextualizes its performance, how it reads its contents—has been shaped by conventions specific to last-words literature.

As it happens, it is precisely at the points where the author of Deuteronomy 31 seems to have misunderstood the song that we can first detect how his interpretation was influenced by the last-words topos. Consider the narrative's claim that the song was composed in anticipation of the future. According to Deuteronomy 31, the song was not composed by Moses himself; it was revealed to him by the Lord as part of a forecast of Israel's future in the land of Canaan.

And the Lord said to Moses, "Soon you will lie down with your ancestors. Then the people will begin to prostitute themselves to the foreign gods in their midst, the gods of the land into which they are going; they will forsake me, breaking my covenant that I have made with them. My anger will be kindled against them in that day. I will forsake them and hide my face from them; they will become easy prey; and many terrible troubles will come upon them. In that day they will say, "Have not these troubles come upon us because our God is not in our midst?" On that day I will surely hide my face on account of all the evil they have done by turning to other gods. Now therefore write this song and teach it to the Israelites; put it in their mouths in order that this song may be a witness for me against the Israelites. For when I have brought them into the land flowing with milk and honey which I promised on oath to their ancestors, and they have eaten their fill and grown fat, they will turn to other gods and serve them, despising me and breaking my covenant. And when many terrible troubles come upon them, this song will confront them as a witness, because it will not be lost from the mouths of their descendants. For I know what they

> are inclined to do even now, before I have brought them into the
> land that I promised them on oath." (Deut 31:16-21)

Nothing within the song itself suggests that it was composed in anticipation
of events yet to come; to the contrary, it refers to Israel's settlement in
the land *as if this had happened in the remote past.*

> Remember the days of old, consider the years long past; ask your
> father and he will inform you; your elders, and they will tell you
> . . . [the Lord] set him atop the heights of the land, and fed him
> with produce of the field; he nursed him with honey from the crags
> and oil from the rock . . . [but the people] sacrificed to demons,
> not God, to deities they had never known, to new ones recently
> arrived whom your ancestors had not feared. (Deut 32:7, 13, 17)

The song's repeated calls to examine the past do not sound like the words
of someone looking ahead to Israel's future. The author of Deuteronomy
31 seems to have been aware of this and to have built into his narrative
an explanation for the song's retrospective cast. God revealed the song to
Moses in advance of the events it describes, but those for whom the song
was really intended are Israel's descendants, those who will one day commit
the sins forecasted by the song. It is only when they have been punished
for their sins, when they realize finally that God has abandoned them,
that the song's words will have reached its intended audience, revealing
to the Israelites why there are suffering: "And when many terrible troubles
come upon them, this song will confront them as a witness." Thus, while
the song was recited by Moses in anticipation of Israel's future in the land,
it was intended to be understood only after this future had been fulfilled.
This is a clever, if somewhat convoluted, explanation for how the song
can be both prophetic and retrospective at the same time, but it raises a
rather basic question: if there is nothing in the song to indicate that it
was recited by Moses in anticipation of Israel's future, one wonders why
it was interpreted in this way. It would seem more logical to have incorporated the song at a point in Israel's history when the events it describes
in the past tense are indeed in the past.

We may never fully understand why the author of Deuteronomy 31
read the song as a divinely revealed prophecy. Once the song was attributed
to Moses, it was almost inevitable that it was understood as a prophecy,
since it refers to events after Moses' death, but it is not clear why it was
attributed to Moses in the first place. There appears to have been something
in or about the song which suggested to the author of the incorporating
narrative that the "I" in the first line ("I will speak") was Moses, but it is
not clear what this something was. Perhaps it was the song's repeated use

of didactic language (e.g., Deut 32:2: "May my teaching drop like the rain," "Remember the days of old"), which suits Deuteronomy's description of Moses as a teacher. Or perhaps it was the song's reference to the wilderness period (vss. 10-12), the time when Moses lived.

Whatever triggered the song's attribution, evidence from ancient Near Eastern last-words literature *does* shed light on why the song—reinterpreted as a Mosaic prophecy—was situated in Moses' final days. I have already mentioned that many ancient cultures believed that the dying were sometimes granted the power to see the future. Consider what Socrates says just before his death in Plato's *Phaedo* 84e-85b, where the sage draws an explicit connection between death, song, and prophecy.

> Evidently you think that I have less insight into the future than a swan; because when these birds feel that the time has come for them to die, they sing more loudly and sweetly than they have sung in all their lives before, for joy that they are going away into the presence of the god whose servants they are. . . . I believe that the swans, belonging as they do to Apollo, have prophetic powers and sing because they know the good things that await them in the unseen world. . . . Now I consider that I am in the same service as the swans, and dedicated to the same god; and that I am no worse endowed with prophetic powers than they are.[6]

It is not known why or when the ancients first concluded that the dying were sometimes granted prophetic powers, but the idea is found in almost every corner of the ancient Mediterranean, surfacing in Greece, in Egypt, and most clearly in Israel, as indicated by the last words of Jacob in Genesis 49 and Joseph in Gen 50:24 and by the forecasts found throughout early Jewish and Christian testamentary literature.[7] In fact, there are signs that early postbiblical Jews were specifically interested in what happened to Moses just before his death and believed that he was granted a vision of the future. In the *Testament of Moses*, a text composed in the first or second century C.E. that purports to be the last words of Moses to Joshua, Moses prophesies much of the history of Israel from the conquest to the end of the Second Temple Period.[8] Similarly, the rabbis claimed that just before his death Moses was given a glimpse of the eschatological Jerusalem.[9] Such evidence testifies that early Jews believed that Moses was granted a vision of the future just before his death. Deuteronomy 31-32 shows that at least one biblical author shared this belief and that it shaped his interpretation of the Song of Moses.

The song's presentation as prophecy is perhaps the most obvious way in which its narrative role bears the imprint of the last-words literary tradition, but it is by no means the only way. Against the backdrop of the

last-words tradition, we can better understand the curious mixture of didactic and legal language which appears in Deuteronomy 31-32, a mixture
which scholars have noticed but never really explained. According to
Deuteronomy 31, the song is at once instructional and incriminatory, functioning both as a teaching which Israel must learn and recite ("teach it
to the Israelites; put it in their mouths") and as a "witness" which accuses
Israel of wrongdoing and justifies its sufferings ("when many terrible troubles come upon them, this song will confront them as a witness"). No one
has been able to account for why the song is represented by Deuteronomy
31 in this way. It is possible, of course, that the narrative's description
simply reflects its author's reading of the song's contents, which itself consists of a fusion of didactic/wisdom and forensic/accusatory elements.
Mixed within the song are didactic terminology and motifs (the song refers
to itself as a teaching in verse 2 and exhorts Israel to remember and
understand in verse 7) alongside the formal characteristics of a lawsuit
(the song contains a summons to heaven and earth as witnesses in verse
1; a formal indictment of Israel for its sins in verses 19-20; an oath in
verse 40; and a pronouncement of sentence in verses 19-29).[10] Even if
this intermingling of didactic and lawsuit elements is what lies behind the
narrative's description of the song, however, this observation does not so
much answer our questions as force us to revise them: How do these
elements relate to one another within the song? Does their fusion serve
the song's narrative role? And why would a song of such content be attributed to Moses in his dying days? Having identified the song as Moses'
final teaching, I believe that the place to look for answers to these questions
is the last-words tradition. What this perspective reveals is that the seemingly
incongruous fusion of didactic and lawsuit strains within the song and its
prologue actually adheres to a conventional literary logic reflected elsewhere in ancient Near Eastern last-words literature.

Let us turn first to the song's role as a teaching. Even a cursory survey
of last-words literature comes up with several texts from ancient Egypt
and Greece where the words of the dying are explicitly represented as
instructions or teachings, as the Song of Moses is. The *Instruction of Ptah-
hotep,* for example, explicitly describes the sage's speech to his son as a
teaching: "Teach thou him first about speaking. Then he may set an example for the children of the officials." Writing several millennia later and
on the other side of the Mediterranean, the Greek historian Xenophon
envisioned the last words of the Persian King Cyrus as a teaching: "My
children and all my friends who are present, the end of my life is near
. . . perchance I teach you sufficiently as to how you are to be to one
another, but if not learn from what has happened in the past."[11] The song
in Deuteronomy 32—both as it is described by the preceding narrative
and in its own right—shares much in common with these texts. God orders

Moses to teach the song to Israel (Deut 31:19) just as the king orders Ptah-hotep to teach his son about speaking; and the song itself makes frequent use of didactic language and motifs, even exhorting its audience to learn from the past as Cyrus does (Deut 32:7 "Remember the days of old, consider the years long ago"). These similarities do not necessarily imply that the song was intended by its original author as a valedictory teaching, any more than it was composed as a dying prophecy. They do nonetheless shed light on why the song was understood in this way by the scribe who inserted it within the narrative. For him, as for the author of *Ptah-hotep* and for Xenophon, the end of life was a time not only for prophecy but for pedagogy as well, the last opportunity for the dying to teach wisdom to the living. This is especially true when the dying person has functioned in life as a sage or teacher. Since Deuteronomy presents Moses as a teacher—it reports that Moses "taught" God's commandments and attributes to him forms of speech typical of pedagogical rhetoric in the ancient Near East[12]—it is not surprising to find that his role as pedagogue carries over into his last words, as is the case with the last words of Ptah-hotep and Socrates. And with its didactic terminology, its exhortations to learn from the past, and its rebuke of the Israelites for their intellectual shortcomings, the song in Deuteronomy 32—whatever its original function and setting—was well suited to play the role of final teaching.

From this vantage point, in fact, we can better understand one of the most puzzling elements within the narrative of Deuteronomy 31. In the midst of its description of the song's origin and purpose, Deuteronomy abruptly shifts its attention to a "torah" which Moses is said to transcribe into a book and deposit next to the ark of the covenant:

> That very day Moses wrote *this song* and taught it to the Israelites. Then the Lord commissioned Joshua, son of Nun, and said, "Be strong and bold, for you shall bring the Israelites into the land that I promised them; I will be with you." When Moses had finished writing down in a book the words of *this torah* to the very end, Moses commanded the Levites who carried the ark of the covenant of the Lord, saying, "Take *this book of the torah* and put it beside the ark of the covenant of the Lord your God; let it remain there as a witness against you. . . . " Then Moses recited the words of *this song*, to the very end, in the hearing of the whole assembly of Israel. (Deut 31:22-30)

The relationship of the "torah" mentioned in verses 24-26 to the "song" described in 19-22 and mentioned again in Deut 31:30 has long perplexed scholars. Do the terms "song" and "torah" refer to the same document? Does the narrative intend two different documents? Has the text of

Deuteronomy 31 been confused or corrupted in some way? Many explanations have been proposed, ranging from hypothetical textual emendation
to complex reconstructions of the narrative's redactional logic, but no
consensus has emerged.[13] I incline toward the view of Von Rad, who concludes that a narrative "originally treating of the law was by a rather superficial revision applied to the song,"[14] with one significant difference: I would
translate the word *torah* not as "law" (a translation which originates with
the Septuagint) but as "instruction" or "teaching," a rendering which is
consistent with the way this word is used throughout Deuteronomy and
other didactic texts, such as Proverbs.[15] The resulting reformulation of
Von Rad's suggestion—a narrative originally treating an *instruction* was by
a rather superficial revision applied to the song—is consistent with the
other evidence which suggests that the song functions within the narrative
as a teaching. It also makes possible an explanation for why the narrative
in Deuteronomy 31 refers to Deuteronomy 32 both as a song and as an
instruction. The label "instruction" is used to introduce a wide variety of
literary genres in the ancient Near East, apparently describing only their
function, not their form. The Egyptian word for "instruction" (*Sb3y.t*), for
example, is used to introduce proverbial collections, laments, autobiogra-
phies, satires, and other literary forms.[16] Something similar appears to be
true of the word for "instruction" in biblical Hebrew ("torah" in the Bible
can refer to laws, proverbs, and other genres). What may be going on,
therefore, is that in the present redactional form of Deuteronomy 31,
"torah" and "song" refer to the same text, the former referring to the
function of the song, the latter to its literary form.

We will have more to say about the song's role as a "torah," but first
we must turn to its role as a "witness against Israel." How does this description of the song relate to its role as Moses' final act of instruction?
And what of the legal and accusatorial elements within the song itself,
elements so prominent that the song is classified by many scholars as a
lawsuit? Do these elements reflect the last-words tradition in any way, or
is this where our comparison falls short?

The Bible itself shows that the phrase "witness against" often appears
in the context of valedictory speeches, especially in the so-called Deuteronomistic History (Deuteronomy-2 Kings). In his farewell speech to the
people (1 Sam 12:1-5), for example, the prophet Samuel invokes both
the Lord and his anointed as a "witness against" Israel lest at some future
time the people deny that it has found Samuel innocent of all wrongdoing
during his tenure as its leader. An even closer parallel to Deuteronomy
31 is the valedictory speech of Joshua spoken just before his death in Josh
24:29, where he invokes a great stone as "a witness against" the people
lest it deal falsely with the Lord (Josh 24:27). In both cases, a dying leader
invokes someone or something that will survive him—the future king, God,

a stone—and will therefore be able to testify against the people should they violate their obligations in his absence. The Song of Moses plays a similar function, according to Deuteronomy 31, serving as a witness against Israel whenever it forsakes God. The people's continual recitation of the song (vs. 21, "It will not be lost from the mouths of their descendants"), along with Moses' preservation of it in writing (vss. 19, 22), ensure that it will survive after Moses' death, ever ready to condemn Israel on the day it violates its covenant. In this sense, the song's role is similar to that of the stone which Joshua sets up in his last days, deposited by Moses to testify against Israel for sins committed after his death.

What remains unexplained by all this is why the Song of Moses is said to function *both* as a teaching and as a witness against Israel. None of the Egyptian, Greek, or biblical texts discussed so far sheds any light on how these two functions relate to one another. There is, however, one other last-words composition from the ancient Near East which may be able to help us. Known as the *Words of Ahiqar* after its hero, the Assyrian sage Ahiqar, this text is preserved in several versions, the oldest of which was discovered on the island of Elephantine in southern Egypt, buried in the ruins of a Persian-period fortress that had been inhabited by Jewish mercenaries.[17] Despite its fragmentary nature, *Ahiqar* appears to have consisted originally of a collection of sayings prefaced by a narrative which introduces it as a teaching from the sage to his heir Nadan.[18] My reason for drawing this text into our investigation is that its narrative section shares many similarities with Deuteronomy 31, similarities which are so striking that they suggest some sort of literary relationship between the two texts. In the context of our investigation, however, these similarities are most important not for what they reveal about Deuteronomy's connection to other ancient Near Eastern texts but for what they reveal about the narrative role of the Song of Moses. For it turns out that *Ahiqar* combines didactic and legal language within the context of a sage's last words in a way that can help us better understand the combination of didactic and legal language within Deuteronomy 31-32.

A comparison of the narratives in Deuteronomy 31 and *Ahiqar* reveals that they share four motifs, the first of which is already familar to us. At the beginning of each narrative, the central figure of the narrative realizes that death is near and appoints—or has appointed for him—a successor. Ahiqar, realizing that he is about to die without an heir, appoints his nephew Nadan as his heir.[19] Although Moses plays a more passive role—his impending death is revealed to him, and his successor is appointed for him by God—he, like Ahiqar, realizes that he is old and is to be replaced (Deut 31:14, 23). This parallel alone does not represent evidence of a specific relationship between *Ahiqar* and Deuteronomy 31, for, as we have seen, other ancient Near Eastern texts begin in a similar way as well. It is possible, however, to supplement this shared motif with parallels between Deuteronomy 31 and *Ahiqar* that are absent in other last-words prologues. Viewed collectively, such parallels strengthen the possibility of a common ancestry behind the two narratives that is not shared by other texts in the tradition.

Consider the second shared motif, the betrayal of the sage by those he has looked after. In both *Ahiqar* and Deuteronomy, the figure or figures to whom the sage issues his final teaching—Nadan in *Ahiqar,* the children of Israel in Deuteronomy 31—prove ungrateful for the many benefactions granted by the author of the teaching, grow spoiled, and eventually betray the benefactor. In the Elephantine version Nadan is said to have executed a plot against his generous uncle after being installed in the palace gate.[20] This plot development has been expanded in later versions of *Ahiqar*. In the Syriac version, for instance, Nadan receives a variety of luxurious privileges from his uncle—eight wet nurses, choice carpets, a diet of honey[21]—and responds by abusing Ahiqar's servants, mistreating his animals, and, finally, accusing the sage himself of senility.[22] The children of Israel, the recipients of God's benefactions in Deuteronomy 31, display a similar ingratitude. Although God treats them to a land of milk and honey, like Nadan's eight wet nurses and diet of honey, Israel's response is to grow fat, turn to other gods, and abandon its covenant with the Lord (Deut 31:16, 20). In both cases, the recipients of the sage's final teaching turn against the patrons responsible for their well-being. Of course, the theme of Israel's ingratitude is by no means unique to Deuteronomy 31—it is found throughout the Bible, even surfacing elsewhere in Deuteronomy.[23] The value of the parallel lies not in the motif of ingratitude itself, however, but in its application to the story of a sage's final teaching. The depiction of the teaching's recipient as unappreciative and resistant to the teacher's authority surfaces only in Deuteronomy 31 and *Ahiqar;* it appears nowhere else in ancient Near Eastern last-words literature prior to the Hellenistic age.[24]

The third shared motif, the disowning of the teacher's heir, is also specific to Deuteronomy 31 and *Ahiqar,* but here there is an added complication, for this parallel surfaces only when Deuteronomy 31 is compared with later versions of *Ahiqar*. According to many of these versions, Ahiqar, realizing that his nephew has grown incorrigibly corrupt, disowns and banishes him. This action resembles God's behavior in Deut 31:17-18; foreseeing that Israel will become incorrigibly corrupt, God predicts that he will have to "forsake them and hide his face from them." Later versions of *Ahiqar* also recount the indignant and uncomprehending response of the now-disinherited Nadan. The Syriac version, for instance, reports that Nadan blames his banishment not on his own profligacy but on his patron's declining intellect: "Ahiqar my father has grown old and his wisdom has diminished;

and he has made foolish his wise words. Has he given his wealth to Nebuzardan my brother, and has he removed me from his house?"[25] In the future described by Deuteronomy 31, the children of Israel likewise realize that God has withdrawn from them, and they also fail to acknowledge that it was their own misdeeds which caused the breach—"Have not these evils come upon us because our God [or "our gods"—the Hebrew allows both translations] is not among us?" (Deut 31:17). Like Nadan, Israel's alienation from its patron reaches a climax when it fails to recognize that this alienation and the concomitant loss of benefits are the result of its own disloyalty.

As I have suggested, this third parallel is problematic because it appears only when one compares Deuteronomy 31 with later versions of *Ahiqar,* which arose long after the composition of Deuteronomy 31 and might themselves have been influenced by biblical literature. There is evidence, however, that the Elephantine text was not the only form of Ahiqar's being circulated in antiquity and that alternative forms of the narrative sometimes surface only in later forms of the tale. According to the Egyptologist Miriam Lichtheim, for example, the *Instruction of Ankhsheshonqy,* a demotic text which was heavily influenced by the *Ahiqar* story, is more closely related to later versions of *Ahiqar* than to that found at Elephantine.[26] There are also signs in the later versions themselves—particularly the Syriac and the Armenian—that they preserve elements from much earlier stages in the story's history.[27] It is thus conceivable that Deuteronomy 31 is most closely related not to the form of the narrative from the Elephantine *Ahiqar* but to an alternative form of the story, now lost but nevertheless dimly reflected in later versions. Given this possibility, there is no inherent reason to dismiss the third parallel on the grounds that it surfaces only when Deuteronomy 31 is compared with later versions of *Ahiqar.*

The fourth and most striking motif shared by *Ahiqar* and Deuteronomy 31 is the transmission of the teaching itself in both written and oral form. Both Deuteronomy 31 and later versions of *Ahiqar* note that the sage issues his final teaching in two forms: in oral form to a contemporary audience and in written form to an audience at a spatial or temporal distance. According to Deut 31:22 and 30, Moses first writes the song down and then recites it "in the ears of all the assembly of Israel," while, according to Syriac *Ahiqar,* before the sage addresses his teaching to Nadan, he orders his servant Nabuel to write what he says on a "writing tablet."[28] Unfortunately, in the Elephantine version of *Ahiqar,* the text immediately preceding the presentation of the sage's words no longer survives, but the "dual transmission" motif does surface quite early in the *Ahiqar* tradition, as attested by the *Instruction of Ankhsheshonqy.* According to this text, the "final teaching" of the sage Ankhsheshonqy is orally reported to Pharaoh and his great men and is also written down on potsherds by the priest himself. It is useful to compare its narrative just before the presentation of

Ankhsheshonqy's teaching with that of Deuteronomy 31 just before the presentation of the song.

> *Ankhsheshonqy:* [Ankhsheshonqy said] "I shall write an Instruction for him [his son] and have it taken to him in Heliopolis to instruct him thereby." The staff-bearer said: "I will report it to Pharaoh first." Pharaoh commanded, saying: "Let a palette be taken to him; do not let a papyrus roll be taken to him." They took a palette to him. They did not take a papyrus roll to him. He wrote on the sherds of jars the matters which he could teach his son. . . . Here follow the words of Ankhsheshonqy son of Tjainufi who wrote on the sherds of the jars that were brought into him containing mixed wine, so as to give them as an instruction to his son, and which was reported before Pharaoh and his great men daily. . . . He wrote on the sherds of the jars the matters that he could teach his son, (as) written. . . . (4:12–5:19)[29]

> *Deuteronomy 31:19–30:* [The Lord said] "Now therefore write this song and teach it to the Israelites." . . . so Moses wrote this song and taught it to the Israelites. . . . When Moses had finished writing down in a book the words of this instruction [torah] to the very end, he commanded the Levites who carried the ark of the covenant of the Lord, saying, "Take this book of the instruction [torah] and put it beside the ark. . . ." Then Moses recited the words of this song, to the very end, in the hearing of the whole assembly of Israel.

Note that both narratives present a fairly detailed description of the physical means used to preserve the written copy of the teaching: potsherds in the case of *Ankhsheshonqy*, a book kept in the ark in the case of Deuteronomy. I suspect that the "written transmission" motif reflected in these texts represents an attempt to explain how the teaching survived after the teacher's death. In each case, after all, the sage cannot count on oral transmission alone to preserve his teaching: Ahiqar's disciple has proven unreliable; Ankhsheshonqy has no direct access to his son; and Moses must ensure the survival of the song even though Israel is destined to break its covenant with God. The purpose of the "written transmission" motif is thus to explain how the sage overcame the unreliability of oral transmission. Whatever the overall relation of Deuteronomy 31 and *Ahiqar,* this is a truly remarkable parallel because the only references to a "book of the torah" in the Pentateuch surface in Deuteronomy, and it now appears that this phrase—at least in Deuteronomy 31—reflects a motif at home in last-words literature.

It is true that the other three parallels are not quite as pronounced or distinctive as the fourth. The first of these parallels can be found elsewhere in ancient Near Eastern literature, and the third surfaces only when Deuteronomy 31 is compared with later versions of *Ahiqar*. As I see it, however, the configuration of similarities—along with the distinctiveness of the last parallel—is sufficiently striking to establish an affinity between *Ahiqar* and Deuteronomy 31-32. The precise nature of this affinity is difficult to determine. *Ahiqar* is known to have been read and recycled by a wide variety of peoples in the ancient Near East—Egyptians, Greeks, and especially Jews. In Egypt, it evidently influenced *Ankhsheshonqy* and was itself translated into demotic, as indicated by demotic ostraca from Roman Egypt which preserve portions of the story.[30] *Ahiqar* also reached the Greek-speaking world. According to Clement of Alexandria (*Stromata* 1.15.69), the fifth-century philosopher Democritus plagiarized the "Babylonian ethical sayings" of one Akikaros, while the *Life of Aesop*, a composition from the first or second century C.E., transforms Ahiqar's story into an episode in the life of the sixth-century Greek fabulist.[31] The story even made its way into Arabic, Indian, and Persian literature.[32] As for the reception of this story among Jews, the Elephantine version indicates that *Ahiqar* was already in their possession by the fifth century B.C.E. The story is also explicitly alluded to in the Jewish narrative of *Tobit* (composed in the Persian or Hellenistic periods), which remakes Ahiqar into a Jew (see *Tobit* 1:21-22, 2:10, 11:18, 14:10) and uses him as a foil for the story's title character.[33] *Ahiqar*'s plot also may have influenced the biblical stories of Daniel and Esther, which center on wise courtiers who, like Ahiqar, fall out of and then back into their patrons' favor.[34] Such evidence suggests that while the story was probably not composed by a Jew, Jews were active appropriators of it, not only reading it but also adjusting it to fit their own culture and literary purposes. This, along with the similarities between Deuteronomy 31 and *Ahiqar*, might lead one to conclude that the author of the former actually borrowed elements from the story of Ahiqar, as did the author of *Tobit*, but there are problems with this explanation. Although both *Ahiqar* and Deuteronomy are thought by many to have been composed around the seventh or sixth century B.C.E., there is no way of knowing which text is earlier.[35] Thus even if one of these works has been directly influenced by the other, it would be very difficult to determine the direction of influence. Indeed, any similarities between the two narratives may as easily stem from a common literary ancestor or an unknown intermediary as from direct influence. In light of these considerations, we must be cautious in proposing any particular explanation for why the two texts resemble one another. At the same time, however, the similarities are sufficiently numerous and in some cases so distinctive that some explanation is required. That is why I tentatively propose that a lost literary ancestor lies behind the two narratives, a conventional story type from which they have inherited their common structure. There may be other ways to account for their parallels, but as I see it, this is the most plausible given the evidence currently available.

That does not mean that one can ignore the many significant differences in how the two narratives arrange and present the four shared motifs I have described. In the *Ahiqar* narrative, the sage's final teaching is issued to Nadan after his betrayal, while in Deuteronomy 31, Moses' final teaching is issued to the children of Israel in prophetic anticipation of their betrayal of God. In *Ahiqar,* the role of thankless child is played by the sage's adopted successor, while in Deuteronomy 31 this role is played not by Moses' successor, Joshua, but by the children of Israel. Finally, in the *Ahiqar* narrative the wronged patron is also the sage issuing the instruction, while in Deuteronomy 31, the instructing sage merely speaks at the behest of the betrayed, who is God.[36] The literary evidence offers no easy way to overcome these differences, and they seriously complicate the relationship of *Ahiqar* to Deuteronomy 31.

Nonetheless, the existence of differences between the two narratives does not eliminate their many striking similarities; nor does it reduce the need to find an explanation for these similarities. Furthermore, if one considers the character of Deuteronomy and the cultural context in which it was composed, one can explain many of the contrasts between the two narratives by arguing that the author of Deuteronomy 31 has drastically reworked the narrative pattern shared by it with *Ahiqar* in accordance with an Israelite or deuteronomic perspective. In later Christian and Muslim versions of *Ahiqar,* the sage is transformed into a pious monotheist who receives oracles from God and hearkens to his commands.[37] There are also indications that Ahiqar was thought of as a prophet at an even earlier stage in the tradition's history: Strabo, the Greek geographer, claimed in the first century (*Geography* 16.2.39) that Ahiqar was a prophet who issued ordinances from the gods. It is conceivable that a comparable (albeit more daring) transformation underlies Deuteronomy 31, where many of the characteristics of the aging sage are transferred to God. Thus God—not the dying Moses—appoints the young successor, suffers the betrayal of those he has benefited, and authors the final teaching. By the same token, many of the characteristics of the treacherous successor are transferred to Israel: it is the children of Israel, not Joshua, who grow spoiled by the patron's benefactions, betray their benefactor, and are punished. While these modifications add up to a radical adaptation of the conventional pattern reflected in the *Ahiqar* narrative, it is worth recalling that this adaptation occurs in the context of Deuteronomy, which itself centers on a theologization of the pedagogue-disciple relationship, casting Israel as a pupil bidden to learn the wisdom of its divine teacher: "You must observe [God's statutes] diligently, for this will show your wisdom and discernment to the peoples" (Deut 4:6).[38] In this context, the differences between Deuteronomy 31 and *Ahiqar* can be explained as theologizing adaptations that transform the story of a dying sage betrayed by his adopted son into a cautionary tale in which a dying sage foretells God's betrayal by God's adopted children, the people of Israel.

Support for this claim comes from the Book of Isaiah. Isa 30:8-9 reads: "And now, go, write it before them on a tablet, and inscribe it in a book, that it may be for the time to come as a witness forever. For they are a rebellious people, lying sons, sons who will not hear the instruction of the Lord." Although this passage does not appear in the story of a final teaching, it shares several characteristics with both Deuteronomy 31 and *Ahiqar*. On one hand, Isa 30:8-9 resembles Deuteronomy 31, since it describes a text that has been preserved on a tablet and is to serve as a "witness" in a future time against "a rebellious people." On the other hand, this passage is reminiscent of *Ahiqar*, since it is concerned with the behavior of "lying sons . . . who will not hear instruction." The correspondence to either composition is not exact, but even so, this passage still sheds light on the relation of Deuteronomy 31 to *Ahiqar*, for it shows how a narrative like that reflected in *Ahiqar* can be "theologized" by an Israelite author. The figure of the "lying son who refuses to heed instruction" is here explicitly equated with "the rebellious people who will not heed the torah of the Lord"—the very equation implied by the attribution of Nadan-like behavior to Israel in Deuteronomy 31. Thus, not only does this passage offer corroboration that Deuteronomy 31 reflects a conventional plot pattern also manifest in *Ahiqar*; it also suggests that the theologization of this pattern was not unique to Deuteronomy 31.

Even if this evidence helps to account for the differences between the narratives of *Ahiqar* and Deuteronomy, however, we are still faced with numerous differences between the teachings themselves. There is simply no denying that both the form and the content of the Song of Moses are quite different from the loosely organized collection of proverbs and fables attributed to Ahiqar. Nonetheless, the two texts do share a highly significant trait: they both intermingle the language of pedagogy with legally tinged language of denunciation. The tone and content of Ahiqar's teaching in the Elephantine version are for the most part didactic, resembling proverb collections such as Proverbs and *Ptah-hotep*. There are a few sayings, however, which cannot be described in this way. In one, Ahiqar cries out for vindication against his slanderous heir: "Before whom will I be found innocent? My own son spied out my house? [Wh]at shall I say to strangers? He was a false witness against me. Who, then, will vindicate me?"[39] Judging from Ahiqar's use of legal language in this passage—particularly the phrases "false witness" and "vindicate," which can be found in Aramaic and biblical legal literature—one is tempted to conclude that the sage wanted to take his heir to court to clear his sullied reputation.[40] Another place where the proverbs decry Nadan's betrayal of Ahiqar is column xi lines 169-70: "My eyes which I have lifted up upon you, and my heart which I gave you in wisdom, [you have despised, and] have brought my name into disrepute."[41] It is true that these sayings, which are so well suited to the preceding narrative, were probably interpolated secondarily into the proverbs to connect them more closely with the preceding story, since almost all of the other proverbs in the collection bear little relationship to the events of the story and perhaps even predate the narrative.[42] It is precisely for this reason, however, that these sayings in the Elephantine version are so important for understanding the proverbs' role in the narrative. For they confirm that within the story the proverbs serve not only to transmit the sage's wisdom to his heir but also to rebuke Nadan for his treachery and to defend against his false accusations. The combination of didactic and legal language within the proverbs thus serves the plot requirements of the surrounding story, which calls for the sage to issue a final teaching to his heir that is at once instructional and incriminatory.

We have seen above that a similar fusion of didactic and legal/accusatory language appears in Deuteronomy 32, a fusion which has never really been explained. Some have sought to discount the didactic elements within the song by treating them as editorial accretions.[43] Others have argued that the lawsuit elements within the song—for example, the song's opening summons to heaven and earth to listen—are really misread didactic motifs paralleled in other wisdom texts, such as Proverbs.[44] Either or both of these approaches may be correct insofar as the composition of the song is concerned. In light of the *Ahiqar* comparison, however, we can see that both the didactic and the lawsuit elements within the song are essential to its present narrative role. After all, the charges laid against Israel are precisely those laid against Nadan: foolishness, moral decline, ingratitude. Indeed, the people of Israel are explicitly described by the song as "perverse," "senseless," and "rotten" children in whom there is no understanding or faithfulness (see Deut 32:5-6, 20, and 28).[45] God, described in the song as a parental figure, has treated them as if they were his own young, nursing them with honey, oil, and milk (11-14); but, fattened by his generosity, Israel forgets its patron and its obligations to him (18). Betrayed and abandoned, God threatens to hide his face from Israel (20), to punish them (21-25), and in the end he cries out for vindication (35): "vengeance is mine and vindication." In short, the song presupposes a relationship between God and Israel very similar to that of Ahiqar and Nadan, merging the language of a teacher instructing his pupil with the language of a betrayed patron rebuking his heir for his prodigality and treachery. That does not mean that the song was composed for its present narrative setting, any more than the proverbs in *Ahiqar* were composed for their present narrative setting. And, indeed, there are elements within the song that do not seem to fit its narrative role as I have described it.[46] What we are now in a position to surmise, however, is why the author of Deuteronomy 31–32 selected this particular song to serve his literary purposes.

The comparison of Deuteronomy 31 to *Ahiqar* has led us to a better understanding of why the song was inserted within Deuteronomy 31, but it has not yet accounted for the larger question of why the narrative of Deuteronomy 31–32 was included in the book of Deuteronomy. Why would a biblical author represent God as a failed pedagogue and the children of Israel as incorrigible students? For an explanation we must consider the place of the Song of Moses within the larger context of Deuteronomy— an issue of some controversy among biblical scholars. The vocabulary of Deuteronomy 31–32 is slightly different from the language used in earlier chapters of Deuteronomy, suggesting that chapters 31–32 were not composed by the author of the rest of the book.[47] According to some scholars, this section of Deuteronomy predates the rest of the book; according to others, it represents a secondary editorial expansion.[48] I have not been able to determine which view is the correct one, but I would agree that these chapters are different from the rest of the book; indeed, the difference is more than linguistic. The intellectual pessimism reflected in Deuteronomy 31–32, its suspicion that Israel will forget and betray God's commandments, cuts against the grain of much of the rest of the book. Elsewhere Deuteronomy seems to operate on the assumption that Israel can learn what it is taught, presenting an assortment of mnemonic devices to help Israel remember God's commandments (e.g., Deut 6:4–9, 11:18– 21); repeatedly warning it not to forget what it has learned (Deut 4:9, 8:11); and, just before the song itself, insisting that God's commandments are easy to master: "this commandment that I am commanding you today is not too hard for you, nor is it too far away . . . the word is very near to you; it is in your mouth and in your heart for you to observe" (Deut 30:11–14). By contrast, the basic story line reflected in Deuteronomy 31 and *Ahiqar* culminates in the failure of a sage to teach the next generation what it needs to know after his death. It is as if the song were seeking to qualify the pedagogical optimism implicit in much of the rest of Deuteronomy by prophesying a time when Israel would forget what it had learned in the days of Moses.

It turns out that there is a way to relate the intellectual pessimism of Deuteronomy 31–32 to the intellectual optimism of the rest of the book. Lurking behind both *Ahiqar* and Deuteronomy 31–32 is a pedagogical problem that troubled teachers throughout the ancient world (and the present world as well): despite their best efforts, some of their students were resistant to learning. In his dialogue *Protagoras* (319–320), Plato describes a conversation between Socrates and the sophist Protagorus in which they debate whether it is possible to teach virtue to another.[49] Socrates' comments are of particular interest to us because in supporting his position that virtue cannot be taught, he refers to an episode that is similar in certain respects to the story line reflected in *Ahiqar* and Deuteronomy 31-32. Pericles, he tells us, was appointed guardian of Cleinias, the younger brother of Alciabiades. Fearing that Cleinias would be corrupted by the immoral ways of his brother, Pericles entrusted him to the wise Ariphron to be educated, but Ariphron was unable to teach Cleinias anything and sent him back within six months. What this anecdote illustrates, according to Socrates, is that even the wisest of men cannot teach virtue to others. There is no reason to believe that the authors of *Ahiqar* and Deuteronomy 31-32 would have agreed with Socrates' conclusion that virtue is not teachable, but their narratives suggest that they too recognized that even great sages were sometimes unable to impart their wisdom to their pupils. Indeed, *Ahiqar* and Deuteronomy 31-32 can be read as responses to this problem, each suggesting a way to overcome pupils' resistance to their patrons' lessons.

The key to understanding these responses is to recognize that the final teachings of both Ahiqar and Moses are addressed to two distinct audiences: a fictional audience within the narrative and a real-life audience reading the narrative. For the audience within the narrative—Nadan in *Ahiqar* and Israel's descendants in Deuteronomy 31—the final teachings of Ahiqar and Moses function principally as chastisement, condemning them for their foolishness and defiance. The angry tone of their teachings, their cries for vindication, and their threats of punishment reflect the frustration and defensiveness of teachers who have failed in their pedagogical missions. That does not mean, however, that the authors of these narratives have given up on their pedagogical missions; to the contrary, the condemnation of the audience within the narrative is but a pretext for admonishing the audience reading the narrative about the consequences of recalcitrance. If the story of *Ahiqar* tells of an incorrigible pupil who betrays his master, it is only to serve its larger pedagogical goal of promoting strict discipline as an effective teaching device—a lesson which the Assyrian sage himself acknowledges only in the proverbs section of *Ahiqar* when it is too late to do him any good but can still benefit others: "Spare not thy son from the rod, otherwise can you save him."[50] So too the portrait of Israel in Deuteronomy 31-32 as a forgetful, spoiled pupil serves a larger pedagogical purpose, though this purpose is a bit more difficult to specify, since it depends on the identity of the narrative's intended audience. If this audience lived at a time when the song's predictions had yet to come true, Deuteronomy 31-32 offered it a chance to avoid this future by revealing what would happen if it continued to behave like the Israel described in the narrative. If, on the other hand, this audience lived at a time after the song's prophecy was thought to have been fulfilled (say, in the Babylonian exile)—if indeed it was meant to identify itself as the very generation prophesied to betray God—the song bears a very different lesson, teaching that Israel's present misfortune, like Nadan's beating by Ahiqar, is its punishment for forgetting what it had been instructed to remember. In either scenario, Israel—that is, the Israel reading Deuteronomy 31-32—is meant *to learn* from the incomprehension of the Israel described within Deuteronomy 31-32, if not to save itself from future punishment, then to understand why it is now being punished.

What this observation suggests is not only that the Song of Moses is integral to its immediate narrative setting in Deuteronomy 31—as I have tried to demonstrate by comparing it with *Ahiqar*—but that it addresses the larger concerns of Deuteronomy, at least as this book appears in its final redactional form. At some point in the editorial history of this text, one of its redactors evidently recognized, as did many other scribes and intellectuals in the ancient world, that pupils often resisted or forgot the instruction of their masters. The narrative of *Ahiqar* demonstrates that the unteachability of certain students was perceived as a serious threat to the continuity of intellectual culture, leaving teachers with no one to pass their wisdom to and students without the wisdom needed to replace their teachers. For the redactor of Deuteronomy, this unteachability also jeopardized the continuity of Israel's relationship with God, which could not survive if it was forgotten. As we have noted, much of Deuteronomy—its repeated exhortations to remember, its mnemonic devices, its assurances that the commandments of God are not too difficult to master—is designed to ensure that this does not happen. We now see that the final teaching of Moses also serves this strategy in a less direct fashion, warning its audience of what will result—or explaining what has already resulted—from Israel's failure to remember God's commandments. The role assigned to the song by its narrative setting is to dramatize the failure of the pedagogical relationship between God and Israel and the consequences of that failure so that Israel's children will never forget the dangers of forgetting. As Moses himself says to Israel when he finishes reciting the words of the song (Deut 32:46), "Take to heart all the words that I am giving in witness against you today; give them as a command to your children, so that they may diligently observe all the words of this teaching."

Our reading of Deuteronomy 32 as Moses' final teaching returns us to the same impasse we encountered at the end of the preceding chapter. There, after relating the narrative roles of the Song of the Sea and the Song of Deborah and Barak to a conventional technique of closure used in ancient Egyptian battle accounts, we noted that this analogy does not work well when extended to songs such as Deuteronomy 32. Having learned now that the narrative role of Deuteronomy 32 reflects the last-words literary tradition, we find that this analogy can likewise not be extended to the songs in Exodus 15 and Judges 5. It seems, therefore, that we have one of two choices: either we must reject both comparisons on the grounds that neither accounts for all the songs within biblical narrative or we must accept one or both as valid. The first option leads one to the conclusion that the incorporation of songs within biblical narrative is not to be understood within the context of ancient Near Eastern literary practice, since to my knowledge this literature offers no other viable analogues. The second option implies that the insertion of songs within Exodus 14-15, Judges 4-5, and Deuteronomy 31-32 reflects distinct scribal practices associated with different kinds of literature, the first two songs reflecting a conventional form of narrative closure specific to military literature and the third bearing the stamp of a didactic/wisdom tradition of "last words."

I believe that the second option is better supported by the evidence and, frankly, more interesting. Better supported by the evidence because even if we set aside the comparative evidence, we can still see that the narrative role of Deuteronomy 32, taught by Moses to the Israelites as a "witness" against their descendants, differs from that of Exodus 15 and Judges 5, which are both recited in celebration of divine victories. More interesting because it forces us to completely rethink biblical scholarship's assumptions about this phenomenon. For if the narrative roles of Exodus 15, Judges 5, and Deuteronomy 32 constitute different kinds of literary behavior, we can no longer assume, as scholars have in the past, that there is a single explanation for the insertion of songs within biblical narrative.

We can find support for this position by looking at other poetic insertions within biblical narrative. In 2 Sam 1:17-27, for example, there appears a lengthy poem introduced by its narrative setting as King David's lament after the death of Saul and Jonathan. The insertion of this lament within the narrative, I feel certain, has been determined by what I call the lament type-scene, another conventional story pattern shared by ancient Israel with a related literary culture, in this case the Late Bronze city-state of Ugarit, located in what is now Syria.[51] The structure of this type-scene, which has left its imprint on several episodes in both biblical and Ugaritic narrative, consists of three elements. It begins by describing the arrival of a messenger, who reports that someone has died. It then cites the messenger's report verbatim and describes the listener's grieved responses, enumerating them as a catalogue of actions—the rending of clothes, weeping, fasting, and so on. The episode culminates with the presentation of the mourner's verbal expression of grief, which, like the messenger's report, is cited verbatim. In appendix A, I present evidence suggesting that the incorporation of David's lament within 2 Samuel 1—following a messenger's report and an enumeration of David's physical gestures of grief—was determined by the third structural requirement of the lament type-scene, the citation of the mourner's verbal expression of grief. Recognizing the conventionality of the lament's narrative role is the key to understanding how it functions both in its immediate setting and as part of the larger narrative depiction of David's reign in 2 Samuel. It also provides corroborating evidence that the insertion of songs and other poetic material within biblical narrative reflects several distinct literary forms used in the composition of different kinds of narrative and serving different rhetorical purposes.

Having reached this conclusion, however, we are far from a complete understanding of why songs appear in biblical narrative. By approaching the Bible as an ancient Near Eastern document, shaped by literary conventions and traditions related to those of cultures from the same era and region, we can explain the insertion of some songs, but not all. Nothing found in ancient Near Eastern literature can account for why this practice endured for so long and appears so frequently in the literature of ancient Israel and its successor religions, Judaism and Christianity. Songs are incorporated into biblical narratives of every conceivable date, from narratives presumably composed long before the fall of the First Temple in 586 B.C.E. (e.g., Judges 4-5) to narratives composed late in the Second Temple period, in the second or first century B.C.E. (e.g., the Greek versions of Daniel 3, which contain the Song of the Three). Songs appear in even greater numbers in postbiblical compositions from the centuries just before and after the fall of the Second Temple in 70 C.E., including narratives within the so-called Apocrypha (e.g. *Tobit, Judith*), the Pseudepigrapha (e.g., the *Apocalypse of Abraham* and Pseudo-Philo's *Biblical Antiquities*), and the New Testament (the Gospel of Luke). Even rabbinic tradition, put in writing long after 70 C.E., often imputes songs to biblical figures, as we will see in the next chapter. While ancient Near Eastern literary practice may shed light on the interaction of song and story in individual episodes like Exodus 14-15, Judges 4-5, and Deuteronomy 31-32, it does not account for the persistence and pervasiveness of this compositional form in biblical and postbiblical literary history.

Something else needs to be explained as well. So far we have focused on the differences between the songs in biblical narrative—the different ways in which they relate to their narrative settings and the different functions which they serve within those settings. But there are also undeniable similarities which cannot be ignored. Many of the songs in biblical and postbiblical narrative celebrate acts of divine intervention—the miraculous birth of a child (the Prayer of Hannah in 1 Samuel 2, the Magnificat in Luke 1) or a miraculous escape from danger (the Psalm of Jonah, the song of Daniel's three friends in the Greek versions of Daniel 3). Many have been placed at the end of literary units, either at the end of an episode (e.g., the Prayer of Hannah, the Psalm of Hezekiah in Isaiah 38) or near the end of a book (the Hymn of Tobit in *Tobit* 13, the Hymn of Judith in *Judith* 16). In some cases, in fact, the narrative position of one song is so similar to that of a second that scholars sometimes conclude that they were inserted by the same hand. The narrative position of the Song of David (2 Samuel 22), for instance, is strikingly similar to the narrative position of the Song of Moses: both appear at analogous points in the books of Deuteronomy and 2 Samuel; both are imputed to a major Israelite leader shortly before his death; and both are immediately followed by a second poetic passage—Moses' blessing in Deuteronomy 33, David's "last words" in 2 Samuel 23.[52] Impressed by these similarities, some scholars have claimed that the insertion of the Song of Moses and the Song of David represents the work of a single editor or school;[53] others, that one song has been inserted in imitation of the other.[54] Whatever the explanation, the narrative role of each song appears to be related in some way to that of the other, and our use of comparative evidence has given us no way to probe this relationship. It has shown us differences in how the songs relate to their narrative settings, but it has little to say about their similarities.

As we proceed with our investigation, therefore, a course correction is required. Thus far we have established that the songs represent different kinds of literary behavior. In the next two chapters we will consider evidence which leads us in the opposite direction, suggesting that the songs reflect a single literary convention. We have seen that the narrative roles of Exodus 15 and Deuteronomy 32 are related to literary forms shared by Israel with other ancient literary cultures. We will now explore why, at the same time, biblical narrative's mixing of song and story can be seen as unique, surfacing in biblical and postbiblical narrative with a frequency and consistency that are without parallel in the ancient Near East. All this may seem to take us in a very different direction from the one we have followed in chapters 2 and 3, but actually it complements our argument there. For what we will discover is that the act of inserting songs within biblical narrative changed over the course of Israelite literary history, evolving from an assortment of disparate Near Eastern scribal practices into a fully formed literary convention unique to the Bible and the later religious literatures which sought to emulate it.

·4·

SING TO THE LORD
A NEW SONG

The evolution of biblical literature took place over a long period, and in rare instances this evolution can actually be observed. What renders its development visible is the existence of several versions of the Bible—especially the Hebrew text in the Masoretic Bible, the Septuagint, and the biblical fragments from Qumran—which differ from one another in thousands of tiny and hundreds of not so tiny ways. Most of the differences arose as the Bible was copied by scribes who, over the course of centuries, introduced myriad errors and deliberate changes into its text. Some differences attest, however, to an early period in the Bible's literary history, originating when biblical compositions were still in the process of formation, revision, and redaction. It sometimes happened that a biblical composition was transmitted in written form before it was considered to be a finished literary product, resulting in two or more versions of the composition which reflect various stages in its development. The Bible itself describes this phenomenon, reporting in Jeremiah 36 that the words of Jeremiah were written on a scroll and recited publicly (vss. 1-10) before they were later recopied and expanded in a second scroll (vs. 32). The original version of Jeremiah's scroll was said to have been burned (vss. 20-26), but in other cases the earlier formulations of a composition survive, having been put into circulation before the final version was completed. These earlier versions can sometimes be recovered from non-Masoretic versions of the Bible (Septuagint, Qumran fragments) or from parallel texts within the Masoretic Bible itself (e.g. 2 Kings 20 = Isaiah 38). We can return to Jeremiah for an example. The Septuagint preserves a shorter text than that reflected in the Masoretic Bible, a text which some scholars believe reflects an earlier edition of Jeremiah.[1] The two versions thus provide us with snapshots of Jeremiah at different stages in its redaction history. By comparing these "snapshots" we can trace the growth of this work from an early stage in its development to the final literary form now venerated as canonical.

Some songs in biblical narrative offer us this kind of opportunity to

observe the Bible in the process of formation. If I am right about the
Song of the Sea and the Song of Moses, they were added by the author
of the incorporating narrative at the time of the narrative's composition
(though the songs themselves may have been composed centuries before
the narrative). The same cannot be said of other songs in biblical narrative,
the Psalm of Hezekiah in Isaiah 38, for instance, or the Song of the
Three in the Greek translations of Daniel 3. These appear to have been
placed in their present literary settings at a late stage in the narrative's
literary development, long after the narrative itself had been composed.
It is true in some cases that this conclusion is based only on the impression
that the song "disrupts" the narrative or renders it incoherent. Some
scholars believe, for example, that the Prayer of Jonah in Jonah 2 was
probably a secondary interpolation because it is "out of place" in the
context of the surrounding narrative.[2] It simply makes no sense, they
claim, that Jonah would recite a song thanking God for deliverance—"with
the voice of thanksgiving I will sacrifice to you. . . . Deliverance belongs
to the Lord" (Jonah 2:9)—when he was still in danger in the belly of the
fish. These scholars conclude therefore that the song constitutes a secondary interpolation imposed upon the text retroactively by someone
who misunderstood or was dissatisfied with the original form of the story.
This would be a compelling analysis were it not that it depends upon a
notion of coherence that other readers of Jonah have come to reject.
Reading the narrative as an ironic parody or satire, these readers argue
that the song is actually integral to the design of the narrative, interacting
with Jonah's other prayers and speeches in a way that sheds light on the
prophet's character and comments upon the central themes of the story.[3]
If the psalm seems "out of place," this is because it was meant to generate
an ironic dissonance between the prophet's pious words, which acknowledge God as the agent of his salvation, and his defiant refusal to obey
God's command. At present there is no way to resolve the debate in favor
of one view or the other, since it really amounts to an argument over
what the Book of Jonah means—whether it is sympathetic to Jonah or
critical; whether it agrees with his viewpoint or wishes to expose its limitations. Faced with forceful arguments from both sides of the debate,
we simply cannot tell whether Jonah's song is an essential component of
the narrative—as I have argued for the songs in Exodus 15, Judges 5,
and Deuteronomy 32—or a secondary addition, offering insight into how
the narrative of Jonah was revised in the course of its transmission.

With other songs, we have more evidence to go on than our own sense
of whether the song fits within the narrative. The conclusion that the song
of Daniel's three companions (often referred to as the Song of the Three)
constitutes a secondary interpolation, for instance, is based on textual
evidence: we have a second and presumably earlier version of this episode,

the Masoretic version of Daniel 3, where there is no song. Similar evidence exists for the Psalm of Hezekiah in Isaiah 38, which does not appear in the parallel version of this narrative preserved in 2 Kings 20, and for the Psalm of David in 1 Chronicles 16, which is not present in the Chronicler's source, 2 Samuel 6. In all three cases, the narrative appears to have been transmitted in two forms: one reflecting an earlier form of the story before the song was interpolated, the other preserving a revised form of the narrative after the interpolation. Such examples confirm that songs were indeed added to preexisting biblical narratives secondarily. They also present us with a rare opportunity to understand what prompted such revisions, for by contrasting each episode as it appeared before and after the interpolation, we can gain insight into *why* songs were added to biblical narrative late in its literary development.

This chapter and the next represent my attempt to make the most of this opportunity. To be specific, I hope to show that the interpolations of songs such as the Song of the Three and the Psalm of Hezekiah represent what I call "scripturalizing revisions." To understand what motivated this sort of revision, we need to recall one of the most significant turning points within the history of Israelite religion, when certain texts from Israel's past—most especially the five books of Moses—came to be perceived as sacred and eternally binding guides for behavior and belief.[4] While the origins of this perception, referred to as "canon-consciousness" by some scholars, are difficult to pinpoint, its consequences are not, for it triggered all manner of changes in the religious, social and literary behaviors of those who claimed the Israelites as their ancestors, most famously the Jews but others as well, including the Samaritans.[5] In the wake of this perception, biblical interpretation first surfaced as a central—perhaps *the* central—religious and cultural activity, as Jews looked to the biblical past for ethical, religious, and political guidance.[6] The rise of canon-consciousness probably explains why Jews began to read texts like the Pentateuch regularly on sabbaths and festivals and to incorporate biblical citations into the words they said during worship.[7] It also accounts for why the names Jews gave their children at this time were increasingly drawn from pentetauchal figures such as Abraham and Joseph, at least in certain areas of Jewish settlement.[8] The dawn of canon-consciousness represented nothing less than a watershed moment in the history of Israelite culture, completely reshaping Jews' relationship to their past, present, and future.

Against this backdrop, it may come as something of a surprise that what we call the Bible was not yet fixed during much of this period. Even as biblical compositions such as Samuel and Jeremiah came to be perceived as scripture, they were subject to revision and expansion, in part because early canon-conscious readers felt the need to clarify the compositions' meaning or to adjust it to their own situation. In such cases, it was precisely the scripturalization of the Bible—the belief in its eternal, inexhaustible relevance—that propelled its literary development as Jews altered its form and content to meet the needs of their present. What I will show in these two chapters is that many of the songs within biblical narrative reflect this kind of revision, having been added to the biblical text in an effort to reconcile its form with its emerging status as scripture.

It is by no means a simple matter to prove such a claim. Scholars such as Isaac Seeligmann, Brevard Childs, Gerald Sheppard, and Michael Fishbane have produced several helpful studies in which they seek to identify the signs of canon-conscious revision, but their research also inadvertently reveals how difficult it is to reach definitive conclusions.[9] Consider what Childs says about the book of Jeremiah. He argues that the "Deuteronomic" speeches within Jeremiah were added to the book in an effort to integrate it more fully with another part of the biblical canon, the book of Deuteronomy.[10] The addition of Deuteronomic material recontextualized Jeremiah's prophecies, explains Childs, preserving them "in conjunction with a commentary which sought to understand his ministry as part of a chain of prophet messengers who were loyal to the law of Moses." The result is that in its present literary form, the book of Jeremiah demands to be understood as part of a larger body of sacred scripture centered on the words of Moses. One problem with this interpretation is that it cannot rule out other equally plausible explanations for the similarity. Perhaps, for example, the Deuteronomic speeches within Jeremiah were added at a time (say the seventh or sixth century B.C.E.) when this particular oratorical style was popular among Israelite scribes.[11] If so, Jeremiah's similarity to Deuteronomy constitutes evidence that the two compositions reflect the same school of rhetoric, not that one composition has been reformed in light of the other. In presenting this alternative explanation, I do not mean to endorse it over others, only to suggest how difficult it is to prove that a given modification of biblical literature was specifically intended as a scripturalizing revision.

In an effort to surmount this difficulty I will turn in this study to a kind of evidence seldom used by those who have investigated the impact of the Bible's canonization on its literary formation: the literature of the so-called postbiblical period, including the Apocrypha and Pseudepigrapha, Jewish Hellenistic literature, the Dead Sea Scrolls, the New Testament, and rabbinic literature. These texts offer fleeting but nonetheless revealing glimpses into how biblical narrative's status as sacred scripture affected the way it was read by canon-conscious Jews living between the second century B.C.E. and the fifth century C.E. Particularly important in this regard are the many passages in these texts that paraphrase or expand upon existing biblical stories—changing details, adding events and characters, restructuring the plot. For, in a sense, these retellings are themselves a kind of canon-conscious revision of biblical narrative—one that did not impinge upon the biblical text itself but that reflects how it was reconceptualized by early canon-conscious readers. The present chapter will bring together some of this evidence to describe four ways in which the scripturalization of the Bible affected early Jewish retellings and imitations of biblical narrative, drawing many of its illustrations from early Jewish "re-representations" of Exodus 15, Deuteronomy 32, and Judges 5. This exercise will reveal that the emerging status of these songs as part of Israel's sacred scripture had several significant implications for how early canon-conscious Jews read and responded to them. Beyond this, it will also suggest why, when early Jewish authors paraphrased biblical narrative, they so often supplied songs for episodes lacking songs in their original form within the Bible. Having in this chapter probed the impact of the Bible's scripturalization on early Jewish perceptions of biblical narrative, I will proceed in the next chapter to show how these perceptions affected the literary formation of the biblical text itself.

This approach is not without its limitations and risks. In the next chapter I will present evidence that the song of Daniel's three friends was added to the narrative of Daniel 3 sometime between the fifth and first centuries B.C.E. (when Daniel was translated into Greek).[12] Given the probable date of the song's interpolation, one may justifiably turn to narratives from around the same time—*Judith,* for example, or *Tobit*—in search of evidence that can help us to reconstruct the motivations and intentions of those who interpolated the song within the narrative. Even rabbinic literature, written down centuries after the Second Temple Period, can shed light on the interpolation, since it preserves related exegetical traditions about Daniel's three friends. For other songs, however—the Psalm of Hezekiah or the Psalm of Hannah—we have no way of knowing for certain when they entered the narrative. They may have been added in the third or fourth century B.C.E.; but then again, their interpolation may have been much earlier. In these instances, our use of literary evidence from the late Second Temple and post–Second Temple periods to illuminate the Bible's literary formation runs the risk of retrojecting the practices and predispositions of a later culture onto the literary behaviors of an earlier age. The risk is even greater when one is trying to reconstruct the effects of incipient canonization on the Bible's formation, since even at the end of the Second Temple period Jews still disagreed sharply over what constituted scripture, and there is no way of knowing which—if any—of the "canons" of early Judaism existed at earlier stages in Israel's history (arguably there were as many definitions of scripture at this time as there were forms of Judaism, though most Jews did seem to agree on the special status of certain biblical texts, especially the

Pentateuch). What follows, therefore, must be judged as something of an interpretive experiment, a tentative probing of early postbiblical literature to see what it might reveal about the literary implications of emergent canon-consciousness.

That said, I would also argue that this sort of experiment is necessary if we are ever to appreciate fully the role of the Bible's canonization in its literary formation. For although we know very little about the formation of the biblical canon prior to the second century B.C.E., we do know that a kind of incipient or protoscripture had begun to take shape long before this time. We thus find in the books of Ezra and Nehemiah, which were probably composed in the fourth century B.C.E., a description of how the scribe Ezra read "the book of the law of Moses" before a public assembly. It is not clear whether this "book of the law" is the same as our own Pentateuch, but if not, it must have been of similar content, since Ezra-Nehemiah is saturated with explicit references and allusions to pentateuchal texts (e.g., see Neh 13:25, which cites Deut 7:3).[13] At the very least, Ezra-Nehemiah indicates that fourth-century Jews, believing that something called the "book of Moses" enjoyed sacred status and authority, sought to disseminate knowledge of its contents, interpret its message, and adhere to its laws. Second Kings 22–23 provides even earlier evidence of incipient scripturalization, reporting that in the days of Josiah (circa 621 B.C.E.) the high priest Hilkiah discovered a "book of the torah" in the Temple in Jerusalem and that its contents prompted Josiah to initiate a reformation of Israelite cultic behavior. Some believe that this event represents the beginning of canonization, but if scholars are right in identifying Josiah's "book of the torah" with some form of Deuteronomy, the idea of scripture probably antedates this event, since Deuteronomy itself cites earlier texts, such as the laws of Exodus, as if they already enjoyed authoritative status.[14] The evidence does not allow us to go much further back into the history of the biblical canon, but the little existing evidence is sufficient to indicate that sacred texts were venerated in ancient Israel perhaps as early as the seventh century B.C.E. and certainly for the duration of the exilic and postexilic periods—precisely the time frame in which much of biblical literature was composed, redacted, and revised. Since, as we will learn, the idea of scripture as it later developed had a profound impact on literary practice and expectations after the third and second centuries B.C.E., it seems reasonable that even in inchoate form it would have some impact on earlier literary behavior as well, affecting the development of Israelite texts eventually included within the canon(s). The analysis presented here represents a first attempt to detect and measure this impact in an effort to understand why songs were interpolated within biblical narrative in the final stages of its literary development.

The Bible as Literary Model

Behind the idea of scripture as it emerged in early Judaism lay a certain conception of Israel's past and its relation to the present. Jews in this period were fascinated by their history—especially that described in the Pentateuch—not simply because it explained where they came from or why God had taken such an interest in them in the past, but also because it bore lessons for how Jews were to live their lives in the present. The most obvious way in which biblical literature served this function was to present the divine commandments that Israel was to observe, but there was another way in which it offered ethical guidance: the great figures of Israel's sacred past—Abraham, Moses, David—were themselves perceived as ethical and religious role models, exemplifying through their deeds and words the kinds of behaviors and attitudes which all Jews should strive to emulate. Perhaps the clearest expression of this attitude appears in Philo's *Life of Moses*. Through the way Moses conducted his life, Philo tells us, the prophet "has set before us, like some well-wrought picture, a piece of work beautiful and God-like, a model for those who are willing to copy it. Happy are they who imprint, or strive to imprint, that image on their souls" (*Life of Moses* 1.158–59).[15] Never mind that Moses as he is presented in the Bible exhibits human frailties. As seen by Philo and other early Jews, the prophet was a model of ethical and religious conduct, exemplifying precisely those virtues to which present-day Jews should aspire in their own conduct.

So deeply rooted was this impulse to emulate the biblical past that it even left its mark on the literary behavior of early Judaism. The form of biblical literature—its stylistic conventions, its stock of images, its range of genres—came to be regarded at this time as a model of literary expression, no less deserving of emulation than the acts of biblical heroes. That is evident from the many texts from the Second Temple Period which strive to imitate "classical" biblical literature in some way. Thus early Jewish narratives such as *Tobit, Judith,* and *I Maccabees* emulate biblical narratives such as Genesis, Judges, and Samuel in the way they tell their stories.[16] Early Jewish psalms and prayers often utilize the genres, imagery, and style of biblical psalms.[17] Early Jewish apocalyptic texts frequently center on biblical figures and reuse biblical language and motifs.[18] And postbiblical testamentary literature such as the *Testaments of the Twelve Patriarchs* and the farewell speech of Tobit in Tobit 14 is modeled upon biblical farewell speeches such as Jacob's final blessing in Genesis 49 and Moses' speeches in Deuteronomy.[19] In different ways, each of these literatures reflects the same aesthetic, an aesthetic that looked to the form of the Pentateuch, the Psalms, and other scriptural texts as *the* model of literary expression.

We can better appreciate the nature of this aesthetic by briefly considering three songs which appear in narratives composed in the Second
Temple or post-Second Temple periods: the Song of Judith in *Judith* 16,
the Magnificat in Luke 1:46-55, and the Hymn of Tobit in *Tobit* 13. In
each text there are clear signs that the song's role within the narrative
has been consciously modeled on a song in the narrative of the Pentateuch
or the Former Prophets.

Let us begin with the hymn of *Judith* 16, sung by Judith and the people
after their miraculous deliverance from their Assyrian oppressors.[20] As several scholars have realized, this song deliberately evokes the songs in Exodus
15 and Judges 5 (which were also sung by women) and the stories with
which these songs are associated.[21] Thus, Jdt. 16:2, "For God is the Lord
who crushes wars," echoes Exod 15:3 as it appears in LXX: "the Lord
crushes wars." In the same verse the verb "pursues" recalls a verb that
appears repeatedly in Exodus 14 to describe the Egyptian pursuit of Israel
across the sea (Exod 14:4, 8, 9, 23). The description in Jdt 16:10 of how
the Persians and Medes trembled in the face of Judith's might parallels
Exod 15:14, where trembling seized the Canaanites in the face of God's
might. And Jdt. 16:6, "But the Lord has foiled them by the hand of a
woman," recalls Judg 4:9: "the Lord will sell Sisera into the hand of a
woman." Forging an intertextual link between *Judith* 16 and Exodus 15
and Judges 5, these biblical echoes help transform Judith's story into a
replay of scriptural history.[22]

The Magnificat, attributed by most versions of Luke to Mary just before
the birth of Jesus, stands in a similar relationship to the Prayer of Hannah
in 1 Samuel 2.[23] Both songs are associated by their narrative settings with
the miraculous birth of a child: the Magnificat celebrates the birth of
Jesus, the Prayer of Hannah celebrates the birth of Samuel. This parallel
has suggested to numerous readers that the former has been modeled on
the latter. It is true that the Magnificat, unlike Judith's hymn, contains no
recognizable echoes of 1 Samuel 2, only general thematic parallels, such
as the motif of God's reversing the fortunes of the prosperous and the
wretched (compare Luke 1:52-53 and 1 Sam 2:7-8).[24] With this evidence
alone, one has little support for the conclusion that the hymn itself was
consciously modeled on Hannah's prayer; in fact, it was probably not created for use in the narrative of Luke at all but was adapted from a preexisting Jewish hymn composed as early as the Maccabean period.[25] What
concerns us here, however, is whether the hymn *as it functions within the
narrative* recalls the Prayer of Hannah, and there is clear evidence that it
does. Almost every recent commentator has observed that the narrative
surrounding the Magnificat, which describes the events leading up to the
birth of John the Baptist and Jesus, is patterned in part upon the narrative
preceding the Prayer of Hannah (1 Samuel 1), which describes the events

leading up to the birth of the prophet Samuel.[26] In both texts, pious wives miraculously conceive future saviors who will initiate a new stage in Israel's history by delivering it from its troubles and preparing for God's kingdom (for an example of a more specific parallel, compare Luke 1:15 with 1 Sam 1:11). Within the context of this broader parallel, the insertion—if not the composition—of the Magnificat seems clearly to have been motivated by the example of the song in 1 Samuel 2. Just as the hymn of Judith links Judith's victory to earlier divine victories against Israel's enemies, the Magnificat helps link Jesus' birth to a similar moment in the history of biblical Israel, the miraculous birth of Samuel.

As I have argued elsewhere, Tobit's "prayer of rejoicing" in Tobit 13 alludes to the Song of Moses in Deuteronomy 32.[27] The first signs of the allusion appear in the narrative just before the hymn in Tobit 12:6-15 in Raphael's farewell exhortation to Tobit and his son Tobias, a passage which resembles instructions given to Moses and Joshua by God in Deut 31:14-30. According to Deuteronomy 31, with Joshua standing by his side, Moses is ordered by God to write down a song (LXX 31:19, 22: καὶ νῦν γράψατε τά ῥήματα τῆς ᾠδῆς ταύτης . . . καὶ ἔγραψεν Μωυσῆς τὴν ᾠδὴν ταύτην); Moses is then said to transcribe the words of a "torah" into a book (συνετέλεσεν Μωυσῆς γράφων πάντας τοὺς λόγους τοῦ νόμου τούτου εἰς βιβλίον); and finally the prophet recites the words of the song to the people of Israel. Similarly, Tobit and Tobias receive a two-part commission from a divinely appointed angel to "praise God" (καὶ νῦν εὐλογεῖτε ἐπὶ τῆς γῆς κύριον καὶ εξομολογεῖσθε τῷ θεῷ) and to "write down all these things that have happened to you" (γράψατε πάντα ταῦτα τά συμβάντα ὑμῖν).[28] Two verses later, according to Vaticanus Tob 13:1, Tobit is said to "write down" his "prayer of rejoicing" (καὶ Τωβὶτ ἔγραψεν προσευχὴν εἰς ἀγαλλίασιν καὶ εἶπεν).[29] Even more suggestive are the parallels between the songs themselves: both are performed by pious sages shortly before their deaths; both are followed by an address from the dying sage to those who will survive him (Deuteronomy 33, Tobit 14[30]); and, most striking of all, the two songs contain similar language. Thus Tobit 13:2, "he leads down to Hades in the lowest regions of the earth, and brings up from the great abyss, and there is nothing that can escape his hand (κατάγει ἕως ᾅδου κατωτάτω τῆς γῆς καὶ αυτὸς ἀνάγει ἐκ τῆς ἀπωλείας τῆς μεγάλης καὶ οὐκ ἔστιν οὐδέν ὅ ἐκφεύξεται τὴν χεῖρα αὐτου), recalls Deut 32:39, "I kill and I make alive . . . and there is none that can deliver out of my hand" (LXX ἐγὼ ἀποκτενῶ καὶ ζῆν ποιήσω . . . καὶ οὐκ ἔστιν ὃς ἐξελεῖται ἐκ τῶν χειρῶν μου).[31] Likewise, Tobit 13:6, "he will not hide his face from you" (οὐ μὴ κρύψῃ τὸ πρόσωπον αυτου ἀφ 'ὑμῶν), calls to mind Deut 32:20, "And he (God) said, 'I will hide my face from them'" (LXX καὶ εἶπεν' Ἀποστρέψω τὸ πρόσωπόν μου ἀπ' αὐτῶν).[32] Finally, both songs culminate with a prophecy of Israel's future

in the land: the Song of Moses anticipates Israel's settlement in the land
of Canaan; the Hymn of Tobit forecasts the ingathering of the exiles in
a restored Jerusalem.[33] These various parallels work together to link *Tobit*
12-13 to Deuteronomy 31-32, as if to suggest that just before his death
Tobit had become a kind of second Moses, ending his life with a song
that prophesied Israel's future in the land promised to it. Like the biblical
echoes in Judith's hymn and the Magnificat, the effect of the allusions is
to suggest that its protagonist's life perpetuates or repeats historical patterns
established in the biblical past.

It is of course impossible to prove the existence of the literary allusions
I have described, much less to know their actual effect on early readers.
In the case of Tobit's hymn, however, a rather interesting piece of evidence
corroborates my claim that it alludes to the Song of Moses. In 1516 an
abridged Hebrew translation of Tobit known as the Münster text was published in Constantinople.[34] The provenance of this text is still unknown,
though it is highly unlikely that it reflects an original Hebrew version of
Tobit (it is more likely that *Tobit* was originally composed in Aramaic, from
which it was later translated into both Hebrew and Greek).[35] Whatever its
origins, this text is significant for our purposes because its version of *Tobit*
12 contains several additions which actually heighten its similarity to
Deuteronomy 31. Thus when Raphael issues his final command to Tobit
and his son Tobias, he says, "Now write for yourselves all these words in
a book" (Neubauer, *Book of Tobit*, p. 34, lines 9-10) — conflating language
from Deut 31:19 ("Now write for yourselves this song") and Deut 31:24
("When Moses had finished writing down the words of this instruction in
a book"). Even more resonant is Raphael's description of the book as a
"witness" (lines 10-11), which recalls the description of the Song of Moses
as a "witness" in Deut 31:19. These additions indicate that the similarity
between Tobit's hymn and the Song of Moses was in fact perceived by
early readers, prompting at least one scribe to weave into *Tobit* 12 additional
links between the two songs.

Having identified the Song of Judith, the Magnificat, and the Hymn
of Tobit as imitations of biblical songs, we would do well to take a step
back to reflect on how we are able to identify them as imitations. What
distinguishes these songs from the songs they emulate is the very fact that
they strive to seem biblical, using scriptural echoes to signal that they are
part of the same literary tradition as the Song of the Sea, the Prayer of
Hannah, and the Song of Moses. The narrative role of *Judith* 16 would
be indistinguishable from that of Exodus 15 and Judges 5 were it not that
in addition to closing a battle account, it uses biblical echoes to relate
itself to earlier scenes in biblical narrative in which God defeated his enemies. So too the Magnificat and Tobit's hymn are only distinguishable
from their literary models because they allude to these models. Beyond

whatever roles they play within their narrative settings, these songs also serve an intertextual function, generating connections between their settings and the Hebrew Bible by imitating its form and alluding to its content.[36]

By describing these hymns as imitations, however, I do not mean to suggest that they are slavishly so. Imitation was simply the literary mode through which early Jewish authors expressed their creativity. We thus find that the biblical allusions generated by *Judith* 16, the Magnificat, and *Tobit* 13 have been skillfully fashioned to serve the specific artistic and rhetorical objectives of the narratives in which they appear. Patrick Skehan has observed that the evocation of the Song of the Sea in *Judith* 16 is one link in a chain of allusions connecting the story of Judith to the larger story of the Exodus, the paradigmatic story of divine deliverance for early Jews.[37] We have seen something similar in the Magnificat's evocation of the Prayer of Hannah, which reflects a larger effort by the author of Luke to draw a connection between Jesus and biblical saviors such as Samuel.[38] Perhaps the most complex example of all is the hymn of Tobit and its evocation of Deuteronomy 32, an allusion that reflects an intertextual strategy also reflected in several other biblical allusions within *Tobit*. Previous scholars have noted that the narrative of *Tobit* alludes to several biblical stories: the patriarchs' betrothals in Mesopotamia in Genesis 24 and 29, Joseph's sojourn in Egypt, the sufferings of Job, and Moses' speeches in Deuteronomy.[39] What these scholars have overlooked is that these seemingly disparate allusions share one trait in common: they all refer to biblical events that took place *outside* the land of Israel. When Abraham instructs his servant to find a bride for his son Isaac, he tells him to return to the land of his kindred in Mesopotamia (Genesis 24; cf. Tob 4:12), and this is where Jacob meets his wives as well. The story of Joseph leads first Joseph and then the children of Israel down into Egypt. The narrative of Job is set in the land of Uz, and although the precise location of this land is unknown, for many readers in the Second Temple period it was located outside the land of Israel.[40] And the Song of Moses—along with all the other speeches of Moses in Deuteronomy—is uttered "beyond the Jordan in the land of Moab," just before Israel enters Canaan. Distributed along the course of the narrative, these allusions imply that the misadventures of Tobit are part of a larger pattern in Israel's sacred history centered on rightous individuals forced to leave or live outside the land of Israel. The author's goal in creating this pattern may have been to suggest to his diaspora audience that their experiences in exile continue a historical pattern that began with the Patriarchs, resurfaced with the Exodus, and will end with Israel's return to the land.[41] The allusion to the Song of Moses in *Tobit* 13 serves this goal by connecting the end of *Tobit*'s narrative with the end of Israel's wanderings in the wilderness, when it has not quite reached the land but has been given a prophetic glimpse of what life there will be like. Indeed, along with other echoes of Deuteronomy in *Tobit* 14, the allusion represents the culminating point of the narrative's intertextual strategy, implying that just as Israel's first exile ended soon after Moses wrote down the song in Deuteronomy 32, so too Israel's present exile will end not long after Tobit writes down his hymn. If the cumulative effect of the biblical allusions in *Tobit* is to suggest that the divinely woven patterns of Israel's past continue into Israel's exilic present, the evocation of the Song of Moses near the end of *Tobit* intimates that the present exile will end in the same way the Pentateuch did—with Israel returning to the land of Israel shortly after the death of Tobit just as its biblical ancestors did after the death of Moses.

What I am trying to suggest through this example is that far from attesting to a lack of creativity, early Jewish imitations of biblical literature were often quite artful in their efforts to recall the biblical past or to extend it into the present. By emulating the past, early Jewish authors were in effect recreating the present, licensing religious and cultural innovations (the introduction of Jesus as a biblical hero, the resignification of exile as a replay of biblical history, etc.) by representing them as continuations of the biblical past. At the same time, however, this example also illustrates how profoundly the Bible influenced the literary and religious imagination of early Jews. In their eyes, the imitation of the Bible was more than a literary practice; it was a religious practice which gave shape to the present by representing it as a repetition of the biblical past.

Canonical Cross-Referencing

Technically, a canon is a collection of sacred texts. In practice, it also represents a claim about how the members of the collection relate to one another. From a canon-conscious perspective, each verse, episode, or book within a scripture is potentially related to every other verse, episode, or book within this scripture, yielding its full significance only when it is read in light of its fellow canonical texts. Thus rabbinic readers of the Bible believed that one could clarify the meaning of works such as the Song of Songs or Psalms by uncovering their connection to events described in the Pentateuch or the Former Prophets.[42] Early Christian readers of the Bible defined the biblical canon differently, but they engaged in a similar exegetical maneuver, using various interpretive strategies—typology, for instance—to link the Old Testament to the New.[43] Even Samaritans, for whom the canon consisted only of the Pentateuch, interpreted individual verses with the help of other verses from remote contexts within the Pentateuch.[44] For each of these traditions, the meaning of any point within scripture was relatable to any other point within scripture, and biblical interpretation often consisted in drawing the lines between them.[45]

We can measure the effects of this "unifying scriptural vision"—to use Michael Fishbane's label for this hermeneutical perspective—by examining how it colored early Jewish readings of the songs in biblical narrative.[46] One tiny but revealing example appears in a paraphrase of the Song of Deborah found in the *Biblical Antiquities* of Pseudo-Philo, a retelling of Genesis through Samuel composed in the first century C.E.[47] As we will see more clearly in the next section of this chapter, Pseudo-Philo has completely reconfigured the song and assigned to it a new narrative role. What concerns us here, however, is a series of small changes which he inserts into the verse introducing the song, Judg 5:1. The original form of this verse reads, "Then Deborah and Barak son of Abinoam sang on that day, saying." Pseudo-Philo's version of this verse contains several unobtrusive but nonetheless significant additions: "Then Deborah and Barak the son of Abino *and all the people* sang *together a hymn to the Lord* on that day" (*Bib. Ant.* 32:1).[48] R. Baukhaum has suggested that Pseudo-Philo's addition of the phrases "all the people" and "to the Lord" may reflect the influence of Exod 15:1 on this verse ("Then Moses and Israel sang this song to the Lord"), a plausible suggestion given what we have seen regarding the paradigmatic status of Exodus 15.[49] In light of a recent study by P. Enns, it also seems likely that "together" was added under the influence of this verse as well, though in a rather roundabout way.[50] Enns's study concerns another Second Temple source, the *Wisdom of Solomon*, which in the course of retelling the events at the Red Sea reports that Israel sang the Song of the Sea "with one accord" (Book 10:20 c).[51] Enns has demonstrated that this detail is not an insignificant flourish but responds to an exegetical problem posed by the first few verses of Exodus 15. In Exod 15:1 the subject of the sentence is plural—"Moses and the sons of Israel"—but the verb "sing" within the same sentence is in the singular ($y\bar{a}\check{s}ir$). Later in the same verse a plural verb is used ("they said"), but then the song itself begins with a singular verb ("I will sing"). According to Enns, the song's perplexing mixture of singular and plural forms led the Jewish Hellenistic author of the *Wisdom of Solomon*, or the exegetical tradition which it preserves, to conclude that the people of Israel sang the song as if they had one voice: "They said, 'I will sing.'" (Other early Jews solved the problem by suggesting that Moses and Israel sang the song responsively, with Moses singing first—hence the singular verb in 15:1—and Israel repeating his words).[52] If Enns's reconstruction is correct, Pseudo-Philo's reformulation of Judg 5:1 may indirectly reflect the same exegetical tradition, having transferred the motif to Judg 5:1 along with all the other motifs drawn from the actual text of Exod 15:1.[53] The resulting modification of Judg 5:1 may be minute, but it exemplifies a much larger phenomenon—the proclivity of canon-conscious readers to read biblical verses or stories in light of other verses and stories within the canon. Indeed, if one reads Pseudo-Philo's song in its entirety—as we will do in the next section—one cannot fail to notice that it is saturated with references to other biblical episodes: the sacrifice of Isaac (*Bib. Ant.* 32:1-4),[54] the birth of Jacob and Esau (5-6), the giving of the Law (7-8), the death of Moses (9), Joshua's battle at Gibeon (10), and, at the song's conclusion, the parting of the Red Sea (17). The impulse to connect disparate biblical texts came so naturally to Pseudo-Philo that he did not merely draw connections between the battle against Sisera and other biblical events; he also claimed that Deborah herself recognized the connections and sought to make them explicit through the words of her song.[55]

It is far from clear when this practice of canonical cross-referencing began. It obviously presupposes some notion of a biblical canon, but as I have indicated, the further back we go in time, the less we know about the nature and status of the biblical canon. In the context of the Second Temple and early post–Second Temple periods, in fact, there appear to have been many different conceptions of scripture. As noted, some worshipers, such as the Samaritans, evidently embraced only the Pentateuch as scripture; others, such as the Christians, expanded the borders of scripture to include the works presently included in the New Testament. This much can be said, however: there is evidence that even in the early Second Temple period, Jews were seeking out connections between disparate parts of scripture as it was defined at that time. Consider the lines drawn between the Psalter and biblical narrative. Many of the psalms in the Psalter are introduced by historical superscriptions, single-line notices that attribute the psalm to an historical figure (usually David) and often refer to the biblical episode in which the psalm was allegedly composed (see, for example, Psalm 51:1: "A Psalm of David, when the prophet came to him, after he had gone into Bathsheba").[56] Scholars have long suspected that these notices are not historically accurate. Like many of the songs in biblical narrative, many of the psalms within the Psalter were evidently composed not on the historical occasions described by their superscriptions but for recitation in a cultic setting as the verbal accompaniment of sacrifices and other rituals.[57] The affixing of the historical superscription thus represents an act of reinterpretation not unlike that created by the incorporation of the songs within biblical narrative. The motivation for this reinterpretation is unknown, though as I suggested in the first chapter, it seems plausible that the loss of cultic sites through centralization and foreign invasion may have been one factor leading ancient Israelites to find noncultic uses for their cultic poetry. In any event, the historization of the Psalms continued and even expanded over the course of the Second Temple and post–Second Temple periods: the Greek, Syriac, and targumic translations of the Psalter contain Davidic superscriptions beyond those in the Masoretic version, and rabbinic tradition eventually attributed the entire book to David.[58] However we explain the origins of this kind of superscription, its proliferation seems connected to the rise of canon-consciousness. Childs, among others, has argued that the purpose of the historical superscriptions was to help situate the psalms in relation to the rest of scripture, correlating their content with the story of the Bible's greatest songwriter, King David.[59] Consider the superscription for Psalm 51—"A Psalm of David, when the prophet Nathan came to him, after he had gone in to Bathsheba." The correlation of the psalm with David's encounter with Nathan in 2 Samuel 12 appears to have arisen from several verbal associations between the psalm and 2 Samuel 12: the verb translated "I have sinned" in verse 5 (MT 6), for example, was evidently linked with the same verb in 2 Sam 12:13.[60] Such associations reflect precisely the kind of canonizing cross-referencing I have described, interrelating the Psalter with other parts of scripture by drawing on its contents to comment upon biblical narrative and drawing on the contents of biblical narrative to contextualize the Psalms.[61] Reflected only sporadically in the biblical text itself—only a few of the Psalms contain historical superscriptions—this reading stategy eventually became habitual among both Jews and Christians, who uncovered within the Psalms countless links to other parts of scripture.

There is evidence that the association of the Psalms with biblical narrative moved in the opposite direction as well, with the songs within biblical narrative being read in light of the Psalms. We can surmise this from the fact that early Jewish paraphrases and imitations of the songs in biblical narrative often incorporate language and motifs from the canonical Psalms. The Song of Judith, for example, interweaves among its allusions to Exodus 15 and Judges 5 several elements borrowed directly from the Psalms. The clearest example occurs in Jdt 16:13, "I will sing to my God a new song," which echoes a famous formula found throughout the Psalter (see Pss 13:3, 40:4, 96:1, 149:1; see also Isa 42:10).[62] Another example appears in the paraphrase of Hannah's Prayer in Pseudo-Philo's *Biblical Antiquities* (51:6), which incorporates a covert citation from Ps 99:6 along with echoes of other biblical texts.[63] The use of psalmic motifs and citations within these songs presupposes the very connection between the Psalms and the songs in biblical narrative I have described. Just as the Psalms were thought of as the prayers and songs of biblical heroes uttered at significant moments in their lives, so too the songs in biblical narrative were reread and rewritten in light of biblical psalmody. So closely were the two bodies of poetry identified that eventually early Christian readers of the Bible gathered the songs within the narratives of the Hebrew Bible, the Apocrypha, and the New Testament into collections of odes (known as canticles in the Western church), which were then sometimes appended to the Psalter.[64] Centuries earlier, the psalms in the Psalter first began to be recontextualized within biblical narrative. The practice of gathering odes or canticles brought this practice full circle, recontextualizing the songs in biblical narrative within a second Psalter of sorts.[65]

The Bible as Liturgical Model

In their wide-ranging study of the sacred book in ancient Mediterranean religion, J. Leopoldt and S. Morenz concluded that one of the clearest signs of a text's canonical status was the ritualized recitation of its contents in the context of communal worship.[66] Though this conclusion begs for refinement—a sacred book can serve many different liturgical functions even within a single religious community[67]—it certainly holds true for the Pentateuch and other biblical books at the end of the Second Temple period. Philo, Josephus, rabbinic sources, and the New Testament all testify that at least by the end of this period the torah and other scriptural texts were read communally by Jews on the sabbath and on other festivals.[68] There is even evidence that the songs of biblical narrative in particular were recited in this way; for example, the songs in Exodus 15 and Deuteronomy 32 and Num 21:17–18 (the Song of the Well) were evidently recited by the Levites during the afternoon sabbath sacrifice at the Temple.[69] We are speaking now of behavior ascribed to the late Second Temple period, but there are hints in the Bible itself that the cultic recitation of sacred texts was inherited from an earlier period in ancient Israelite history. Thus Deuteronomy prescribes the recitation of the words of a "torah" during the festival of booths (Deut 31:9–13), and later biblical books describe occasions when a leader publicly recited the "book of the covenant" (2 Kings 23:1–3) or the "law of Moses" (Neh 8:1–12). Such evidence has suggested to at least one scholar that the motivation for canonization was cultic, that is, the decision to "canonize" a work was tantamount to the decision to recite it in the cult.[70] This view has been criticized because for many of the books within the canon (e.g., Proverbs) there is no evidence that they were ever recited in the temple cult.[71] Whatever the precise relationship between the liturgical recitation of the Bible and the history of its canonization, however, the evidence indicates that they became thoroughly intertwined over the course of the Second Temple period, their interaction affecting how Jews perceived the Bible, their own liturgical practice, and the relation of these to one another.

To illustrate this interaction, let us consider how early Jews related the songs in biblical narrative to the praise they themselves recited during public worship. There is scattered but nonetheless revealing evidence that early Jews regarded the songs in biblical narrative as models of liturgical praise to be emulated in contemporary worship. Judging from the Babylonian Talmud, for instance, the rabbis appear to have believed that their singing of the so-called Egyptian Hallel, the liturgical recitation of Psalms 113-118 on Passover and other festivals, emulated the Israelites' performance of the Song of the Sea. They claimed, for example, that the Hallel was first recited at the Red Sea by Moses and Israel,[72] and they regularly referred to the Hallel as *šîrâ* = "song," the very word used by the Bible to introduce Exodus 15 and other songs.[73] Implicit in these traditions is the belief that the Hallel continued a practice initiated by the song in Exodus 15, as if when Moses and the Israelites sang the Song of the Sea, they set a precedent for how Jews in all ages should praise God for his intervention in their lives. The testimony of Philo of Alexandria suggests that earlier Second Temple period Jews also perceived a connection between the Song of the Sea and contemporary liturgical praise. In his treatise *On the Contemplative Life*, Philo describes the practices of a mysterious sect of Jews known as the Therapeutae, including a periodic vigil conducted once every fifty days in which "they sing hymns to God composed of many measures, sometimes chanting together, sometimes undertaking antiphonic harmonies" (1.84).[74] Reporting that both men and women participate antiphonally in this choral performance, Philo explains that their singing is in "imitation" of the "hymns of thanksgiving" sung long ago by those who stood at the Red Sea.[75] We have no way of verifying the accuracy of Philo's report or of determining whether the behavior of the Therapeutae was typical of Jewish liturgical practice at this time, but Philo's remarks do seem to indicate that at least some prerabbinic Jews believed that certain forms of liturgical praise emulated the songs of their biblical ancestors. The leap from present-day liturgical praise to the songs of the biblical past was possible only because by the Second Temple period the Song of the Sea at least was perceived as a model for how Jews were to praise God in their own divine worship.

Not only did early Jews view their own liturgical behavior in light of the songs in biblical narrative; they also viewed the songs in biblical narrative in light of their own liturgical behavior. One finds, for example, that just as the songs in biblical narrative shaped Philo's understanding of liturgical behavior, so too his assumptions about liturgical behavior shaped his understanding of the songs within biblical narrative. Consider his retelling of the Song of Moses in Deuteronomy 32. As we know from the preceding chapter, the narrative in Deuteronomy 31 is quite explicit about the song's function: it was taught by Moses to Israel as a "witness" against it after the prophet's death. As Philo retells the song in *On the Virtues* 72-75, however, the Song of Moses serves a very different function.

Having discoursed on topics suitable for his subjects and to the one appointed for leadership, he began to hymn God with an ode, rendering to him the final thanksgiving of his bodily life for the strange and exceptional acts of grace with which he had been benefitted from his birth to his old age. And he assembled a divine gathering of the elements of all (the universe) and the foremost portion of the cosmos, earth and heaven, the first the home of mortals, the second the house of the immortals. In their midst he composed hymns with all the forms of harmony and symphony so that both men and the ministering angels might hear. The men as disciples were to learn to be of a similar thankful disposition, while the (angels) as overseers, watching in accordance with their own skill lest the song be discordant, were at the same time not able to believe that a man confined to a mortal body could in the same manner as the most holy choir of sun, moon and the other stars attune his soul to the divine instrument, heaven and all the cosmos. So taking his place among the heavenly choir-members, the revealer of holy things blended strains of thanksgiving to God with his true sentiment of good will towards the nation, mixing reproof for ancient sins with admonitions and chastisements for the present, along with counsel for the future . . .

Philo's paraphrase makes clear that he detected both the didactic and accusatory elements within Deuteronomy 32 (he reports that Moses performed the song "so that men as disciples [would] *learn* to be of a similar thankful disposition," and he mentions that the song included "admonitions and chastisements"). According to this passage, however, Moses' basic motivation for performing Deuteronomy 32 was neither to teach Israel nor to castigate it but to thank God for "the strange and exceptional acts of grace with which he had been benefitted from his birth to his old age." Why would Philo assert that Moses sang the song in gratitude to God when biblical narrative reports that God ordered Moses to perform the song in order to witness against Israel? Philo's reading may have been triggered by verses within the song that praise God for his greatness (see Deut 32:3, "I will proclaim the name of the Lord. Ascribe greatness to the Lord"), but this does not explain why Philo would give more weight to such verses than to the many verses within the song that are castigatory in tone. Nor does it reveal why he would ignore the information provided by Deuteronomy 31, which clearly indicates that the song was addressed not from Moses to God but from God via Moses to Israel. The true answer, I think, lies in Philo's understanding of hymnody as a form of divine worship. Philo's use of the word translated "thanksgiving" (*eucharistia* in Greek, the ancestor of the word *Eucharist*) to describe the song has clear liturgical connotations in the context of Philo's other writings, in which he uses the same word to describe the function of sacrifice, prayer, and other forms of divine service.[76] As a matter of fact, Philo explicitly groups the singing of hymns together with other liturgical acts (sacrifice, prayer, etc.) as ways in which one should praise and thank God for his benefactions (*The Special Laws* I.275). Philo's understanding of hymnody as a form of liturgical praise evidently affected his reading of Deuteronomy 32, trans-forming it in his eyes from a witness against Israel into a song of thanks-giving. If Philo seems unaware that this reading violated the plain sense of the biblical text, it was because he assumed that the songs of the biblical past were sung for the same reason that hymns were sung in the liturgical present—to thank and praise the Lord for his benefactions.

A similar assumption is reflected in Pseudo-Philo's *Biblical Antiquities*. As we saw in the preceding section of this chapter, Pseudo-Philo introduces several tiny changes into Judg 5:1, probably under the influence of Exodus 15. It is time now to consider the much more substantial changes which he introduces into the Song of Deborah itself. Pseudo-Philo's paraphrase of the song is too long to reproduce here, so I present only those sections of the song relevant to my argument.

> Then Deborah and Barak the son of Abino and all the people sang together a hymn to the Lord in that day, saying, "Behold, the Lord has shown us his glory from on high, just as he did from the upper region, sending forth his voice in order to confuse the languages of men. And he chose our people and rescued Abraham our father from the fire and chose him before all his brothers and protected him from the fire and freed him from the bricks for the building of the tower. He gave him a son in the extremity of his old age and delivered him from a sterile womb. And all the angels were jealous of him, and the worshippers of the ranks (of angels) became envious. Since they had become jealous, God said to him, 'Slay the fruit of your body for me and offer for me what was given to you by me as a sacrifice.'. . . And when the father had offered his son on the altar and bound his feet in order to slay him, the Most Powerful hastened to send his voice from on high saying, 'Do not murder your son or destroy the fruit of your body.'. . . And he gave Isaac two sons . . . Jacob and Esau. And God loved Jacob, but Esau he hated on account of his deeds. And it happened that when their father became an old man, Isaac blessed Jacob and sent him into Mesopotamia, and he begat there twelve sons. And they went down into Egypt and settled there. And when their enemies began to ill-treat them, the people cried out to the Lord, and their cry was heeded, and he led them out from there, and led them to Mount Sinai . . .

All his creation convened in order to see the covenant granted by the Lord to the children of Israel. And all the words which the Most Powerful said, these he observed, having Moses his beloved as a witness. And when he was about to die, God laid at his disposal the Heavens, and showed him those witnesses which we now have, saying, 'Let the Heaven into which you now enter and the Earth upon which you have been walking until now be witnesses between me and you and my people, for the sun, moon and stars shall be servants to you.' And when Joshua arose to rule the people, it happened on the day in which he was fighting against the enemy that the fighting was still going strong when evening approached. Joshua said to the sun and moon, 'You, who have become ministers between the Most Powerful and his sons, behold, the battle is going strong and are you derelict in your duty? So stand still this day, provide light for his sons and darkness for his enemies.' And so they did. And now in these days Sisera has risen up to enslave us. And we cried out to our Lord, and he commanded the stars and said, 'Leave your positions and burn up my enemies, so that they will know my strength.' And the stars descended and destroyed their camp and protected us without effort. Therefore, we will not cease to sing hymns, nor will our mouth be silent in narrating his marvelous deeds, because he has remembered both his recent and his ancient promises and shown his saving power to us. And so, Jael is glorified among women, because she alone took the good path, slaying Sisera with her own hands. Go earth; go heavens and lightnings; go, angels of the host; go and report to the fathers in their repository of souls and say, 'The Most Powerful has not forgotten the smallest of his promises that he has granted us, saying, "Many marvelous deeds will I do for your sons".'" And now from this day on let it be known that whatever God has said to men that he will do, so he will do, even if man delays in singing hymns to God. Sing, O Deborah, and let the grace of the Holy Spirit awaken in you, and begin to praise the works of the Lord because there will not again arise such a day in which the stars will give notice and subdue the enemies of Israel as it was commanded them. From this hour, when Israel falls into distress, it will call upon those witnesses along with (these) servants, and they will form a delegation to the Most High, and he will remember that day and send the saving power of his covenant . . .

"Slow up, you hours of the day, and do not hurry on, so that we may set forth what our mind can contrive, for night is coming upon us. It will be like the night when God struck the firstborn of the

Egyptians for the sake of his firstborn. And then I will cease my hymn, for the time will be prepared for his acts of judgement. So I will sing a hymn to him in the renewal of creation, and the people will remember this salvation, and this will be a testimony for it. And let the sea with its abyss be a witness for it, because not only has God dried it up in the presence of our fathers, but he has also diverted the stars from their courses and subdued our enemies." And when Deborah ceased her words, she together with the people went up to Shiloh, and offered sacrifices and holocausts, and they sang to the accompaniment of trumpets. And when they were singing and the sacrifices had been offered, Deborah said, "This will be as a testimony of trumpets between the stars and their Lord."

Pseudo-Philo's retelling of the song drastically revises the original. He has deleted the tribal catalogue altogether (Judg 5:13-23), abbreviated the song's tribute to Jael (vss. 24-30), added a long historical résumé of events from biblical history, and appended a new conclusion in which Deborah looks forward to singing a second song "in the renewal of creation" (*in innovatione creature*).[77] Pseudo-Philo had a number of reasons for making so many modifications. Some additions were triggered by small exegetical problems posed by the text of Judges 5. For instance, Deborah's desire to finish the song before nightfall—"Slow up, you hours of the day . . . for night is coming upon us . . . then I will cease my hymn"—solves a difficulty created by an overly literalist reading of Judg 5:1: "Then Deborah . . . sang on that day." With all that had happened on "that day"—the mustering of the Israelites, the battle itself, Jael's slaying of Sisera—it was astonishing to early interpreters that there was time to sing so long a song before the onset of night. Rabbinic tradition attributes the feat to a miraculous prolonging of the day which provided the time needed to finish the song "on that day."[78] Pseudo-Philo does not mention such a miracle explicitly, but he has rewritten the song to accommodate the problem of "on that day" by noting that Deborah asked the day to slow down.[79] Other changes reflect Pseudo-Philo's attempt to harmonize the song with the preceding narrative in Judges 4, which presents a different—and sometimes contradictory—version of the battle. According to Judg 4:10, for instance, Barak mustered only the tribes of Zebulun and Naphtali to fight the battle, whereas according to the song's account the tribes of Ephraim, Benjamin, Machir (possibly Manasseh), and Issachar were also involved in the fighting. Pseudo-Philo has eliminated the apparent contradiction by deleting all references to specific tribes from both the prose account and the song and reporting that the battle was fought by "all the people."[80] Both this and the previous example show that Pseudo-Philo's modifications were neither fanciful nor capricious but represent the author's deliberate attempt to expand upon the implications of the biblical text as he read it and to integrate the song more fully with the prose account in Judges 4.

I would suggest, however, that not all the modifications introduced by Pseudo-Philo reflect an attempt to solve exegetical problems posed by the biblical text. Also detectable within his retelling of Judges 5 is another kind of change that reconfigures the song in light of contemporary liturgical practice. Within the biblical text itself, the Song of Deborah functions as a victory song, praising God and Israel for their respective contributions to the battle against Sisera, rebuking those tribes which failed to help, and celebrating Jael's exceptional act of heroism. Pseudo-Philo's version of the song serves a very different function. The song still celebrates the victory over Sisera, but it is no longer concerned with Israel's role in the battle (it eliminates the tribal catalogue) and scarcely mentions Jael's contribution. As presented by Pseudo-Philo, its function is to present Israel's praise of God for his wondrous acts both in the present and in the past. (It will be recalled that in his version of Judg 5:1 Pseudo Philo added the phrase "to the Lord," thus making explicit the audience to whom he thought the song was addressed.) Behind this change lies the same assumption that colored Philo's reading of the Song of Moses, the assumption that the songs in biblical narrative functioned as liturgical/cultic praise did in Philo's own day. It was this assumption that predisposed Pseudo-Philo to read the song as an act of communal worship performed by all the people. It also prompted him to report that after the song Deborah and the people went up to Shiloh to offer "sacrifices and holocausts"—yet another detail which does not appear in the story's original form. Indeed, this assumption so thoroughly saturated Pseudo-Philo's thinking about the song that it appears to have led him to reshape it in light of a liturgical genre in use in the Second Temple period.

As I have already indicated, until recently scholars knew almost nothing about liturgical poetry in the Second Temple period, and much of what they claimed to know was actually reconstructed from the literary songs in narratives such as *Judith* and *Tobit* or from rabbinic literature.[81] Thanks to evidence provided by Qumran liturgical poetry, however, we are now in a position to identify the conventional characteristics of several genres of liturgical poetry.[82] What this evidence reveals in the present case is that Pseudo-Philo's rewriting of Judges 5 appears to have been influenced by a specific genre of petitionary prayer preserved in the *Words of the Luminaries* and the *Festival Prayers,* two liturgical compositions found at Qumran.[83] Consider the following parallels:

First, the petitionary prayers found within the *Words of the Luminaries* and the *Festival Prayers* typically begin by asking God to remember: "Remember, Lord." What is to be remembered is often a divine action performed in the past (4Q 504, Frags. 1 and 2, col. ii, lines 11–12: "Remember your marvels which you performed in view of the peoples") or, in the case of the *Festival Prayers*, a festival (4Q 508, Frag. 2, line 2: "Remember, Lord, the feast of your compassion and time of the return"). The prayers in both compositions also periodically refer to earlier instances when God has remembered something: 4Q 504, Frags. 1-2, col. v, lines 9-10: "You remembered your covenant, for you redeemed us in the eyes of the nations"; 1Q 34, Frag. 3, col. ii, line 5: "you have chosen a people in the period of your favour, because you have remembered the covenant"; 4Q 508, Frag. 3, line 4: "you have remembered the times of . . ." Pseudo-Philo's version of the song does not begin by asking God to remember, but it does refer to God's memory in ways that are similar to what one finds in the *Festival Prayers* and the *Words of the Luminaries*. The song praises God for remembering his promises in the past (*Bib. Ant.* 32:12): "nor will our mouth be silent in narrating his marvelous deeds, *because he has remembered both his recent and his ancient promises.*" And as the song draws to a close, it looks forward to a time when God will remember Israel again (14): "From this hour, when Israel falls into distress . . . *he will remember that day* and send the saving power of his covenant . . ."

Second, after the formulaic opening, the prayers in the *Words of the Luminaries* and the *Festival Prayers* almost always make specific reference to an event or a series of events from biblical history in preparation for the petition itself. Among the events alluded to in the *Words*, for example, are the creation of Adam, the revelation at Sinai and other events from the life of Moses, the establishment of the Davidic kingship, the exaltation of Jerusalem as God's holy city, the Babylonian exile, and the sin and atonement of Israel in the postexilic period. As rewritten by Pseudo-Philo, the Song of Deborah also makes reference to events from the biblical past, moving chronologically from the life of Abraham to Sisera's defeat, a similarity which suggests that the song's historical prologue was one of the formal elements borrowed from the petitionary prayer genre found in the *Festival Prayers* and the *Words of the Luminaries*. This conclusion is reinforced by one other similarity: like several of the historical prologues in the *Words of the Luminaries*, Pseudo-Philo's song employs the first-person plural in recounting biblical history: "Behold the Lord has shown *us* his glory from on high. . . . And he chose *our* people and rescued Abraham *our* father" (*Bib. Ant.* 32:1). Compare 4Q 504, Frags. 1-2, col. ii, lines 7-15: "You, who did forgive *our* fathers when they made your mouth bitter . . . for *our* faults were *we* sold, but in spite of *our* failings you did call *us*."[84]

Third, in addition to structural similarities, certain more sporadic motifs surface in both the Qumran petitionary prayers and Pseudo-Philo's version of the Song of Deborah. One such motif is the petitioner's promise that God's wonders will be recounted in the future. In the *Words*, this idea appears several times: 4Q 504, Frag. 7, lines 2-3: "the marvels which you have done . . . Israel / so that the everlasting generations can tell . . . ; Frags. 1-2, col. vi, lines 9-10: "so that we can recount your mighty works to everlasting generations." A similar idea appears in the *Festival Prayers*, where the petitioner promises to sing eternally of God's wonders: 4Q 509, Frags. 1-4, col. i, line 22: "[And we, we will sing] your wonders from generation to generation"; 1Q 34, Frag. 3, col. i, line 6: "And we, we will celebrate your name forever [and ever]." These motifs are by no means unique to the petitionary-prayer genre. Similar language can be found in the Psalms, as in Psalm 145: "One generation shall laud your works to another, and shall declare your mighty acts." Even so, it is striking that this motif, found so often in the Qumran petitionary prayers, surfaces in Pseudo-Philo's Song of Deborah in such close proximity to other motifs characteristic of this genre (*Bib. Ant.* 32:12: "we will not cease to sing hymns, nor will our mouth be silent in narrating his marvelous deeds").

The final parallel is functional rather than formal. The primary rhetorical objective of the prayers in the *Words of the Luminaries* and of some of the festival prayers as well is to petition God for some favor—for deliverance from danger, for forgiveness, or for knowledge of torah; for example, 4Q 504, Frags. 1-2, col. ii, lines 11-12: "May your anger and your rage for all their sin turn away from your people Israel. Remember your wonders which you performed in view of the peoples. . . ." Given the narrative context of the Song of Deborah, which is sung *after* Israel is rescued from Sisera's army, one would not expect to find within it a petition for help. Significantly, however, the song's final section in Pseudo-Philo's version does refer to the petitioning of God, describing how Israel should seek God's help in the future (*Bib. Ant.* 32:14); "From this hour, when Israel falls into distress, it will call upon those witnesses [probably referring to the heaven and earth] along with these servants [probably the sun, moon and stars], and they will form a delegation to the Most High, and he will remember that day and send the saving power of His covenant."

In light of all these parallels, it appears that many of Pseudo-Philo's additions to the Song of Deborah can be traced to the influence of a single liturgical genre in use in Palestine in the final centuries of the Second Temple period, the time and place in which the *Biblical Antiquities* is believed to have been composed. In making this assertion I do not mean to dismiss the differences between the song and the petitionary prayers of Qumran. The historical prologue in the song is longer than anything found in the *Words of the Luminaries* and the *Festival Prayers,* and the song is missing motifs oft-repeated in the prayers (e.g., the phrase "Remember, O Lord"). As significant as these differences are, however, they are the kind that can be explained without having to invalidate the comparison altogether, since some can be understood as concessions to the song's original narrative role as a victory hymn, while others may reflect the fact that the petitionary prayer was itself a pliable genre that was adapted to different occasions. Moreover, I am arguing not that the song should be classified as a petitionary prayer but that the elements of the petitionary-prayer genre have been woven into the song alongside elements drawn from the original song in Judges 5 and the preceding narrative in Judges 4.

Whatever specific motivation prompted Pseudo-Philo to fuse elements from the supplicatory prayer genre into his retelling of Judges 5, his decision to do so presupposes a belief shared by many other early Jews—that there was no clear line between the biblical past and the liturgical present. We have seen evidence that when early Jews praised God in liturgical contexts, they believed that they were behaving as their biblical ancestors had when they sang songs to the Lord in the sacred past. Philo's paraphrase of Deuteronomy 32 and Pseudo-Philo's rewriting of Judges 5 suggest further that this belief also affected the way early Jews understood the songs in biblical narrative themselves, leading them to reconceptualize the songs' form and function in light of contemporary liturgical praise.

Canonical Self-Correction

A kind of cognitive dissonance emerged when early Jews began to notice that the contents of biblical narrative did not always live up to its reputation as sacred scripture. Those who perceived the Bible as an authoritative guide for ethical, literary, and liturgical conduct were liable to feel scandalized if a biblical hero failed to adhere to the standards they thought the Bible itself had established. We have seen, for instance, that early Jews saw in Exodus 15 the ideal response to a divine miracle: whenever God delivers Israel from danger or does it some other favor, the proper and pious response is to thank and praise him. Against the backdrop of this literary/behavioral norm, it was puzzling that Abraham, who had received so many benefactions from God throughout his life, never once sang a song in praise of God. One could even infer from his silence that the patriarch was ungrateful were his reputation for piety not so firmly established. As we will see, this dilemma was a source both of anxiety and of creativity in the early history of the Bible's interpretation, as Jewish interpreters and authors sought ways to reconcile the contents of biblical narrative with the norms they had derived from it.

Rabbinic literature preserves one kind of response to the absence of songs at certain points in biblical narrative. The rabbis sometimes explicitly acknowledged that they were disappointed by the "failure" of certain biblical heros to sing God's praises for his intervention in their lives. Believing as they did that it was obligatory to thank God for his benefactions, the rabbis could only interpret this silence as a mark of arrogance, ingratitude, or immaturity. Consider the following comments:

> Rabbi Berekiyah said in the name of Rabbi Elazar: "Israel ought to have sung a song over the fall of Sihon and Og, and Hezekiah ought to have sung a song over the fall of Sennacherib, as it is written: 'But Hezekiah did not make return according to the benefit done to him' (2 Chr 32:25). Why? Because 'his heart was proud.' You might object that Hezekiah was both king and righteous man, so how could his heart be proud? Rather, his heart was too proud to sing a song.". . . Rabbi Joshua son of Levi said, "If Hezekiah had sung a song over the fall of Sennacherib, he would have become the Messiah, and Sennacherib—Gog and Magog. He did not do so, however." (*Cant. Rab.* 4.19).[85]

> Why did they (the Israelites) not recite a song over the manna as they did over the well? Because concerning the manna they spoke words of disrespect, as it says: "But now our strength is dried up; and there is nothing at all" (Num 11:6). The Holy One blessed be He said, "I desire neither your complaints nor praises." Therefore, He permitted them to recite a song only over the well which they loved, as it says "Spring up, O well—sing ye unto it." (*Exod. Rab.* bəšallaḥ 25.7).

> From the day that the Holy One Blessed Be He created the world until Israel stood over the Sea, we do not find a man who sang a song to the Holy One Blessed Be He, except for Israel. He created Adam, and he did not sing a song. He saved Noah from the Flood, and he did not sing a song. He saved Abraham from the furnace and from the kings, and he did not sing a song. He saved Isaac from the knife, and he did not sing a song. He saved Jacob from the angel, and from Esau, and from the men of Shechem, and he did not sing a song. When Israel approached the Sea and He split it for them, however, immediately they sang a song before the Holy One blessed be He (*Exod. Rab.* bəšallaḥ 23.4).

The first passage identifies two biblical episodes where biblical figures did not sing a song after they were delivered from their foes: the defeat of Sihon and Og in the days of Moses (Num 21:21-35; Deut 2:26-3:7), and Hezekiah's escape from the Assyrian army of Sennacherib (2 Kgs 18-19). Hezekiah's silence was particularly disturbing for the rabbis because both biblical narrative and postbiblical tradition portray him as one of Israel's most righteous kings; indeed, there are even hints in rabbinic literature that he was viewed as a potential messiah.[86] It was all the more troublesome, therefore, that Hezekiah did not thank God for saving him from the Assyrians. The example set by the Song of the Sea and other songs in biblical narrative left such a deep imprint on the rabbis' sense of how biblical figures ought to behave after a miracle that it was impossible for them simply to excuse the king's silence. They concluded that while Hezekiah was a righteous leader, he was apparently afflicted with a streak of arrogance that prevented him from acknowledging God's help at a vulnerable moment in his reign. His failure to sing a song thus represents a blemish in his career; in fact, according to rabbi Joshua, Hezekiah's silence is the sin that ultimately prevented the king from becoming the messiah. The rabbis' commitment to the principle of thanking God for his benefactions was so deeply rooted that they were willing to tarnish the reputation of one of their most revered heroes in order to uphold it.

In the second passage, Israel is not permitted by God to sing a song after the miracle of the manna because earlier it had dared to complain about it: "If only we had meat to eat . . . our strength is dried up, and there is nothing at all but this manna to look at" (Num 11:4-6). Here again, the absence of a song in biblical narrative is interpreted as a deviation from the behavioral norm which biblical heroes were expected to exemplify—though this time it represents punishment for arrogance rather than the expression of it. This is made explicit by the contrast which the rabbis draw between Israel's silence after the miracle of the manna and the song it sings after the miracle of the well (Num 21:17-18). The contrast confirms that early Jewish readers of biblical narrative sometimes consciously measured its contents against the ethical and literary standards which they had derived from biblical narrative itself, in this case, from the Song of the Well.[87] What this tradition suggests, in fact, is that the elevation of the songs in biblical narrative to paradigmatic status had the effect of transforming biblical episodes without songs into a kind of antiparadigm, the way Israel was *not* to respond to God's generosity.

A similar response is implicit in the third passage, which contrasts the silence of Adam, Noah, and the three patriarchs with Israel's song at the Red Sea. Here we find the claim that Israel's ability to praise God with song was a kind of honor so special that not even Adam and the patriarchs were considered worthy of it. Israel should thus be grateful to God, not only for the miracles he has done for it but also for the opportunity to express its gratitude to God through song. We have in this passage additional evidence that Exodus 15 was assigned a special status by early Jews. Of interest here, however, is what this passage says about the Book of Genesis and its lack of songs. The silence of Adam and the patriarchs is not interpreted here as ingratitude, as is the silence of Hezekiah; it is taken as an indication that the heroes of Genesis do not fully exemplify the way Israel should relate to God. In my view, there is no better evidence that the paradigmatic status of songs such as Exodus 15 affected the way early Jews read biblical episodes without songs.[88]

There appears to have been another way in which early Jews—both rabbinic Jews and earlier Jews in the Second Temple period—responded to the lack of songs in biblical narrative. We have seen from Pseudo-Philo's *Biblical Antiquities* that early Jews often retold biblical narrative, adding or subtracting details and events in the process. By means of such changes it was possible to suppress those elements within the Bible that clashed with its status as sacred scripture—to whitewash the character flaws of biblical heroes, to credit them with additional acts of righteousness and faith, and to ensure that they always adhered to biblical standards of piety. Thus in both rabbinic and Second Temple period literature one can find a number of traditions which allege that biblical heroes such as Abraham and Hezekiah actually sang a song to the Lord in gratitude for his help. Rather than admitting that these figures failed to live up to the ethical and religious standards established by the songs in biblical narrative, these traditions simply supply the missing song when retelling biblical narrative. To document how widespread this phenomenon was, I have gathered several examples of it, culled from the Pseudepigrapha, Philo, the Dead Sea Scrolls, and rabbinic literature:

- Rabbinic tradition describes Psalm 92 as a song sung by Adam in gratitude for the Sabbath.[89] According to *Midrash Psalms* and *Pesikta Rabbati,* the psalm's superscription—"a song for the Sabbath day"—implies that Adam first addressed the psalm to the Sabbath. These texts then go on to read the next line—"It is good to give thanks to the Lord"—as an indication that Adam immediately readdressed the song to God at the Sabbath's suggestion.
- A song of Abraham is mentioned in several sources. In his treatise *On Drunkenness* (105-121), Philo describes Gen 14:22 as a song sung by Abraham after he defeated the kings who had taken Lot captive.[90] A song of Abraham is also presented in full in the *Apocalypse of Abraham,* an apocalyptic retelling of Genesis 15 probably composed in the first century C.E., which reports that an angel taught the song to the patriarch as he ascended to heaven to view its mysteries.[91] I have argued elsewhere that this song may also have been derived from Gen 14:22-23, the same verse from which Philo derives his version of the Song of Abraham.[92] The *Genesis Apocryphon,* an Aramaic paraphrase of Genesis found at Qumran, does not mention a song of Abraham per se, but it infers from the phrase "he called on the name of the Lord" in Gen 13:4 and elsewhere that Abraham praised and thanked God for his benefactions. Thus, at a point in its para-

phrase corresponding to Gen 13:4, the *Genesis Apocryphon* reports
that Abraham "praised," "blessed," and "gave thanks" to God "for
all the flocks and the good things which he had given me . . . because
he had brought me back to this land in safety" (col. xxi lines 2–3).[93]
Finally, rabbinic literature and at least one early Christian source
refer to a song of Abraham as well.[94] Significantly, one of these
references (*Gen. Rab.* 43.9) associates the song with Gen 14:22, as
did Philo and possibly the *Apocalypse of Abraham,* thus providing additional evidence that the Song of Abraham was originally associated
with this verse in particular.[95] I will discuss the origins of this tradition
at greater length below.

- Philo mentions in passing that Jacob "offers a hymn" when he dis-
covers that Joseph is still alive (*On Joseph* 253). In what appears to
be an unrelated tradition, one rabbinic source, a manuscript of *Midrash Tanhuma* published by Solomon Buber, ascribes a song to Jacob
after he wrestles with the angel in Gen 32:25–33.[96] According to this
tradition, Jacob's song replaces the song which the angel is supposed
to sing to God but cannot because he is being restrained by Jacob
(see appendix B for more on the Song of the Angels). The existence
of this song was evidently derived from the consonantal form of
Hos 12:4 (MT vs. 5) *wayyāśar ʾel-malʾāk* = "He strove with an angel."
Here it is important to note that traditional biblical manuscripts
contain only the consonantal form of the biblical text (the reader
was expected to provide the vocalization orally). It was therefore
possible to change the meaning of a word simply by inventing a
new pronunciation consistent with its consonantal form, something
that the rabbis delighted in doing. In the present instance, a rabbinic
reader revocalized the consonantal form of Hos 12:4 (MT vs. 5) to
read "he sang for an angel" *(wayyāšar ʾel-malʾāk)*.

- A hymn is attributed to Joseph's wife Aseneth (mentioned in Gen
41:45, 50–52, 46:20) in some versions of *Joseph and Aseneth* (21:10–21),
a Greek text which describes how Aseneth, daughter of the Egyptian
priest Potiphera, converted to the God of the Hebrews before mar-
rying Joseph (the story was apparently motivated by the need to
explain why a chaste Israelite like Joseph would marry the daughter
of an Egyptian priest). Composed sometime between the first century
B.C.E. and the second century C.E., the narrative reports that Aseneth "began to confess to the Lord and gave thanks, praying, for
all the good (things) of which she was deemed worthy by the Lord."[97]
In one manuscript (MS c 37 in the University Library, Uppsala),
she is joined by Joseph: "And it happened after this that Joseph
entered to the song of confession which Aseneth sang to the Lord
most High after she gave birth to Ephraim and Manasseh."

- The rabbis impute a song to Moses after he escapes from Egypt.[98]
- Targum Pseudo-Jonathan, an Aramaic translation of the Pentateuch, translates "It was then she (Zipporah) said" in Exod 4:26 as "It was then she praised" ("praise" = *šbḥ* is the word normally used in Aramaic biblical translations for "sing" in biblical Hebrew).[99] The translation appears to reflect an association of the word *ʾāz* ("then") in Exod 4:26 with the same word in Exodus 15:1: "*Then* Moses and the Israelites sang."
- A text from Qumran published in 1992—4Q 365 frag. 6b—contains an expanded version of Miriam's song in Exod 15:21.[100] Unlike many early interpreters who understood Miriam's singing as an antiphonic response to the Song of the Sea, the author of this text seems to have believed that Miriam sang a song with its own distinct lyrics. At one point in this song (which is quite fragmentary), its contents bear a resemblance to Judith's Hymn (line 3 of the song "You are great . . . " resembles Jdt 16:13, "O Lord, you are great . . . "), suggesting a possible literary relationship: perhaps Judith's Hymn was modeled on an expanded form of Miriam's song or Miriam's song was reshaped in light of Judith's hymn.
- Rabbinic tradition ascribes a song to Joshua when he stops the sun and moon during the battle at Gibeon. The song is represented in most sources as a replacement for the praise of the sun and moon when they cease "moving" at Joshua's command (compare Jacob's song cited earlier).[101] As was true of Zipporah's praise, the existence of Joshua's song may have been derived from an assocation of the word translated "then" in Josh 10:12 with the word translated "then" in Exod 15:1. It may also have been suggested by the word *Yāšār* in 10:13 (appearing in the sentence "Is it not written in the Book of Yashar?"), which can be revocalized as "he sang."[102] No extant Second Temple period source attributes a song to Joshua on this occasion, but two sources refer to a song or praise uttered by Joshua. Pseudo-Philo ascribes a song to Joshua and the people after the former recites the law (*Bib. Ant.* 21:8-9), and the fragmentary *Psalms of Joshua* from Qumran, which combines prose narrative, speeches, and poetic prayers in what is perhaps a retelling of Joshua's life, contains the following sentence: "When Joshua finished extolling and confessing praise with his praises . . ." (4Q 379 22 ii line 7).[103] It seems likely that this line once followed a song of praise of some sort (compare Deut 32:45 just after the Song of Moses, "When Moses had finished reciting all these words . . .").
- Several rabbinic sources, including *Pesikta de Rav Kahana* 17.1 and *Lamentations Rabba* 1:1 sec. 23, allude to a song sung by Gideon after he defeated the Midianites (Judges 7).

- Rabbinic tradition imputes a hymn to the cows who lead the ark from the Philistines back to Israel in the days of Samuel (1 Sam 6:10–12).[104] The rabbis infer the existence of the song from the verb *wayyišarnâ* ("And they went straight") in 1 Sam 6:12, which they revocalize as "And they sang." The rabbis propose several possible lyrics for the song. One proposal by Rabbi Nappaḥa was made famous by Gershon Scholem's suggestion that it represents one of the earliest examples of "Hekhalot hymnody," a genre of Jewish mystical poetry.[105] Other proposals deserve mention as well. One rabbi claims, for example, that the cows recited the Song of the Sea, apparently inferring this from an aural similarity between the phrase translated "he has triumphed gloriously" (*gāʾōh gāʾâ*) in Exod 15:1 and the verb translated "they mooed" (*wĕgāʿōh*) in 1 Sam 6:12. A similar pun underlies the proposals of Ps 93:1 and Isa 12:5, which both contain a word (*gēʾût* = "majesty") that sounds like "moo" in Hebrew.[106]
- King David's reputation as a musician and singer is already established within biblical literature itself. Several songs and poems are attributed to him by biblical narrative (2 Samuel 2, 2 Samuel 22, 2 Samuel 23, 1 Chronicles 16), and many of the psalms within the Psalter are imputed to him as well (recall the historical superscriptions described earlier). Nevertheless, it is worth noting that in the Second Temple period his reputation as a songwriter grew to immense proportions. Not only do the Septuagint and the Pšhitta (a Syriac translation of the Bible) attribute additional psalms to David, but literally thousands of songs and hymns are imputed to King David in Qumran literature, the Pseudepigrapha, and post–Second Temple sources as well.[107] Note the following examples: Pseudo-Philo ascribes two songs to David not mentioned by the Bible—one sung after he is anointed king (*Bib. Ant.* 59);[108] the other to exorcise Saul from demons (*Bib. Ant.* 60).[109] In addition to this, a prose passage in the *Psalms Scroll* found in cave 11 at Qumran reports that David composed 3,600 psalms and 450 songs, 446 to accompany offerings and festivals and four to heal the sick.[110]
- King Solomon's reputation as a songwriter is also well established within biblical literature. Thus 1 Kgs 4:32 mentions that he composed 1,005 songs (expanded to 5,000 in the Septuagint), and he is given credit for the Song of Songs as well (Song of Songs 1:1). Like David's, however, Solomon's repertoire of songs grew considerably in the Second Temple period, when the king was credited with the *Psalms of Solomon* and the *Odes of Solomon,* the first composed around 100 B.C.E., the second around 100 C.E.[111]
- Rabbinic tradition remedies Hezekiah's silence after he has been rescued from Sennacherib by associating the psalm in Isaiah 38

(performed by the king when he recovers from illness) with this episode. For example, the late midrashic collection *Aggadat Bereshit* reads, "*When Sennacherib came,* Hezekiah said, 'We will sing to stringed instruments'" (Isa 38:20).[112] Commenting on 2 Kings 20, the midrashic anthology *Yalqut Shimʿoni* preserves a clever development of this tradition, reporting that when Hezekiah did not sing a song after Sennacherib's defeat, God afflicted him with illness until he sang; the result is the song in Isaiah 38.

- Near the end of the *Testament of Job,* an early Jewish composition thought by some to have been composed by the Therapeutae, Job's companion Eliphaz recites a "hymn" responsively with Bildad and Zophar when they "knew that the Lord had granted them forgiveness for their sin but did not consider Elious [Greek for Elihu] worthy."[113] Their hymn consists largely in castigation of Elihu, "who did not acquire the Lord for his own" (43:9), but it also praises God for his justice (43:13).

- According to *Ag. Shir-hashirim,* p. 29, Daniel sings a song after he is delivered from the lion's den.

- *Esther Rabbah* 10.5 and other rabbinic texts report that as Mordecai is led around on a horse by his foe Haman, he offers praise to God accompanied by his students, by Esther, and by all Israel.

This list is incomplete. It does not include, for example, a song mentioned in both the Greek Apocrypha and rabbinic literature—the song sung by Daniel's three companions after God delivers them from the fiery furnace in Daniel 3—because, as we will see in the next chapter, this example represents a special case. That said, the list does show that early Jews believed that many more songs were sung in biblical history than are actually recorded in the biblical text. In part, this belief reflects an exegetical phenomenon which we discussed in connection with the historical superscriptions in the Psalter. The attributions of additional psalms to David and of the *Odes of Solomon* and the *Psalms of Solomon* to Solomon represent attempts to scripturalize postbiblical poetry, to situate it within the context of biblical narrative.[114] I wish to stress, however, that this was not the only reason that songs and psalms were attributed to biblical heroes. Many of the songs listed here serve to "reform" the contents of biblical narrative in light of the example set by the Song of the Sea and other songs in biblical narrative. In the eyes of early Jewish readers of the Bible, biblical heroes such as Abraham and Hezekiah personified piety and were thus expected to acknowledge God for his benefactions, even as the descendants of these heroes—Jews living in the present—acknowledged God in their communal worship. This expectation led early Jews to discover songs in biblical narrative either by reading its contents in a certain way or by drawing out the narrative's implications through biblical paraphrase. Each discovery had the effect of confirming for early Jews that the heroes of biblical history consistently adhered to the religious and literary standards of the Bible's canon-conscious readers.

We can observe this process at work by listening more closely to the song sung by Abraham. The earliest reference to the Song of Abraham appears in the writings of Philo, who describes Abraham's statement in Gen 14:22 as a victory song—a reading shared by later rabbinic tradition (see *Gen. Rab.* 43.9).[115] Although Philo himself does not seem to realize it, his description of Gen 14:22 contravenes the plain sense of the verse, which clearly indicates that the patriarch's statement was an oath: "I have raised my hand to the Lord Most High, maker of heaven and earth, that I would not take a thread or a sandal thong or anything that is yours . . ." To recognize what it was about this verse that led Philo to read it as a song, we must first understand Philo's attitude toward oath-taking. Philo makes it abundantly clear in his writings that he was highly suspicious of oaths which invoke God's name, for not only does the mere act of swearing call into the question the oath-taker's credibility, but the invocation of God's name subjects the oath-taker to the risk of profanation (see *Leg. Alleg.* III.207, *Spec. Leg.* II.4–5, *Decal.* 84).[116] Philo was not alone in this view, for other Second Temple and rabbinic sources adopt a similar posture toward oaths, especially those which invoke God's name (see Ben Sira 23:7–11; Matt 5:35; b. Ned. 20a, 22 a–b, 28a).[117] For such Jews Abraham's oath in Gen 14:22 violated a basic ethical norm, creating the impression that the patriarch was guilty of irreverence. Reading this verse as a song not only eliminated this problem; it also transformed Abraham's speech into yet another example of his renowned piety.[118] This stratagem evidently had some success in rehabilitating Abraham in this episode, for centuries after Philo, Rabbi Berachiah claimed that Moses was so impressed by Abraham's song that it influenced his composition of the Song of the Sea.[119] This was exactly the kind of response that the Song of Abraham tradition was meant to elicit, since one of the principle motivations for its invention was the scripturalizing impulse to adjust Abraham's behavior to fit the expectations of those who regarded the patriarch as a model of piety.

There is something else to be learned from Philo's reference to the Song of Abraham. There is no indication that Philo realized that he was misinterpreting the biblical text or for that matter that he was even interpreting it. As far as he was concerned, the Song of Abraham was there in the text in Gen 14:22 where the patriarch raises his hand to the Lord. As far as we can tell, Philo makes no distinction between it and the Song of the Sea or the Song of the Well in Numbers 21, which he mentions in the same passage. The same appears to be true for the songs mentioned in rabbinic tradition: the Song of Jacob, the Song of Joshua, even the

Song of the Cows. If rabbinic readers believed in the existence of these songs, it was not because they realized how reassuring it was to do so, but because they thought that they had uncovered references to these songs in Josh 10:12, Hos 12:4-5, and 1 Sam 6:12. Of course, the readings that led to these discoveries violated the text's plain sense—they were frequently triggered by no more than a superficial resemblance of some word in the verse to a form of the verb "to sing"—but for those who accepted these readings, the songs of Abraham, Jacob, Joshua, and the Cows were as much a part of the biblical past as was the Song of the Sea. Early Jews did not realize, or at least they did not act as if they realized, that in their attempts to recover the songs of the biblical past they were in fact reshaping that past in light of their own literary and liturgical expectations.

I have sought to describe how the scripturalization of biblical literature affected early Jewish literary practice. The rise of the Pentateuch and certain other texts as sacred scripture represented a crucial turning point in Israelite literary history, triggering new behaviors among both authors and readers. Jews now sought to emulate biblical genres and styles in their own literary and liturgical compositions, as if the Bible's form was as sacred as the events which it described. Ironically, it was this very effort to recover the biblical past by imitating the form in which it was told that marked the emergence of a new literary culture, a culture that expressed its values, its expectations, and its creativity through the way it remembered—and tried to relive—the biblical past.

What I hope to demonstrate next is that this culture left an imprint on the biblical text itself. The Bible's status as a model of literary and liturgical practice created a problem for early Jewish readers when they realized that the heroes of biblical history did not always live up to their responsibilities as sacred role models. Some Jewish exegetes and authors responded to this problem by retelling biblical narrative in their own way. Other Jews, as I will show in the next chapter, responded to it by revising the actual text of the Bible, weaving their religious norms and literary expectations into biblical narrative itself. We will discover that many of the songs in biblical narrative represent this kind of revision, having been inserted into the biblical text to transform the Bible into what it was perceived to be by the scripturalizing imagination of early Judaism.

·5·

SELF-FULFILLING POETRY

Early Jewish readers of the Bible did not fail to recognize that many of its stories lacked songs, a silence they found disquieting. For some rabbinic readers, the reticence of the Israelites after God's gift of the manna or of Hezekiah after his miraculous deliverance from the Assyrians was a sign of thanklessness. Other rabbis responded to the silence of biblical figures in the way that their Second Temple predecessors did. Unwilling to believe that pious figures like Abraham had failed to thank God for his benefactions, early Jews uncovered hints in the biblical text that their ancestors had really sung his praises after all; in some cases, they even believed that they knew the words of their songs. What prompted this kind of response was the need to reconcile the behavior of biblical heroes to the literary, ethical, and liturgical norms which the Bible itself was thought to have established. The greater the authority of biblical narrative as a model for conduct and expression, the greater the need to eliminate the dissonance between its actual content and what was expected of that content by those who saw it as scripture. One way in which early Jews did this was to reimagine the biblical past as it was supposed to be, a past in which biblical heroes regularly praised God for his generosity just as early Jews did themselves during their own worship.

In this chapter we will see that early Jewish reimaginings of biblical history actually had an effect on the development of the biblical text itself. I mentioned at the beginning of the preceding chapter that several of the songs in biblical narrative appear to have been added at a late stage in its compositional history, having been interpolated into episodes already long in existence at the time of their addition or appearing in episodes which were themselves composed at a late date. I should now like to suggest that the addition of these songs represents an effort—or series of efforts—to reconcile the Bible with its own scriptural status. In form and textual position, these songs are quite similar to songs such as Exodus 15 and Deuteronomy 32 (deliberately so, as we will see), but their insertion within the narrative represents a fundamentally different kind of literary act—one designed to fill in disturbing lacunae in the biblical text which became perceptible when it was read as scripture. The interpolation of these songs reflects an attempt to rewrite biblical narrative which is similar to the revisionist biblical paraphrases from the Second Temple period, only here biblical history is corrected through a reshaping of the biblical text itself.

Before we proceed to the evidence for this claim, we must address two methodological problems with significant implications for our argument. The first is the problem of dating. We can date with relative precision the interpolation of a few songs within biblical narrative. We know, for example, that the Song of the Three in the Greek versions of Daniel 3 must have been placed in its present narrative setting before 100 B.C.E., the approximate date of Daniel's translation into Greek and after the composition of the original form of Daniel 3 in or after the Persian period (Daniel 3 contains Persian loanwords which indicate that it could not have been composed before this time).[1] This is still not as precise a dating as one would like, but it is specific enough to indicate that the song was added at a time when canon-consciousness was exerting its influence on literary practice. Unfortunately, the interpolation of other songs is not so easy to date. As we will see, while the textual evidence clearly indicates that the Psalm of Hezekiah in Isaiah 38 was a secondary interpolation, it does not reveal when the interpolation occurred. In this and in other cases where the evidence is comparably ambiguous, we must again reason by analogy, appealing to the known to illuminate the unknown. Beginning with datable examples such as the Song of the Three and the Song of David in 1 Chronicles 16, which were clearly added to biblical narrative in the post-exilic period, I will show that other songs in biblical narrative share with them the signs of canon-conscious revision. In the end we may still be unable to pinpoint the century in which these songs were added to the biblical text, but we will have good reason for concluding that their narrative roles reflect the workings of the scripturalizing imagination.

That brings us to the second problem: how to identify the signs of canon-conscious revision. In the preceding chapter I suggested that songs were included within early postbiblical narratives such as *Judith* and *Tobit* in conscious emulation of Exodus 15 and Deuteronomy 32. In this chapter I will be making a similar claim for songs interpolated into biblical narrative itself late in its literary development: that they were added in an effort to emulate the literary characteristics of "classical" biblical narratives such as Exodus 15 and Deuteronomy 32. Such a claim is not altogether new. Some scholars already suspect, for instance, that the Song of David in 2 Samuel 22 emulates the Song of Moses in Deuteronomy 32, a reading that will be supported by evidence presented later in this chapter. The problem is how to distinguish between the act of emulation and the object being emulated. Given the similarities between 2 Samuel 22 and Deuteronomy 32, how does one know that it is the former which is the imitation and not the latter? And why should one not conclude that the insertions of the two songs simply represent independent manifestations of the same literary practice rather than the imitation of one song by the other? These are difficult questions to answer. As a matter of fact, there are indications that early Jewish readers themselves had difficulty distinguishing the songs actually in biblical narrative from those which which had been fashioned in emulation of biblical narrative. We have seen, for instance, that one rabbinic source (*Genesis Rabbah*) asserts that when Moses composed the Song of the Sea, he had in mind the Song of Abraham in Genesis 14, a conclusion that was only possible for someone who did not recognize that the Song of Abraham tradition only emerged in the wake of Exodus 15. Since we cannot know with certainty when most of the songs in biblical narrative were placed in their narrative settings, how are we to avoid mistaking the copy for the original and the original for a copy?

The solution to this problem lies in what we learned in the preceding chapter. There we saw that the scripturalization of biblical narrative had far-reaching implications for early Jewish literary practice. New kinds of literary behaviors emerged as Jews began to emulate the form of biblical narrative, as they forged links between its content and that of other scriptural compositions, and as they sought to extend the biblical past into their present through liturgical practice. These behaviors have left recognizable fingerprints all over postbiblical literature, as we have seen, and I now propose that these very fingerprints can be used to identify the songs in biblical narrative that were added as scripturalizing revisions. If a song seems consciously modeled on a song within the Pentateuch, if it cites a psalm within the Psalter, if it incorporates forms and motifs characteristic of early Jewish liturgical poetry, or in cases where the song has been interpolated to a preexisting text, if it noticeably alters the behavior of a biblical hero to better suit the religious and ethical norms of early Judaism—these are all marks of a scripturalizing imagination. Of course, none of this evidence is without its complications. A song that appears to cite a canonical psalm, for example, may simply preserve a formulaic expression independently surfacing in the psalm. Admittedly, there is little one can do to overcome the equivocal nature of some of the evidence. Nevertheless, I do not think it a coincidence that signs of canon-conscious literary activity almost always appear *in songs suspected to be late in any event*—either because the songs appear in narratives dated for linguistic or historical reasons to the postexilic period or because there is textual evidence that the songs were interpolated secondarily into preexisting narratives. This corroborating evidence makes it much harder to dismiss alleged signs of scripturalizing literary activity, since it places the insertions of these songs after the rise of incipient canon-consciousness

To further clarify this approach, let us look more carefully at the Song of the Three inserted into Daniel 3 between verses 23 and 24 in the Old Greek and Theodotian Greek translations.[2] The song is actually part of a much larger addition which has three components: the so-called Prayer of Azariah, which includes a confession of sin and a petition to God for deliverance;[3] a brief prose narrative, which describes how Daniel's companions were miraculously rescued by an angel from the fire into which they had been cast; and the Song of the Three itself, sung by Daniel's three friends in praise of God after their deliverance from danger. It is theoretically possible that these components were original to the narrative and somehow fell out of the Aramaic version preserved in the Masoretic Bible; but that is highly unlikely, for the Aramaic version is completely coherent without the additions, and indeed, the additions disrupt the surrounding story in a number of ways. Thus the additions use Hebrew names for the friends (Hananiah, Azariah, and Mishael), whereas the Aramaic version of Daniel 3 consistently uses their Aramaic names (Shadrach, Abednego, and Meshach). Moreover, in verse 46=23[4] it is reported that after the servants threw the martyrs into the furnace, they continued to stoke its fires—a claim that contradicts information already presented in verse 22 that these very servants had been burned to death as they cast the martyrs into the furnace.[5] And the additions have Azariah praying for salvation from the fire *after* the three friends are already walking around unharmed in its midst, rendering its petition superfluous.[6] It is of course possible that the prayer, the prose inset, and the song were not all placed in the text at the same time—in fact, there is reason to believe that the prayer may have been added only after the song and prose inset were already in place.[7] In whatever manner the additions entered the text, however, both the textual evidence and the disruption caused by the additions clearly indicate that all three components were added secondarily, not that they were removed secondarily. The question before us then is not *whether* the song was added to the narrative in Daniel 3 at a late stage in its compositional development, but *why*.

For an answer, it is helpful to compare the Song of the Three with the Song of Abraham as described by Philo. Whether Philo himself realized it or not, his reference to the Song of Abraham resolved the cognitive dissonance generated by the patriarch's oath in Genesis 14 by transforming it into an act of piety. So too the addition of the Song of the Three helps to reshape the narrative in Daniel 3 to fit the religious values and literary expectations of a canon-conscious audience. In the original form of Daniel 3 the narrative's focus is actually on Nebuchadnezzar. To be sure, the narrative recounts God's deliverance of the friends, but its description of the miracle is quite brief, and the narrative immediately shifts its attention to the king's response, as if it were more interested in how the miracle was perceived by the king than in the miracle itself.

The three men, Shadrach, Meshach, and Abednego, fell down, bound, into the furnace of blazing fire. Then King Nebuchadnezzar was astonished and rose up quickly. He said to his counselors, "Was it not three men that we threw bound into the fire . . . but I see four men unbound, walking in the middle of the fire, and they are not hurt; and the fourth has the appearance of a god. . . . Blessed be the God of Shadrach, Meshach, and Abednego, who has sent his angel and delivered his servants who trusted in him. They disobeyed the king's command and yielded up their bodies rather than serve and worship any god except their own God . . . there is no other god who is able to deliver in this way." (MT Daniel 3:23-28)

It is not altogether clear why the author of Daniel 3 placed so much emphasis on the king's response to the miracle. His objective may have been to promote the social benefits of belief in God by providing an example of how such belief shielded Jews from oppression by a foreign ruler. Alternatively, the king's praise of God may have served a missionizing agenda by illustrating how an act of Jewish piety led to the conversion of a non-Jewish ruler.[8] Whatever the explanation, the original form of the narrative fails to cite the response of the three friends themselves, precisely the kind of omission that would have troubled early canon-conscious readers. Their silence is all the more disturbing when contrasted with the pious response of the evil Nebuchadnezzar, who explicitly praises God for the miracle. For an audience that expected such praise from their Israelite heroes, the contrast between the pagan king's affirmation of God and the friends' silence would have made the latter appear all the more impious.[9] Rabbinic tradition solved the problem with its claim that the friends recited the Hallel after the miracle.[10] The Greek versions offer evidence that an earlier reader in the Second Temple period found another solution, rewriting the narrative to include the missing song.

The Song of Abraham tradition sheds light on the interpolation of the Song of the Three in another way as well. We discovered that Philo's reference to the song was not an arbitrary act of imagination. As far as Philo was concerned, the biblical text itself described the patriarch's song in Gen 14:22, where it reports that Abraham raised his arm to the Lord. Similarly, the praise attributed to Abraham in *Genesis Aprocryphon* turned out to be a reading of the phrase "Abraham called on the name of the Lord" in passages such as Gen 13:4. Still other songs mentioned in rabbinic sources—the song sung by Jacob after he wrestled with the angel or the Song of the Cows—were inferred from words in the biblical text which seemed to imply the performance of a song. Even if the literal meaning of the word in question had nothing to do with singing or song, it was enough that its consonantal form resembled a form of the verb translated "to sing." It is possible that a similar exegetical process underlies the addition of the Song of the Three. Much of what happens in the Greek additions appears to have been inferred from information provided by the narrative in its original Semitic form. For instance, the Greek additions contain a description of how the friends were saved by an angel who came down into the furnace and cooled the flames with a moist breeze (vss. 49-50=26-27). No such event is described in the original Aramaic version, but it could be inferred from the statements of Nebuchadnezzar, who claims to see a fourth "god-like" person in the furnace (vs. 25), and who later praises God for sending an angel to deliver the friends (vs. 28). In this instance at least, the author of the Greek additions has simply elaborated upon an event which, in his view, was mentioned in the original form of the story. So too the singing of the friends in the furnace may have been inferred from a "clue" hidden in the original. In Dan 3:25, the king reports that he sees "four men unbound, walking in the middle of the fire." The Aramaic word for "unbound" in this passage is the plural passive participle *šĕrayin*. The various Greek translations of Dan 3:25 translate this word with its original meaning, but an early reader familar with both Aramaic and Hebrew could very well have understood its unvocalized form as a plural active participle of the Hebrew verb meaning "to sing," which has virtually the same consonantal form.[11] Such a reading violates all the rules of modern philology but not the interpretive principles of early biblical interpretation, which often took great liberties with the consonantal form of the biblical text. Understood in this way, verse 25 could be translated as "I see four men singing and walking in the midst of the fire," a rendering which is close to what one actually finds in the Theodotian version of the Greek translation (vs. 24=1): "They walked around in the midst of the flames, singing hymns to God and blessing the Lord" (note that the verb translated "to sing" here is in the participial form, which supports my claim that it reflects the consonantal form of *šryn* read as an active participle).[12] This explanation is conjectural, of course, but it is consistent with the behavior of Philo and other early Jews, who assumed the existence of songs not actually found in biblical narrative itself because they, or the exegetical tradition which they had inherited, had detected references to the songs somewhere within the biblical text.

Even if this proposal proves to be correct, however, it describes only the trigger for the insertion, not the literary and religious factors that predisposed early readers to find songs within episodes like Daniel 3. What ultimately prompted the song's interpolation was the basic perception that the salvation of the three friends from the fiery furnace is analogous to other biblical stories of divine miracles. The existence of such a perception is not a matter of supposition; it was articulated in Second Temple period sources from as early as the second century B.C.E. that list the fiery furnace episode alongside other miraculous events from biblical history. Thus in 1 *Macc* 2:51-60, after Mattathias instructs his sons to "remember the deeds of the ancestors," he recalls the faith of the three friends in the furnace in a list of biblical heroes that includes Abraham, Joseph, and David. Clearly by this time, Jews believed that Daniel 3 continued a pattern in biblical history in which God delivers pious Israelites from danger. Similarly, in 3 *Macc* 6:2-9 (probably composed in the first century C.E.), the priest Eleazer recalls several events from Israel's past in which God delivered the people from danger, including the destruction of the Egyptian army in the Red Sea, the destruction of Sennacherib's army in the days of Hezekiah, the deliverance of Jonah from the belly of the fish, and the miraculous dousing of the flames that threatened the lives of Daniel's companions.[13] This passage is even more illuminating than 1 *Macc* 2:51-60 because it testifies that early Jews consciously associated the miracle in Daniel 3 with other biblical miracles celebrated afterward by songs of praise, such as Exodus 14-15, 2 Kings 18-19/Isa 37-38, and Jonah 2. It was precisely this association that probably suggested to early Jews that there was something missing in Daniel 3. At other times when God delivered Israel from danger, Israel responded by praising God. If Daniel 3 continued the pattern established by these episodes, it too should contain a song of praise after the description of the miracle—all the more so since the friends had already proved themselves so pious. The insertion of the Song of the Three conveniently supplied the missing element and in so doing aligned Daniel 3 with early Jews' sense of how biblical history should proceed.

We probably would not have surmised any of this were it not for the textual evidence which proves that the song was interpolated into the narrative secondarily. If we had only the Greek version of Daniel 3, after all, there would be little reason to suspect that its use of a song was any different from the use of songs in episodes such as Exodus 14-15 and Judges 4-5, which also describe acts of divine intervention. Once alerted by the textual evidence that the Song of the Three represents a revision of biblical narrative, however, one can recognize within the song itself further evidence that it was added "to scripturalize" Daniel 3, that is, to transform it into what biblical narrative was expected to be by canon-conscious Jews.

Let us return to the references to the fiery furnace episode in 1 *Maccabees* 2 and 3 *Maccabees* 6. The passages in which these references occur not only demonstrate that early Jews identified certain patterns running through biblical history but that they sought to extend these patterns into the present day. If Mattathias instructed his sons to remember the zealous heroism of their biblical ancestors, it was to encourage them to behave similarly in their struggle to resist Antiochus IV: "Remember the deeds of the ancestors . . . and *you* will receive great honor and an everlasting name" (1 *Macc* 2:51). If Eleazar reminds God of how he saved Israel in the past, it is to convince God to act again in the present to save the Alexandrian Jews from the persecution of Ptolemy IV Philopater. Each speech reflects a fundamental tenet of the scripturalizing imagination, that the heroes of the biblical past represent *exempla* to be emulated in the present-day conduct of Jews. As we saw in chapter 4, it is this perception which accounts for why the songs in biblical narrative were treated as models of contemporary liturgical conduct. Less directly, it also sheds light on why they were assigned new functions by authors such as Philo and Pseudo-Philo, who interpreted them in light of contemporary liturgical conduct. There is reason to believe that the scribe who interpolated the Song of the Three read Daniel 3 through the filter of this perception and that it affected his choice of lyrics for the song.

Scholars have long believed that the lyrics of the Song of the Three were drawn from or were modeled upon a song once recited in the Jerusalem Temple or in a synagogue.[14] They note, for example, that in the first six lines (52-56=29-34), the song makes repeated references to the temple and to God's throne within the temple: "the temple of your sacred glory," "you who sit upon the cherubim" (winged creatures who guarded God's throne), "your royal throne" (note also the mention of priests in vs. 84=62).[15] Within the same section of the song, line 52=30—"Blessed is your glorious and holy name, to be highly praised and highly exalted forever"—resembles a doxological formula recited by the high priest in the Second Temple: "Blessed be the name of the glory of his kingship forever."[16] Later in the song, verses 57-90=35-68 alternate between calls to bless the Lord and the refrain "sing his praise and highly exalt him forever," suggesting that this section of the song at least was originally composed for responsive recitation in a congregational setting (compare the structure of Psalm 136).[17] Finally, the song's last line—"give thanks to him for his mercy endures forever"—resembles yet another doxological formula which was recited in cultic/congregational settings in the postexilic period (see Jer 33:11; 1 Chr 16:34, 41; 2 Chr 5:13, 7:3, 6, 20:21; Ezra 3:11; 1 *Macc* 4:24; Ps 100:5, 106:1, 107:1, and 136:1; and the last psalm of the Egyptian Hallel, Ps 118:1, 29).[18] All this evidence suggests either that the song was itself once recited in a liturgical context before being incorporated into Daniel 3 or that it was modeled on such a song.[19] In either case, the addition of the song represents the same kind of change we saw reflected in Philo's description of the Song of Moses and Pseudo-Philo's paraphrase of the Song of Deborah, a reshaping of biblical history in light of contemporary liturgical genres and style. The scribe who interpolated the song did not recognize that its references to the temple and the temple cult were anachronistic in the context of Daniel 3 (at the time of Daniel's three friends, the Babylonian exile, the temple was not standing) because from his perspective the heroes of the biblical past and Jews worshiping in the present day adhered to the same liturgical norms.

A similar fusion of biblical past and liturgical present surfaces in a second song within biblical narrative that can be also be demonstrably dated to the postexilic period: the song attributed to David in 1 Chr 16:7-36. Like the Song of the Three, the song in 1 Chronicles 16 appears within a rewriting of an earlier biblical narrative that does not contain a song, the story of how David transported the ark of the Lord to Jerusalem in 2 Samuel 6. The original form of the narrative in Samuel reports that David "brought up the ark of the Lord with shouting, and with the sound of the trumpets" (2 Sam 6:15), after which the king "offered burnt offerings and offerings of well-being before the Lord . . . and blessed the people in the name of the Lord" (vss. 17-18). The Chronicler has completely transformed this episode by inserting an elaborate description of how David appointed "certain of the Levites as ministers before the ark of the Lord, to invoke, to thank, and to praise the Lord" (1 Chr 15:25-16:42). The song is presented in the midst of this larger addition, appearing as one of the cultic practices instituted by David at this time. According to the narrative, David does not actually sing the song himself; rather, he orders Asaph and his kindred, professional levitical singers, to perform the song as part of their official responsibilities as ministers before the ark. Evidently the reader of the narrative is to understand that the Levites first performed the song at this time (the Chronicler stresses in verse 7 that David commanded the performance of the song on the very day he brought the ark to Jerusalem—"then on that day."),[20] but the Chronicler also implies that the Levites regularly recited the song afterward as well, claiming just after the song in verse 37 that "David left Asaph and his kinsfolk before the ark of the covenant to minister regularly before the ark as each day required."[21] What the narrative seems to be describing is not merely the recitation of a song at a significant moment in the biblical past but also the institution of a ritual performed continuously by the Levites.

It is for this reason that the song in 1 Chronicles 16 is unique among the songs in biblical narrative. Other songs may have originated within a cultic context, but no other song is *explicitly* assigned a cultic role by its present narrative setting. In 2 Samuel, for example, David is credited with several songs and poems—the lament for Saul and Jonathan in 2 Samuel 1, a song of thanksgiving in 2 Samuel 22, and "last words" in 2 Samuel 23—but these songs are not placed within a cultic context; nor are they said to have served a cultic function. It is only in Chronicles 16 that biblical narrative explicitly credits David with composing cultic poetry. Many recent scholars believe that the Chronicler was making a claim about contemporary cultic practice through his attribution of the psalm to David—perhaps in response to rival claims about the nature of the the temple cult.[22] There are hints here and there in biblical literature that some in the postexilic period were opposed to the participation of Levites in the cult. J. Wellhausen argued, for example, that P (which he dated to the postexilic period) sought through its presentation of Israel's history to exclude non-Aaronide Levites from the priesthood.[23] When the Chronicler wrote in 1 Chronicles 15-16 that David established the Levitical cultic rite in the temple, he may have been responding to such anti-Levite posturing, justifying the Levites' participation in the temple cult of his own day by attributing their role to Israel's greatest king.[24] Another possible motive is that the Chronicler may have been trying to convince his readers that cultic practice in the Second Temple represented an authentic continuation of cultic practice in the glory days of David and Solomon *despite the destruction of Solomon's Temple by the Babylonians in 586 B.C.E.* According to the Chronicler, David assigned the Levites their cultic responsibilities before the temple was actually contructed in the days of his son Solomon. The Chronicler's version of Israel's cultic history effectively freed Israel's cultic worship from dependence upon the temple's physical structure, with the implication that even after its destruction, the temple's organizational infrastructure and the practices performed within it could survive. This is consistent with the observation of Sara Japhet that the Chronicler sought through his rewriting of biblical history to minimize the scope and significance of events that disrupted Israel's habitation of the land, especially the Exodus and the Babylonian exile.[25] Indeed, Japhet cites the song in 1 Chronicles 16 as an example of how the Chronicler manipulated his biblical sources to promote his distinctive view of Israelite history. The song cites Psalm 105, which recounts Israel's history from Abraham to the Exodus, but it interrupts its citation just before the psalm reaches Joseph's descent into Egypt and the Exodus (vs. 16), as if the Chronicler wanted to delete these events from his audience's memory of its past.[26] In this way the song reinforces the impression of uninterrupted continuity in Israel's occupation of the land. If scholars are right that the contents of 1 Chronicles 16 reflect postexilic conventions of liturgical praise, the song also helps to create the impression that the ritual practices of the Second Temple—if not the physical structure of Second Temple itself—represent a direct continuation of ritual practices begun even before the construction of the First Temple.

Whatever claim the Chronicler was trying to make by inserting the song, our interest lies in the literary and religious assumptions that licensed the attribution of a contemporary liturgical act to a hero from biblical history. First Chronicles 16 offers evidence that even early in the Second Temple period the biblical past was being reinvented in light of the liturgical present; indeed, the Chronicler actually claims that David *intended* the song to be recited cultically, as if the king knew that what he did would later serve as a model for liturgical conduct. For the Chronicler, David was not merely a poet or a musician—roles he already plays in Samuel—he was a liturgist who composed psalms for recitation in the temple even before there was a temple. Perhaps the Chronicler invented this role for David to serve his own agenda, but such a role would have seemed credible only to an audience whose members were already predisposed to identify their own ritualistic speech with the historical speech of their biblical ancestors.

There is another way in which the song in 1 Chronicles 16 reflects a canon-conscious perspective. As I have hinted, the song cites psalms found in Psalter; indeed, it is constructed entirely from psalm citations drawn from three psalms: Pss 105:1-15 (= 1 Chr 16: 8-22); 96:1-13 (= vss. 23-33), and 106:1, 47-48 (= vss. 34-35).[27] We have already seen evidence that these citations have been carefully edited to serve the Chronicler's ideology, with all references to the Exodus excluded from his song. Further evidence for this conclusion is the way in which the citations have been selected so as to echo the preceding narrative. As scholars have long noted, the song repeatedly employs the verbal roots found in 1 Chr 16:4, "He appointed certain of the Levites as ministers before the ark of the Lord, *to invoke, to thank, and to praise* the Lord." Thus the verb "invoke" = *zkr* in this sentence appears in vss. 12 and 15 of the song (translated in NRSV as "remember");[28] "thank" = *ydh* appears in vss. 8, 34, and 35; and "praise" = *hll* surfaces in vss. 10 (translated as "glory"), 25, and 36. All this is evidence that the author of the preceding narrative in 1 Chronicles 16, presumably the Chronicler himself, was responsible for the selection of psalm citations within the song. But what made this author turn to the Psalms in the first place? The most likely answer is that at the time of the Chronicler, the psalms in the Psalter and the narrative in 1-2 Samuel were already being read in light of one another, an association triggered by the presence of these two bodies of literature within the same scriptural corpus. Hence, just as the author or authors of the historical superscriptions in the Psalter reinterpreted the psalms in light of 1-2 Samuel by using biblical narrative to reconstruct the circumstances in which David recited the psalms, the Chronicler rewrote David's story in light of the Psalter by using the psalms to construct the words of his song in 1 Chronicles 16. Both behaviors signal that the scripturalization of biblical narrative had completely altered the context in which it was read, expanding its literary borders to include whatever else was included within scripture at the time. As we know, a similar kind of behavior became habitual among later rabbinic and Christian readers of the Bible, who would draw myriad connections between even far-flung verses within their respectives canons. While it is not clear what the Chronicler's canon consisted of—indeed the term "canon" in the sense of a closed corpus of sacred writings is likely to be somewhat anachronistic for his period[29]—his choice of lyrics represents precisely the kind of scriptural cross-referencing which is so central to how canon-conscious readers perceive biblical literature.

In light of 1 Chronicles 16 we now know that the interpolation of the Song of the Three was not an isolated literary act but was part of a larger revisionist trend which sought to reformulate biblical narrative in light of canon-conscious assumptions. The question now before us is whether there are other songs in biblical narrative which also reflect this revisionist trend. Even a century ago scholars were claiming that many of the songs in biblical narrative—the Psalm of Hezekiah in Isaiah 38, the Prayer of Jonah in Jonah 2, the Prayer of Hannah in 1 Samuel 2, the Song of David in 2 Samuel 22—represent secondary interpolations added to biblical narrative at a late date. Might these songs also reflect scripturalizing revisions?

To answer this question we must be willing to speculate a bit. As we have seen, the Song of the Three was probably inserted into Daniel 3 at around the same time as the authors of *Judith* and *Tobit* were inserting songs into their narratives, and so it is no stretch to conclude that it reflects the same literary culture which produced the hymns of Judith and Tobit. As for Chronicles, though it was probably composed two or even as many as three centuries earlier than Daniel 3 (it was probably written in the fourth century),[30] we have already seen that it too reflects a time when the scripturalizing imagination was already at work. The insertion of other songs in biblical narrative is much more difficult to date, however. In the case of the songs in the Greek versions of Daniel 3 and 1 Chronicles 16 we can date the addition of these songs to the postexilic period because we can date the narratives in which they have been placed to this period. In the case of the songs in Isaiah 38, Jonah 2, 1 Samuel 2, and 2 Samuel 22, on the other hand, the evidence is much more equivocal. At least three of these songs—Isaiah 38, 1 Samuel 2, and 2 Samuel 22—appear in narrative compositions probably composed in the First Temple period. If these songs were added secondarily, however, the date of the original narrative's composition may tell us nothing about the date of the song's addition: the two events could be separated by centuries (compare the chronological gap between First Isaiah in Isa 1-39, parts of which were evidently composed in the eighth century, and Second Isaiah in chapters 40-55, probably composed in the sixth century). So far as I can tell, the language of the songs themselves exhibits none of the signs of postexilic Hebrew found throughout late biblical books such as Chronicles and the Hebrew sections of Daniel—perhaps another clue that they were added in the First Temple period—but this evidence may also be irrelevant. First Chronicles 16 proves that postexilic authors sometimes recycled earlier poetry for use in a narrative setting. Hence, while the songs of Hezekiah, Hannah, David, and Jonah may have been composed in the First Temple period—after all, each is attributed to a figure living in that period—their insertion within their present settings may not have occurred until the Second Temple period, after the dawn of canon-consciousness. With the linguistic and historical evidence currently available, there is no way to prove that these songs were placed in the narrative at a late date, but neither is there any way to prove that they were added earlier.

If definitive conclusions are beyond our reach, however, provisional hypotheses are not. The narrative settings of the songs in Isaiah 38, Jonah 2, 1 Samuel 2, and 2 Samuel 22 may have originated in the First Temple Period, and the songs themselves may have been composed in this period as well, but in each case *the relationship* between narrative and song bears some of the distinguishing marks of scripturalizing revisionism. Regarding the songs of Hezekiah and Jonah, their position in the textual sequence and the effect of their contents on the surrounding narrative are so similar to what we have found for the Song of the Three, 1 Chronicles 16, and early postbiblical songs such as the Hymn of Judith and the Hymn of Tobit—and at the same time so different from the roles of Exodus 15 and Deuteronomy 32—that one can date *their insertion* (not, I stress, their composition) to the age of emergent canon-consciousness with a high degree of confidence. Turning to the songs in 1 Samuel 2 and 2 Samuel 22, the literary evidence is less straightforward, but even here one can detect the effects of the scripturalizing imagination. Proof may be impossible, but the weight of the evidence tilts the scales in favor of the conclusion that the elevation of biblical narrative to scriptural status did not merely affect the formation of late biblical books like Daniel and Chronicles but was a major force in the reshaping of biblical narrative as a whole, leaving its imprint even on episodes composed before the emergence of canon-consciousness.

Nowhere is this imprint more clearly recognizable than in the Psalm of Hezekiah in Isaiah 38, imputed to the king after God miraculously cures him from mortal illness. As was true for the Song of the Three and 1 Chronicles 16, the narrative in Isaiah 38 survives in two forms: one with the psalm (Isaiah 38) and one without (2 Kings 20). Scholars still differ over which of these two versions reflects the original form of the narrative. Gesenius was the first of many scholars to argue that the narrative in Isaiah 36–39 was borrowed from 2 Kings, observing that a similar phenomenon is reflected in Jeremiah 52, which reuses the narrative in 2 Kings 25 as a kind of historical epilogue for Jeremiah's prophecies. More recent commentators have begun to question this view, arguing that the arrangement of episodes in these chapters better suits the structure of Isaiah than that of the Deuteronomistic History.[31] Whatever the precise relation of these versions to one another, most scholars agree that the psalm at least represents a secondary interpolation added to the narrative at a late stage in its literary development.[32] This explanation is more convincing than the opposite conclusion—that the psalm was original to the narrative and was later removed from the version preserved in 2 Kings 20—because, along with the absence of the psalm in 2 Kings, there are at least two other reasons to suspect that the psalm was added at a late date.

First, the verse introducing the psalm—verse 9—interrupts the narrative's flow with the kind of syntactical structure characteristic of the historical superscriptions used in the Psalter to impute psalms to David. It begins with a generic label ("a writing"),[33] ascribes the psalm to a historical figure ("of King Hezekiah of Judah"), and concludes with a temporal phrase describing the circumstances of the song's performance ("when he was sick and had recovered from his sickness")—exactly the form of superscriptions found at the beginning of psalms such as 3 and 63.[34] If, as Childs argued, the use of the historical superscription is a canon-conscious literary activity, the use of this form to introduce Hezekiah's psalm must have occurred after the rise of canon-consciousness; indeed, one could argue that the appearance of this kind of superscription *in a narrative setting* reflects the same equation of the Psalms with the songs in biblical narrative that we detected in 1 Chronicles 16 and other early Jewish sources.

Second, there are signs that the narrative in Isaiah 38 has been subject to other kinds of secondary interpolations. Consider Isa 38:21-22. These verses were apparently part of the original form of the episode (they appear as verses 7-8 in 2 Kings 20), but they surface at a different point in the narrative in Isaiah 38. In 2 Kings 20 Hezekiah's request for a sign in verse 8 is what elicits Isaiah's description of the sign in verse 9. In Isaiah 38, on the other hand, the king's request for a sign is placed in verse 22 *after* Isaiah's description of the sign in verse 7, a sequence which obscures the causal relationship of these events to one another. Moreover, in Isaiah 38, Hezekiah is no longer asking for a sign that he will be healed as he does in 2 Kgs 20:8: "What is the sign that the Lord will heal me and that I will go up to the House of the Lord on the third day?"; in Isa 38:22 he simply wants to know when he is supposed to go up to the House of the Lord— "What will be the sign that I shall go up to the House of the Lord?"—a request which never receives a response in Isaiah 38. These verses fit so poorly within the narrative of Isaiah 38 that some scholars believe that they were added as a kind of clumsy emendation by a scribe seeking to remedy the omission of these verses earlier in the narrative. This hypothesis is supported by a manuscript of Isaiah found at Qumran, where vss. 21-22 appear in a different hand and spill into the margin of the text.[35] The textual evidence still allows for other possible interpretations—it is possible that the original copyist of the Qumran manuscript simply forgot to write down vss. 21-22 by accident and a later proofreader tried to squeeze them back in[36]—but it certainly lends support to the hypothesis that these verses were added as a secondary revision of the narrative in Isaiah 38 and, by extension, to the claim that other parts of Isaiah 38—specifically the psalm—were added as secondary revisions as well.

In truth, neither of these arguments is the kind that can prove that the psalm was added secondarily to the narrative. One must keep in mind, however, that the absense of the psalm in 2 Kings 20 allows for only two possibilities: either the psalm was added to the narrative secondarily or it was removed from it secondarily. Within the confines of this choice, the arguments presented here lend greater credibility to the first possibility.

Having reached this conclusion, however, one may well wonder why a scribe would disrupt an originally coherent narrative with a song. Given what we have seen in this and the preceding chapter, the answer is clear: the interpolation of Hezekiah's Psalm represents precisely the kind of scripturalizing revision detectable within the Greek versions of Daniel 3 and 1 Chronicles 16. The interpolation of the song may make the narrative appear less coherent in our eyes, but the evidence suggests that it made the narrative *more* coherent in the eyes of early Jewish readers who believed that no miracle story was complete without a song of praise from those delivered by God. The original form of narrative reflected in Isaiah 38 = 2 Kings 20 reports that Hezekiah became deathly ill, prayed to God to remember his past righteousness, and was granted a sign by God that he would recover, but it mentions no response from Hezekiah, no act of praise or acknowledgment of God for his intervention. This was precisely the kind of omission that troubled early canon-conscious Jews. As a matter of fact, one postexilic source, Chronicles, actually expresses disappointment with Hezekiah for not thanking God as he should have after his recovery. In his retelling of this episode in 2 Chr 32:24-25, the Chronicler reports that after the king's recovery Hezekiah "did not make return according to the benefit done to him, for his heart was proud." If this verse seems familiar, it is because we have already had occasion to look at it in the preceding chapter. There we saw that it was cited by the rabbis to explain why Hezekiah did not sing a song after he was rescued by God from the Assyrians.[37] Because the rabbis' biblical canon included Hezekiah's Psalm in Isaiah 38, they had to explain the verse in light of another episode in the life of Hezekiah when the king failed to sing a song in response to a miracle— Hezekiah's miraculous deliverance from Sennacherib. When the Chronicler first composed this verse, however, he seems to have had in mind Hezekiah's failure to acknowledge the Lord after his recovery from illness, the episode which he has just described in 1 Chronicles 32.[38] I would argue that the interpolation of a psalm in Isaiah 38 responds to the same interpretive problem that troubled the Chronicler—the seeming ingratitude of a biblical hero—but it offers a different kind of solution, restoring Hezekiah's pious reputation by ascribing to him a song of thanksgiving. The fact that the

Chronicler makes no reference to the psalm—as if he did not know about it—represents additional circumstantial evidence that its interpolation did not occur until after the composition of Chronicles in the early Second Temple period.

This interpretation of the evidence assumes that the psalm in Isaiah 38 functions within the narrative as an expression of gratitude, an assumption that not all scholars would accept. To be sure, most scholars see Isa 38:9–20 as a typical psalm of thanksgiving, resembling psalms such as Psalm 30 which praises God for delivering the speaker from illness: "You have held back my life from the pit of destruction . . . the living, they thank you, as I do this day" (Isa 38:17–19).[39] A few commentators have concluded, however, that the psalm should actually be classified as a petition for help.[40] The tenses of many of the verbs used in the psalm are ambiguous, so that one can read the psalm as a lament for troubles currently suffered, not as a recollection of troubles now overcome. Moreover, noting that the psalm is introduced as a "letter," William Hallo has likened it to Sumerian inscriptional "letter-prayers" addressed to deities by kings in need of their intervention (one such letter-prayer was evidently occasioned by illness).[41] If, as this evidence suggests, the psalm constitutes a petition and not a thanksgiving song, are we right to liken its interpolation to that of the Song of the Three? There may be no way to settle the debate over the psalm's genre once and for all, but I would note that the psalm's actual genre is not as relevant for understanding its present narrative role as one might think. What is relevant is the psalm's function as perceived by the scribe responsible for its insertion in the narrative, and while we can never know for certain how this scribe read the psalm, we do know that other early Jews read it as a thanksgiving song performed in response to the king's miraculous recovery. Note, for example, how the psalm is represented in the Aramaic translation of Isa 38:9: "A writing *of thanks for the miracle* that was wrought for Hezekiah king of the tribe of Judah after he had been sick and had recovered from his illness." This evidence is not decisive, for the targum may reflect only how the Aramaic translator saw the psalm, not the way it was intended to function within the narrative by the scribe who interpolated it. It does show, however, that even if the Psalm of Hezekiah was originally composed as a petition or as a "letter-prayer," it was eventually reread as a song of thanksgiving by early Jewish readers. Also keep in mind that Hezekiah is criticized by early Jewish interpreters not because he forgot to complain about his health but because he failed to behave gratefully after God delivered him from danger. In my view, it was precisely this disappointment that predisposed an early Jewish scribe to insert the psalm in the narrative as the king's missing act of thanks even though this may have involved a misinterpretation of the song's contents.

Disappointment also may have prompted the insertion of the Prayer of Jonah in Jonah 2. As is true of Hezekiah's Psalm, scholars disagree over the genre and function of the prayer. It was once common for scholars to read it as a petition through which Jonah seeks deliverance from the belly of the fish.[42] They based this interpretation in large part on Jonah 2:1, which reports that Jonah *"prayed* to the Lord his God," since the verb "to pray" in biblical Hebrew often refers to acts of petition (compare Jonah 4:2, "He prayed to the Lord and said . . . please take my life from me"). The problem with this interpretation is that the prayer itself has many attributes of a thanksgiving song. It begins in the first five verses by recalling the distress of the speaker as he sinks into the water (e.g., vs. 3, "You cast me into the deep . . . and the flood surrounded me"), but it soon slips into praise of God for sparing the life of the speaker (vs. 6, "you brought up my life from the pit") and then ends with a promise to celebrate God's deliverance with the "voice of thanksgiving" in verse 9 (translated as "the voice of praise" in the targumic translation of Jonah). This evidence is hard to ignore, and indeed many recent studies have concluded that Jonah's prayer represents not a cry for salvation from the belly of the fish but a song of thanksgiving for deliverance from drowning.[43] This is how some early Jewish and Christian interpreters understood the prayer, and it is consistent with the penchant of early Jews to place songs of praise near the end of stories of divine deliverance (though it is true that they occasionally added petitionary prayers as well; recall the Prayer of Azariah added to Daniel 3).[44] In light of recent advances in the understanding of early Hebrew lexicography, it appears that even the verb translated "prayed" in Jon 2:1 may support this interpretation—or at least is not inconsistent with it—since the word meaning "prayer" (*tĕpillâ*) could be used interchangeably with the word meaning "praise" (*tĕhillâ*), especially in the postexilic period.[45] Because of such evidence, most recent studies understand the prayer as praise offered by Jonah to thank God for saving him from drowning in the sea.

Now to understand why I claim that the insertion of this prayer was motivated by disappointment, one must first recognize that of all the prophets in the Hebrew Bible, Jonah is the most consistently disappointing—at least from the vantage point of an early Jew. At several points in the narrative, the prophet stubbornly refuses to behave as a pious biblical hero should, fleeing from a divine command (Jonah 1:1-3) and chastising rather than praising God for his mercy (4:1-4). If the prayer was interpolated into the narrative secondarily, its addition may reflect an attempt to reconcile the behavior of Jonah with the ethical and religious norms of canon-conscious readers, to make him behave in accordance with their expectations of biblical heros. Brevard Childs has made precisely this point, suggesting that the prayer was added after the Book of Jonah came to be accepted as canonical.[46] He argues that its insertion was intended to "typify" Jonah, to transform him from an antihero into a hero whom a canon-conscious audience could relate to and emulate. If from our point of view the prayer does not quite fit in its narrative setting, this was the cost of resolving the larger incongruity created by the book's canonization, which forced the defiant prophet into the role of moral exemplum.

But what if more recent scholars are right in claiming that the prayer is actually integral to the surrounding story? As we saw at the beginning of chapter 4, many recent readers of Jonah acknowledge that the prayer fits awkwardly into its present narrative setting, but they believe this awkwardness serves the larger literary purposes of the Book of Jonah.[47] They maintain that the prayer adheres to a pattern reflected in other instances of direct discourse within the narrative in which the prophet's declarations are consistently undermined by the surrounding narrative. Much of what the prophet says in the narrative *sounds* pious, after all, but his words are often accompanied by deeds which reveal that Jonah does not fully understand the implications of what he says. Thus Jonah flees from God across the sea even as he declares that God is the one who made the sea (1:9), and a bit later, he rebukes God for saving the Assyrians even as he acknowledges God's merciful nature (4:2). The dissonance is intentional, this approach argues, serving to expose the narrowness and vindictiveness of a religious perspective that confines the reach of God's compassion to the borders of Israel. To the extent that the prayer contributes to the overall dissonance generated by the narrative, it helps to make this point. In the prayer Jonah criticizes those who forsake their "loyalty" = *hisdām* to God (2:8=MT 2:9), but later in the story he uses similar language to criticize God himself for being steadfast: "I knew that you were abounding in steadfast love" = *rab-hesed* (4:2). In the prayer he thanks God for saving his life (2:7), but later in the story he becomes angry with God for saving the lives of others (so much so that he pleads with God to take his life in 4:3). As these examples show, the sentiments of the prayer clash with the prophet's actions in the narrative that follows, forcing a reconsideration of both. In the light of the prophet's later actions, the prayer appears artificial, sanctimonious, even insincere, but at the same time it also articulates certain religious principles—the value of "steadfast love," God's concern for the living—in the light of which the prophet's later actions seem vindictive and impious. From this perspective, the prayer's "inappropriateness" is not an accidental by-product of the book's canonical revision, as Childs claimed; it makes a subtle contribution to the narrative's efforts to expose the limitations of the prophet's piety.

An alternative reading of the narrative developed by M. Sternberg and A. Hauser offers another way of understanding the role of the prayer within the narrative's overall design.[48] This approach argues that the first two chapters of Jonah, including the prayer, are carefully crafted to mislead the reader into sympathizing with the prophet. In the first chapter, the author conceals Jonah's motivation for fleeing from God because he does not yet wish the reader to realize how vindictive the prophet really is. Later in the same chapter Jonah seems downright selfless when he offers to sacrifice himself to save the sailors from the storm: "Pick me up and throw me into the sea; then the sea will quiet down for you; for I know that it is because of me that this great storm has come upon you" (1:12). The prayer in chapter 2 reinforces this positive first impression by presenting Jonah as grateful and devout. It is only in the last two chapters that the author begins to overturn the reader's first impressions. Chapter 3 springs two surprises. First, the evil Assyrians decide to believe Jonah's prophecy and change their ways (to the prophet's chagrin), fasting, putting on sackcloth, and turning "from their evil ways and from the violence that is in their hands." Second, God himself does an about-face, turning away from his decision to destroy the Assyrians. These two surprises lead to a third in chapter 4 when the prophet, angry with God for changing his mind, reveals the real reason he had fled to Tarshish: it was not because the prophet would rather suffer than see the suffering of others, or because he feared the Assyrians' wrath, but because he knew God was so forgiving that he would probably change his mind about destroying the Assyrians: "O Lord, is this not what I said while I was still in my own country? That is why I fled to Tarshish at the beginning, for I knew that you were a gracious God and merciful . . . and ready to relent from punishing." This final twist forces the audience to reconsider its first impression of Jonah and his religious perspective just as it has had to abandon its preconceptions about the Assyrians. The narrative, it turns out, represents an exercise in changing one's mind—the very behavior that led Nineveh to abandon its evil ways, that allowed God to relent from destroying the Assyrians, and that in the end proved impossible for the unyielding Jonah. Like the interpretation described in the preceding paragraph, this reading asserts that the prayer is not out of place at all but is actually essential to the narrative as part of its sly game of bait and switch. Working in collusion with chapter 1, it helps lure the audience into making up its mind about the prophet early on so that later in the narrative, when all the principal characters have changed their minds but Jonah, the audience will have something to change its mind about as well.

If either of these interpretations is correct, the insertion of Jonah's prayer does not represent the kind of scripturalizing revision reflected in Daniel 3, 1 Chronicles 16, and Isaiah 38. The intended effect of its insertion was not to adjust the narrative to the expectations of its audience but to manipulate those expectations in support of the author's rhetorical goals. As I see it, however, such behavior—which really represents an attempt to parody the songs in biblical narrative—was only possible in a literary culture that expected biblical heroes to sing to God after he delivered them from danger. My argument has been that such a culture surfaced in ancient Israel with the emergence of canon-consciousness. H. R. Jauss, the historian of literary expectation, has written that texts

> predispose [their] audience to a very specific kind of reception by announcements, overt and covert signals, familiar characteristics, or implicit allusions. . . . [They] awaken memories of that which was already read, [bring] the reader to a specific emotional attitude, and [their] beginning arouses expectations for the "middle and end" which can be maintained intact or altered, reoriented or even fulfilled ironically in the course of the reading according to specific rules of the genre or type of text.[49]

According to the readings I have described, Jonah's prayer represents one of the "covert signals" within the narrative of Jonah that predisposes its audience to read it within—or against—the tradition of biblical narrative. If the prayer is secondary, the signal it sends reflects the interpolator's effort to assimilate the narrative of Jonah to the literary norm established by earlier biblical stories of divine deliverance. If, on the other hand, the prayer is an original component of the narrative, the signal it sends reflects the author's effort to evoke the literary norm in order to mislead his readers about Jonah's character and satirize their literary and religious assumptions. Both readings point to a time when readers could recognize when a biblical episode failed to behave as a biblical episode "should," and the only question left open is whether the prayer was added to satisfy the expectations of such readers or to exploit them. I would argue, therefore, that whether the prayer is original or secondary, its role within the narrative points to the age of emergent canon-consciousness, when biblical narratives were first expected to include songs of praise.

Several considerations strengthen this interpretation of the evidence. One such consideration is that the language and syntax of Jonah exhibit a number of traits characteristic of postexilic Hebrew, the time when canon-conscious literary culture was already busy imitating, alluding to, and re-shaping biblical narrative (many scholars place Jonah between the sixth and fourth centuries B.C.E., roughly the time frame within which Chronicles was composed).[50] Also indicative of canon-conscious literary culture is Jonah's well-known tendency to evoke stock biblical texts and motifs in scenes such as Jonah 1:1-3, where Jonah's flight from God recalls the resistance of other biblical prophets to unwanted commissions from God (see Exod 4:1-10; Jer 1:6), and Jonah 4:1-3, which cites a famous description of God's nature first presented in Exod 34:6-7 and later cited in variant form in Num 14:18, Jer 32:18, Joel 2:13, Nahum 1:3, and elsewhere. The prayer in Jonah 2 appears to reflect this tendency as well, reading like an anthology of citations drawn from canonical psalms. Note, for example, the parallels between Jonah 2:4 and Ps 42:7 [MT 8], Jonah 2:6 and Ps 69:2, and Jonah 2:10 and Ps 3:8 [MT 9].[51] The scriptural echoes within Jonah suggest a text striving to situate itself in relation to other biblical texts, drawing biblical elements into itself with the goal of being drawn into the tradition of biblical literature. All this is consistent with what we have observed about canon-conscious literary compositions and their efforts to relate themselves to scripture.

Such evidence does not exist for the final two songs that we will examine in this study—the Prayer of Hannah in 1 Samuel 2 and the Song of David in 2 Samuel 22. These songs appear in a narrative, 1-2 Samuel, that probably originated in the preexilic period and in any event lacks the telltale signs of canon-consciousness found in the Chronicler's paraphrase of 1-2 Samuel. Nevertheless, I would argue that the insertions of Hannah's Prayer and the Song of David within the narrative of Samuel represent scripturalizing revisions not unlike the insertion of the Song of David in 1 Chronicles 16. Since the nineteenth century, biblical commentators have often concluded that the songs in 1 Samuel 2 and 2 Samuel 22 represent secondary interpolations added to Samuel in the final stages of its literary development. Consider first the Prayer of Hannah.[52] The prayer celebrates a divinely wrought reversal of fortune—a sentiment appropriate for Hannah, whom God has just healed from barrenness—but there are no specific references within the prayer to the events of the surrounding narrative. It is true that one verse (1 Sam 2:5) refers to a barren woman who has given birth to seven children (perhaps it was this verse that led to the prayer's association with Hannah), but even this reference does not quite fit Hannah's situation, for according to 1 Sam 2:21 she is said to bear a total of only six children. By itself, this observation is insufficient to show that the prayer was interpolated secondarily—after all, the author of the surrounding narrative could have adapted a generic hymn to serve his literary purposes just as easily as a later interpolator. But if the prayer is original to the narrative, it is difficult to account for what one finds when one compares the Masoretic version of 1 Samuel 2 to other versions of the text preserved in Greek translation and Qumran fragments. The Masoretic version of 1 Samuel 2 introduces the prayer with this line: "And he (Elkanah) worshipped there before God. Hannah prayed and said . . ." (1 Sam 1:28b-2:1a). The Greek version of the narrative in Codex Vaticanus reports a slightly different sequence of events; there the prayer is *followed* by the report that Hannah "left him there before the Lord and returned to Ramah," a statement which is absent in the Masoretic version. This extra line, which implies that Hannah performed the prayer prior to leaving

Samuel at Shiloh, resembles the narrative *before* the psalm in a fragment of Samuel found at Qumran (4QSam[a]: "[And she left] him there and bowed . . ."), which has Hannah performing the prayer *after* leaving Samuel at Shiloh.[53] It is hard to understand why the prayer would have moved from one textual position to another if it was an original part of the narrative. All the textual traditions seem to agree that a prayer belongs near the end of the episode, but each places it at a slightly different point in the story—as if the communities which transmitted these different texts agreed that Hannah recited the song after the birth of Samuel but came to slightly different conclusions about where exactly in the text it belonged. This is consistent with a scenario in which first an extrabiblical tradition arose associating the song with 1 Samuel 1 (we know this kind of tradition existed in the Second Temple period; recall that Philo *assumed* that Abraham sang a song in Genesis 14) and then later, once this tradition insinuated itself into readers' perceptions of 1 Samuel 1, various communities sought to integrate the song into the biblical text through interpolation, splicing it in at different points in the story.[54]

There is no way to prove this is what happened, but one can find corroborating evidence in other biblical stories of miraculous births (Gen 29:31–30:24, Judges 13, Ruth 4:13–17). Sharing a number of motifs and their basic plotline, these episodes reflect what Robert Alter has described as a "type-scene," a conventionally structured story type used repeatedly in biblical literature to depict certain recurrent dramatic situations (compare the last-words topos discussed in chapter 3, and see appendix A for yet another kind of type-scene).[55] Among the type-scenes used by the biblical authors was one that described the miraculous birth of a biblical hero to a barren mother, a scene that is used to describe the birth of several of the Patriarchs in Genesis and Samson. The story in 1 Samuel 1 exhibits many of the traits of this type-scene, but it is the only instance of this scene in the Hebrew Bible to conclude with a song (the only other birth scene which contains a song is in Luke 1, but as we have seen, this episode was deliberately modeled on 1 Samuel 1–2). Considered alongside the arguments presented in the preceding paragraph, the absence of songs in similarly structured biblical episodes is yet another sign that the prayer was not an original part of the story of Samuel's birth.

Even if this evidence establishes that the Prayer of Hannah constitutes a secondary interpolation, however, it sheds little light on what motivated this interpolation or what literary purpose it was intended to serve. The story of Samuel's birth is perfectly coherent without the prayer; indeed, we have just seen that the Hebrew Bible contains many other stories of miraculous births, none of which ends with a song of praise. Why would someone want to disrupt the narrative of 1 Samuel 1 by adding a song of praise, and why add a song that has only the slightest connection to

Samuel's birth? I believe the song's contents may shed light on these questions. It is well known that verses 7 and 8 in 1 Samuel 2, "He raises up the poor from the dust; he lifts up the needy from the dunghill, to make them sit with nobles," are virtually identical to Ps 113:7-8.[56] This parallel, I suggest, is of great significance for understanding when and why Hannah's Prayer was placed in its present narrative setting. As we have seen, canon-conscious readers eventually came to equate the songs in biblical narrative with the Psalms in the Psalter, an equation that led early Jews to incorporate psalmic motifs and citations within their attempts to emulate the songs in biblical narrative and to relate the Psalms to events described by biblical narrative. With all the evidence that Hannah's Prayer was added to 1 Samuel late in its literary development, I conclude that the prayer is actually citing Psalm 113, just as Judith's hymn echoes common psalmic motifs and as 1 Chronicles 16 draws directly on canonical psalms for its content. After all, we know from rabbinic sources that early Jews perceived a connection between Psalm 113 in particular and the songs in biblical narrative. Psalm 113 was the first psalm in the Egyptian Hallel (Psalms 113-18) which early Jews associated with the Song of the Sea and with many other biblical episodes featuring songs (see chapter 4). Some rabbis even believed that their biblical ancestors recited part of Psalm 113 *to celebrate miraculous births*, deriving this conclusion from the final verse of the psalm, which reads, "He sets the childless woman among her household as a happy mother of children." For example, *Pesikta Rabbati*, a collection of rabbinic homilies, reports that the Israelites celebrated Moses' birth by singing Pss 113:9-114:1.[57] This evidence dates from long after the Second Temple period, but it is conceivable that Second Temple Jews also read the Hallel into the biblical past. In fact, one song within a biblical narrative from this time, the Song of the Three, echoes a line found in Ps 118:1 and 29, the final psalm of the Hallel. Since early Jews believed that the Hallel was recited in biblical times to celebrate God's miracles (including miraculous births) and since one song in a Second Temple narrative may actually cite the Hallel, it is at least plausible that the interpolation of Hannah's Prayer reflects the same kind of literary behavior, ascribing to a biblical heroine a song of praise which echoes the Hallel. Such behavior would not be exceptional in the age of emergent canon-consciousness, when Jews often fused elements from their own liturgical praise into the songs they supplied for their biblical ancestors.

Adding to the plausibility of this claim is the fact that Hannah's story was actually associated in the Second Temple period with Passover, one of the festivals during which the Hallel was recited. In his retelling of 1 Samuel 1-2, Pseudo-Philo (*Bib. Ant.* 50:2) situates some of the events of 1 Samuel 1 on Passover, probably deriving this detail from an association of the temporal phrase "year by year" in 1 Sam 1:3 with the same phrase

used in reference to the first Passover in Exod 13:10.[58] Of course, the
Prayer of Hannah was already long in place when the *Biblical Antiquities*
was composed in the first century C.E.; indeed, the latter contains an
expanded paraphrase of the prayer in *Biblical Antiquities* 50.[59] It is possible,
however, that Pseudo-Philo preserves a much older exegetical tradition
associating Samuel's birth with Passover or that some earlier scribe coin-
cidently recognized the verbal link between 1 Sam 1:3 and Exod 13:10. If
so, it makes all the more sense that Hannah's Prayer echoes the first psalm
of the Hallel. Perhaps the prayer was added not simply to supply the story
with the requisite song of praise but also to assimilate it to the normative
pattern of biblical history exemplified (in the minds of early Jews) by the
Exodus story, in which God first delivered the people of Israel from danger
and Israel first praised God with song. In the reformulated version of the
story, Samuel's mother celebrates the miraculous birth of her son with
the very language used—or rather thought by early Jews to have been
used—by Israel after its miraculous exodus from Egypt.

Even as I propose this reading I am ready to admit that it depends
on a number of assumptions. In the cases of the Song of the Three, the
song in 1 Chronicles 16, and the Psalm of Hezekiah, we have versions of
the narratives without the songs—compelling evidence that they represent
secondary interpolations. We do not have such evidence in the case of
Hannah's Prayer, and even if the diverse placements of the prayer in the
different versions of Samuel convince us that it was interpolated secondarily,
there is still no way to know for certain when the interpolation occurred.
The fact that the language of both the narrative and the song shows no
sign of postexilic Hebrew may be irrelevant for identifying when story and
song were combined—we have seen, after all, that most of the materials
used by the postexilic Chronicler originated in the preexilic period—but
it certainly does not offer any support for the thesis that the interpolation
of Hannah's Prayer represents a scripturalizing revision.[60] Concerning my
claim that Hannah's Prayer cites Psalm 113, it is entirely possible that 1
Samuel 2 and Psalm 113 parallel each other not because Hannah's Prayer
cites Psalm 113 but because it is being cited by Psalm 113, or because
both psalms independently employ the same poetic cliché. Furthermore,
we have no way of knowing whether Psalm 113, or the Hallel generally,
was recited liturgically at a period sufficiently early for it to have played
the role assigned to it by my hypothesis. Several sources attest to the singing
of praise at the festival of Passover during the days of the Second Temple
(see 2 Chr 30:21; *Jub 49:6;* Matt 26:30), and it is possible that these refer
to the recitation of the Hallel; but there is no way to confirm this conjecture.[61] Despite the limitations of the evidence, what has impressed me
about the interpretation of Hannah's Prayer proposed here is its ability
to integrate seemingly unrelated data—from the evidence of interpolation,

to the parallel between 1 Samuel 2 and Psalm 113, to the rabbinic association of Psalm 113 with the birth of Moses—into a single viable hypothesis. While there is no denying that this interpretation depends on reasoned conjecture, there is also no denying that everything about the prayer—its genre, its unstable position within the narrative, its echoes of other biblical texts—is consistent with the hypothesis of scripturalizing revision. If we imagine that a version of 1 Samuel without the song somehow found its way into the hands of early canon-conscious Jews, it is now clear that these readers were perfectly capable of revising the narrative to include the song. And given what we have observed in the songs in Chronicles and other canon-conscious works, one can further surmise that this hypothetical song would likely have contained elements borrowed from canonical psalms, contemporary forms of liturgical praise, or both. There may be no way to prove that this is what happened in the case of 1 Samuel 1-2; but if it did, we would expect to find in this episode a song similar in form, content, and textual position to what we actually find there.

The evidence that the Song of David represents a scripturalizing revision is equally controvertible, and also no less striking. The song in 2 Samuel 22, which functions in the narrative as a thanksgiving song sung by David to the Lord after he is delivered from all his enemies,[62] is part of a loosely organized collage of narratives, catalogues, and poetic passages appended to the end of the book of Samuel (2 Samuel 21-24). It has long been believed that the material in these chapters is arranged not chronologically but concentrically or chiastically, consisting as it does of two narratives (2 Sam 21:1-14 and 24:1-25)[63] that frame two catalogues (21:15-22 and 23:8-39), which in turn frame two poetic passages (22 and 23).[64] One can only speculate about why these materials were organized in this way, but what is clear is that thematic and structural concerns seem to have played a greater role in their disposition than the need to present events in chronological order. Consider the relationship of David's song to the catalogue preceding it in 2 Samuel 21. The verse introducing the song in 2 Sam 22:1 reports that David sang the song "on the day when the Lord delivered him from the hands of all his enemies and from the hand of Saul" (2 Sam 22:1).[65] This function requires the song to be placed somewhere near the end of Samuel, after David emerges from all the rebellions and battles that threatened his rule, but it does not account specifically for the song's placement after the catalogue of David's heroes in 2 Samuel 21. In fact, the song bears no connection at all to 2 Samuel 21, except perhaps for a faint verbal similarity between 2 Sam 22:1 and 2 Sam 21:22 (the phrase "from the hand of all his enemies and from the hand of Saul" in 2 Sam 22:1 dimly echoes the phrase "by the hands of David and his servants" in 21:22). Perhaps representing some kind of editorial seam used to sew these materials together, the echo only reinforces the impression that we are dealing here with a mode of redactional organization very different from the chronological organization governing the disposition of literary materials in 2 Samuel 1–20 (including poetic material such as David's lament in 2 Samuel 1; see appendix A). It is this very difference that has led many scholars to conclude that chapters 21–24 were not an original part of the narrative of David's life in 1–2 Samuel but were appended to it, either piecemeal or en masse, at a late date in its compositional history.[66]

Additional support for this conclusion is the fact that 2 Samuel 22 gives a very different impression of David than the one given by the rest of 2 Samuel. The David of 2 Samuel 1–20 is a great but sinful leader who, through adultery and murder, falls under God's curse in chapters 11–20. By contrast, the David of the song claims to have lived a life of sinlessness.

> The Lord rewarded me according to my righteousness; according to the cleanness of my hands he recompensed me. For I have kept the ways of the Lord, and have not wickedly departed from my God. For all his ordinances were before me, and from his statutes I did not turn aside. I was blameless before him, and I kept myself from guilt. Therefore the Lord has recompensed me according to my righteousness, according to my cleanness in his sight. (2 Sam 22:21–25)

The David who sings this song is not the morally ambiguous ruler who, after murdering Uriah, confesses that he "has sinned against the Lord (2 Sam 12:13); rather, he is a paragon of righteousness and piety, the glorious figure reflected in 1 Chronicles and in the psalm superscriptions. The difference is so stark that one wonders whether the song was added as a kind of damage control to restore the reputation of Israel's greatest king. Certainly it is striking that it is just after 2 Samuel 11–20, at a moment in the narrative when its portrait of David bears little in common with the pious king imagined by early Jews, that the song in 2 Samuel 22 appears, as if to rehabilitate David after all his moral lapses in 2 Samuel.

We have observed similar behavior in 1 Chronicles, where the Chronicler also used a song in his effort to rehabilitate the figure of David. There is also another point of correspondence no less significant for contextualizing the insertion of the song in 2 Samuel 22. We have seen that the Chronicler drew on Psalms 96, 105, and 106 as the source material for his Song of David, a literary act rooted in the canon-conscious association of biblical narrative with Israel's sacred psalmody. It appears that the scribe responsible for the song in 2 Samuel 22 may have engaged in similar behavior, since 2 Samuel 22 is virtually identical to Psalm 18.[67] If, as some scholars believe, the author of 2 Samuel 22 lifted the song directly from the Psalter—as the Chronicler seems to have done to construct his

song of David in 1 Chronicles 16—we have here a clear sign of scripturalizing behavior involving the use of a canonical psalm to revise a biblical
narrative. In this case, it appears that the interpolator's goal was not simply
to reconcile biblical narrative and the Psalms but to reconcile the ruthless
David of Samuel with the much more pious and poetic David of the Psalms.
Of course, it is also possible that Psalm 18 is drawn from the narrative of
2 Samuel, a move which is also consistent with the canon-conscious association of the Psalter with the songs in biblical narrative but which tells
us nothing about why the song was first inserted in Samuel. Even if the
insertion of the song was not intended to connect the story of David to
the psalms in Psalter, however, its effect on the surrounding narrative still
smacks of canon-conscious revision, transforming David into the idealized
king he was believed to be by canon-conscious Jews.

There is one final piece of evidence that supports this interpretation,
a clue that we uncovered at the end of chapter 3 without realizing its
significance. There I noted briefly that the insertion of 2 Samuel 22 shares
rather striking similarities with the insertion of the Song of Moses in
Deuteronomy 32: the two songs are placed at analogous points in their
narrative sequences (shortly before the death of the singers); both are
immediately followed by a second poetic insertion (the Blessing of Moses
in Deuteronomy 33 and the "last words" of David in 2 Samuel 23); and
both are introduced with similarly structured statements (compare Deut
32:1 with 2 Sam 22:1).[68] The similarities are so pronounced that some
scholars have concluded that the Song of David was inserted within Samuel
in conscious emulation of the Song of Moses. In light of our study, we
now know that such behavior would make sense in the age of emergent
canon-consciousness, when the Pentateuch was perceived as a literary model
and when Jews were predisposed to draw connections between disparate
parts of scripture.[69] The only problem with identifying 2 Samuel 22 as an
imitation of Deuteronomy 32 is that its narrative role is not exactly analogous to the Song of Moses. In contrast to Deuteronomy 32, which is
introduced by its narrative setting as God's "witness against Israel," 2 Samuel
22 is said by its narrative setting to have been sung by David to the Lord
"on the day the Lord delivered him." The difference is great, but a closer
look reveals that even so it is consistent with the hypothesis that 2 Samuel
22 represents a scripturalizing revision. We have seen that the Song of
Moses was perceived by early Jews not as an act of chastisement from God
against Israel but as a song of thanksgiving uttered by Moses in gratitude
to God. Recall especially Philo's paraphrase of Deuteronomy 32 (*Virt* 72–
75), which he describes as a "hymn of thanksgiving" sung by Moses "for
the rare and extraordinary gifts with which he had been blessed from his
birth to his old age." Philo's reading of the song provides us with a way
to account for the differences between Deuteronomy 32 and 2 Samuel

22, for it suggests that the latter emulates the Song of Moses not as it appears to us but as it once appeared to early Jews, who saw it as a paradigmatic thanksgiving song. Though obviously impossible to prove, this hypothesis nonetheless has impressive explanatory power, shedding light not only on the parallels between 2 Samuel 22 and Deuteronomy 32 but on their discrepancies as well. The difference is tantamount to the difference between the ancient Near Eastern culture that first construed the song in Deuteronomy 32 as a castigatory teaching and the canon-conscious culture that reconceptualized it as a paradigmatic act of praise addressed to God. (A similar argument can be made for David's last words in 2 Samuel 23, which resemble Moses' final blessing in Deuteronomy 33, but that is a story for another day.)

At first glance, this reading of the Prayer of Hannah and the Song of David as scripturalizing revisions directly contradicts a view which has grown increasingly popular in recent years. Many commentators now believe that the two songs work in conjunction with one another to form a kind of *inclusio,* or interpretive framework, around the narrative of 1-2 Samuel, making explicit God's role in the early history of the monarchy.[70] This interpretation has proved so appealing because it accounts both for the position of the two songs within their narratives (they bracket the canonical books of Samuel like two parentheses) and for the fact that 2 Samuel 22 echoes Hannah's Prayer at a number of points, as if David's song were sung in antiphonic response to the Prayer of Hannah.[71] These—argue Brevard Childs, Walter Brueggemann, H. G. Reventlow, and several other recent biblical scholars—are indications that the insertions of the two songs manifest the same overarching redactional design that seeks to shape the reader's interpretation of the events in 1-2 Samuel by enfolding them within two proclamations of God's power. As compelling as this interpretation is, I am not quite satisfied with it because it leaves one question unresolved: why would the redactor of Samuel have settled upon the literary form of the song to connect the beginning of his narrative to its end? The hypothesis I am proposing here provides an answer. We have seen that the songs in Second Temple narratives such as *Judith* and *Tobit* often served an intertextual—or perhaps one should say intertemporal—function, linking the events they celebrate to pivotal events in the biblical past, like the Exodus, the death of Moses, and the birth of Samuel. Samuel's songs evidently serve a similar role, linking two defining moments in the narrative of Samuel to one another and perhaps to other biblical events as well (i.e., the death of Moses). What I have been arguing here, in other words, is actually consistent with the claim that the Prayer of Hannah and the Song of David serve a single redactional design, only adding the suggestion that this design was imposed upon the narrative of Samuel in the age of canon-consciousness when authors often exploited the literary form of the song to relate their stories to other events in biblical history. In fact, one wonders whether the interpolation of the Prayer of Hannah and the Song of David was not an attempt to restructure the narrative of Samuel in imitation of the Pentateuch, an account which also features songs near its beginning (Exodus 15) and end (Deuteronomy 32). I can detect no clear parallels between the Prayer of Hannah and Exodus 15 except that women play a central role in the performance of the two songs, but we now know that early Jews, including Pseudo-Philo, linked 1 Samuel 1 to the Passover and, even more significantly, that Hannah's Prayer may cite a line from the Hallel, which some Jews believed was first recited when Israel escaped from Egypt.[72] It is possible, therefore, that Hannah's Prayer was meant to recall the song sung by Israel when it escaped from Egypt—not the Song of the Sea but the other song of praise thought to have been performed at that time, the Hallel. As for the Song of David, we have already seen how closely it corresponds to the Song of Moses in Deuteronomy 32. Perhaps the intended rhetorical effect of these songs was to suggest that the historical events described in Samuel replayed pentateuchal history (as perceived by early Jews), beginning with praise of God for a miraculous act of salvation and ending with praise of God from a Moses-like leader. It would not be the only time that a biblical book was redacted in imitation of the five books of Moses; the Pentateuch's influence evidently led to the division of the Psalter into five books.[73] The insertion of songs in Samuel may well represent the same kind of canon-conscious redaction, connecting the story of the early monarchy with earlier sacred history by giving it the literary shape of the Pentateuch.

With this we have exhausted the evidence supporting the hypothesis that the insertions of the Prayer of Hannah and the Song of David represent scripturalizing revisions added to biblical narrative late in its literary development. There is, however, one final piece of evidence showing that whether or not canon-conscious literary assumptions prompted the interpolation of these songs, it did affect how they were perceived by early Jews. One can see this by comparing the Masoretic version of Hannah's Prayer with its Greek translation in LXX. The Greek translation repeats the word "holy" (קָדוֹשׁ) three times (two times in LXX 1 Sam 2:2, one time in verse 10), whereas this word appears only once in verse 2 of the Masoretic version. Moreover, the Greek version expands the psalm's conclusion by adding several lines from Jer 9:22–23. Both differences, I believe, reflect the workings of the scripturalizing imagination. H. St.-J. Thackeray suggested over eighty years ago that the threefold repetition of the word "holy" in Hannah's Prayer reflects the influence of the trisagion, for which Isaiah 6:3, "Holy, holy, holy! the Lord of Hosts!" is cited as a biblical prooftext.[74] The earliest reference to the ritual recitation of the trisagion, which became an important liturgical practice in both rabbinic and Christian liturgy, is found in rabbinic sources (see Tosefta Berakhot 1:9),[75] but the evidence of LXX 1 Samuel 2—now supported by Qumran fragments of Hannah's Prayer[76]—suggests that it may have originated in the Second Temple period. Some scholars even believe that its ritual recitation began in the temple itself, since in Isaiah 6:3 Isaiah had claimed to hear the line proclaimed by angels in the heavenly throne room. (If so, it may also be relevant that in LXX Hannah recites the prayer *before* leaving the temple at Shiloh, a setting which may have predisposed early Jews to associate the prayer with liturgical praise recited in the temple.) Whatever led early Jews to modify the prayer in light of the trisagion—whether it was simply the use of the word "holy" in the original form of the psalm or some other exegetical link between 1 Samuel 1-2 and the trisagion that can no longer be reconstructed—the alteration indicates that by the time of the prayer's translation into Greek it was being adjusted to fit canon-conscious assumptions about biblical narrative and its relation to liturgical practice of the day.

The expansion of 1 Sam 2:10 with a line from Jer 9:22-23 appears also to have been a result of canon-conscious assumptions. So far, no scholar has been able to determine what triggered this addition. Some scholars believe that Jeremiah 9 may have once served as a haftarah reading (the liturgical recitation of a biblical text from the Prophets) in the season of the autumnal New Year, and that this led to its association with Hannah's Prayer, which was also apparently recited as the New Year's haftarah (see b. *Meg.* 31a). This explanation is highly conjectural, however since we know so little little about the public reading of biblical texts in the prerabbinic period. What we do know is that the scripturalizing imagination of early Jews inclined them to read 1 Samuel 2 in light of other texts within the biblical canon. In paraphrasing Hannah's prayer, for example, Pseudo-Philo incorporates citations from Isa 51:4 and Ps 99:6 into the prayer (see *Bib. Ant.* 51:4 and 6 respectively). The Aramaic translation of Targum Jonathan links the prayer to the rest of scripture by transforming it into a prophecy that forecasts events in the history of Israel. Whatever the specific trigger for the addition of Jer 9:22-23, it reflects this broader exegetical trend, modifying the prayer in light of a remote biblical text from Jeremiah. Together with the piece of evidence presented in the preceding paragraph, this example shows that whether or not the Prayer of Hannah was itself added as a scripturalizing revision, its form and function were eventually modified by scripturalizing revisions on a smaller scale which sought both to liturgicize the prayer and to link it to other biblical texts.

This brings us to one final point. My goal in this chapter has been to demonstrate that many of the songs in biblical narrative—perhaps as many as six—represent scripturalizing revisions added to preexisting biblical episodes to accommodate the assumptions and expectations of a canon-conscious audience. Even if I am correct in each and every case, however, we would not have exhausted the ways in which the songs in biblical narrative were affected by the scripturalizing imagination. For this imagination is not only responsible for the occasional interpolation; it left its mark on all the songs within biblical narrative, if not literally rewriting them, then reshaping them in the minds of early Jewish readers. Some of these songs bear no visible imprint of canon-conscious revision, unlike the Song of the Three and other interpolated songs, but their narrative roles were indirectly affected by such revisions because they were now read not as discrete literary acts but as instances of a pattern running throughout biblical narrative. The Song of the Sea, for example, came to mean something different once it was recontextualized within the scriptural corpus that contained the songs in 1 Samuel 2, 2 Samuel 22, Isaiah 38, and so on. In this context, it was no longer simply an expression of Israel's joy after its deliverance from the Egyptians; it now appeared as the initiating member of a tradition of praise and thanksgiving that Israel would repeat consistently throughout its history. To impose this role upon the song, the scripturalizing imagination did not have to change a single word in Exodus 15, for it had changed the literary context in which Exodus 15 was read, expanding its borders far beyond the story told in Exodus 14–15 to encompass all of the biblical past and the liturgical present as well.

What we have discovered, then, is that what I call the scripturalizing imagination did not merely modify an existing literary practice; it created this practice anew from raw materials inherited from the biblical past. Songs were inserted into biblical episodes before the rise of canon-consciousness, but as we saw in chapters 2 and 3 these insertions were the products of unrelated practices that Israel shared with other ancient Near Eastern literary cultures. They gave canon-conscious Jewish authors something to emulate, but it was the impulse of these authors to emulate—and to interrelate, to liturgicize, and to contemporize—that led them to forge from the occasional song in biblical narrative a full-fledged literary convention. It is easy to miss the originality of their response in large part because it expressed itself through imitation, interpolation, and the resignification of existing literary materials. What I have tried to establish in this study is that through its effort to perpetuate the patterns of biblical history, the scripturalizing imagination created new literary expectations, new literary practices, and a new conception of that sacred past it sought to emulate.

CONCLUSION: A
BIBLICAL FUGUE

This book has approached its subject—the fusing of song and story within biblical narrative—from several directions. At some points in our investigation we have looked at the songs from a comparative perspective, viewing their narrative roles in light of literary practices reflected in ancient Egyptian and Aramaic texts. At others we have taken a diachronic approach, explaining the songs as interpolations added to the biblical text in the final stages of its literary evolution. Sometimes we have viewed a song as integral to the narrative's structure and rhetorical objectives; at other times, it made more sense to treat a song as a secondary interpolation that reshapes the narrative in light of canon-conscious assumptions. All this has demanded of us a tactical flexibility, a willingness to use whatever method best accounts for the evidence. I hope to have persuaded the reader that the result of this approach—or, rather, grafting of approaches—is a reading of the Bible's fusion of song and story that recognizes the many functions served by this practice.

I do not want the reader to be misled by the eclecticism of this study, however, for the various methodologies employed all serve a single argument. Beyond what each chapter reveals about the narrative roles of individual songs, in its entirety this book presents a comprehensive history of the practice of incorporating songs within biblical narrative, tracing its development from the earliest recoverable stages of Israelite scribal convention to the scripturalizing imagination of Judaism in the Second Temple period. The songs in biblical narrative relate to their respective settings in different ways in part because their insertions occurred at different stages in this history, sometimes reflecting practices shared by Israel with other ancient Near Eastern cultures, sometimes reflecting emergent canon-consciousness. Although I have fashioned each of my analyses as a self-supporting argument, the reader can fully appreciate their significance only by viewing them as part of a larger construction of biblical narrative's compositional development.

To clarify this point, I would like to briefly review some of the major implications of our investigation. In the first half of our study we found that the narrative roles of the songs in Exodus 15, Judges 5, and Deuteronomy 32 resemble—and are perhaps related to—literary behaviors manifest elsewhere in ancient Near Eastern narratives composed in the first half of the first millennium B.C.E. In chapter 2 I argued that the narrative role of the songs in Exodus 15 and Judges 5 parallels an often-used technique of closure employed in ancient Egyptian battle accounts (most clearly in the Piye inscription from the eighth century B.C.E.) to acclaim the conquering king for the victories depicted in the preceding narrative. Quite different is the narrative role of the Song of Moses in Deuteronomy 32, which, as we learned in chapter 3, is presented as the last teaching of Moses before his death. Its narrative role represents an Israelite adaptation of a preexistent literary topos which has shaped at least one other text composed at around the same time as Deuteronomy, the *Words of Ahiqar*. Each of these arguments confirms the other's claim that at least some of the songs within biblical narrative are integral to their narrative settings, functioning not merely as ornaments or exclamation points but as essential components in the narrative's overall argument. Yes, it is likely that these songs were composed before their present literary settings—perhaps long before—but we have seen how the authors of biblical narrative resignified their form and content so that they might play key roles in their surrounding stories, whether they serve to draw God into the action of a battle or to present the final teaching of a dying sage. The *Ahiqar* analogue is especially pertinent because it too draws on preexisting literary material—a collection of proverbs, admonitions, and fables—which it recontextualizes within the story of Ahiqar. This example illustrates what students of ancient Near Eastern literature have long realized, that the art of storytelling in the ancient Near East often lies in how preexisiting materials and traditions have been recycled and recombined into new compositions. It now appears that episodes such as Exodus 14-15, Judges 4-5, and Deuteronomy 31-32 also reflect this mode of storytelling, welding song and story into integrated wholes.

This brings us to a second lesson implicit in chapters 2 and 3, that the insertion of songs within biblical narrative is a practice—or rather a conglomeration of practices—rooted in ancient Near Eastern literary culture. For those familar with modern biblical scholarship, there is nothing particularly surprising about this conclusion, because for well over one hundred years, scholars have been continually discovering affinities between the Bible and ancient Near Eastern literature. Still, in the present instance it is a conclusion that was hard won, for before reaching it, we had to confront our own literary presuppositions about prose and poetry. As we saw in chapter 1, while modern biblical scholarship has had relatively little difficulty in recognizing parallels between biblical prose and poetry and the prose and poetry of other ancient Near Eastern documents, it has less readily accepted the flip side of this observation, that its own sense of prose and poetry is contingent and culture-bound. We thus found that biblical scholars are in fact imposing their own literary culture onto the Bible when they interpret its mixing of story and song as a mixing of reason and emotion, of objectivity and subjectivity, or of the sublime and the mundane. In discovering how the conclusions reached by these scholars have been shaped by modern conceptions of how prose and poetry relate to one another, we have seen that the decipherment of a literary document from the ancient Near East is comparable to the decipherment of an ancient Near Eastern language: not only do the words differ from our own, but the rules which govern the relationships between words are different as well. This does not mean that biblical and other ancient Near Eastern literatures are forever inaccessible to a modern reader, any more than the languages of ancient Mesopotamia, Egypt, and Ugarit proved to be inherently indecipherable. But to read them as ancient Near Eastern literatures requires one to acknowledge that the syntax of literary expression is no more universal than its morphology.

Of course, this is not the only reason it is difficult to recognize the links between the insertions of songs in biblical narrative and compositional practices employed elsewhere in the ancient Near East. One of the most pervasive claims made by biblical literature is that the influence of foreign cultures represents a threat to Israel's belief in God. We detected this claim within Exodus 14-15, which represents Egypt not merely as a dangerous foe but as God's rival for Israel's loyalty. So too in Deuteronomy 31-32 the narrative associates Israel's moral corruption with its worship of "strange gods" (see Deut 32:16). With such an attitude toward foreign culture, the authors of biblical narrative are not likely to have admitted—to others or to themselves—that they shared literary practices with non-Israelite literary cultures. A clear (albeit late) example of this is provided by the book of *Tobit*, which borrows directly from the story of Ahiqar—even mentioning the Assyrian sage by name—but disguises its indebtedness to this text by transforming Ahiqar into a Jewish sage and imputing much of his story to Tobit. The same process of assimilation appears to have occurred at earlier stages in Israelite literary history as compositional forms were taken over by biblical authors without any acknowledgment that these forms were shared with—and perhaps derived from—other cultures. The claim to cultural uniqueness implicit in biblical narrative makes it very difficult to discern its resemblance to other ancient Near Eastern texts, but not impossible. For despite its aspiration to be culturally impermeable, ancient Israel was an engaged participant in the larger literary culture of the ancient Near East. I would suggest, in fact, that there is no better illustration of Israel's self-masking indebtedness to its literary environment than the mixtures of song and story in Exodus 14-15, Judges 4-5, and Deuteronomy 31-32, episodes which share their form with narratives from other Near Eastern cultures even as they seek to sever Israel's dependency upon foreign culture.

Having uncovered several parallels between the use of songs in biblical narrative and literary forms found in other ancient Near Eastern literatures, our use of comparative evidence has also revealed significant differences. Some of these differences can be explained as deliberate modifications introduced by the authors of biblical narrative to serve their literary and ideological agenda. Thus many of the differences between Deuteronomy 31-32 and *Ahiqar* can be explained as "theologizing" adaptations introduced by the author of Deuteronomy 31-32, who imagined the relationship between God and Israel as a relationship between a teacher and his pupil. A similiar theologizing adaptation is reflected in Exodus 14-15, where motifs conventionally associated with the king in Egyptian battle literature are transferred to God. There is nothing unique about the act of adaptation itself: the story pattern reflected in *Ahiqar* was tranferred by Greeks to Aesop, by Egyptians to Ankhsheshonqy, and by Jews to Tobit. What is unique is the religious imagination directing Israel's adaptation of these conventions, an imagination which saw God as the hero of all its stories.

Not all the differences between the songs in biblical narrative and ancient Near Eastern literary practice can be explained as conscious theologizing adapations, however. In chapters 4 and 5 we observed that over time the insertion of songs within biblical narrative appears to have developed a life of its own. Many of the narratives composed in the Second Temple period or shortly thereafter—works such as *Tobit, Judith, Joseph and Aseneth*, the *Apocalypse of Abraham*, the *Testament of Job*, and the Gospel of Luke—attribute songs of praise to biblical heroes or to characters modeled on biblical heroes who have been rescued by miracles. Living centuries after the end of the Second Temple period, the rabbis also invented songs for their biblical heroes by creatively revocalizing the biblical text. Most striking of all, some early Jews appear to have revised the biblical text itself by adding songs to miracle scenes which do not feature songs in their original form. The evidence suggests that early Jews expected their biblical heroes to break into song whenever they were delivered by miracles. When biblical figures failed to do so—as they often do—some early Jewish readers expressed disappointment, and others responded by re-imagining and even rewriting biblical history so as to provide the missing song. In our investigation, we were unable to explain these behaviors in the context of ancient Near Eastern literary practice. We found instead that they were related to a development specific to the literary history of ancient Israel, the formation of a new aesthetic that regarded the form of the Hebrew Bible, especially the Pentateuch, as a model of literary expression. The rise of this aesthetic represented a turning point in the literary history of ancient Israel, completely reshaping both the act of reading and the act of writing in early Judaism. The purpose of chapters 4 and 5 was to show that, among its effects, this aesthetic reconfigured the practice of inserting songs in biblical narrative, transforming an assortment of literary practices shared by Israel with other ancient Near Eastern cultures into a self-conscious literary convention.

The origins of this aesthetic are intimately bound up with the rise of canon-consciousness, the belief among early Jews that certain texts which they inherited from their past enjoyed a special sanctity and authority. In its most fully developed form this belief resulted in the establishment of the biblical canon—or canons, since different forms of Judaism evidently differed in how they defined scripture—but it is reflected in behaviors which predate canonization (in the strict sense of the word) by centuries, surfacing in sources from the exilic and postexilic periods that emulate, allude to, and interpret what we now call biblical literature. At present, it is not clear whether this belief was the product of a gradual process or a single historical event, whether it reflects foreign influence or is the result of internal processes within Israelite culture. As we saw in chapter 4, however, it had far-reaching consequences for literary behavior in ancient Israel, triggering new attitudes, practices, and conventions. The scripturalization of biblical literature led early Jews to emulate its genres and stylistic characteristics in their own literary and liturgical compositions. The originality of these compositions is easy to miss because, just as ancient Israelite literature masked its conventionality, early Jewish literature masked its originality, expressing its imagination through the imitation of the biblical past. Even as early Jewish writers emulated the Pentateuch and other biblical texts, they departed from their models by synthesizing elements from distinct biblical genres and by fusing together literary and liturgical forms. While it is true that all these innovations were fueled by early Jews' self-effacing reverence for their biblical past, this very reverence was itself an innovation, one of the characteristics that distinguishes canon-conscious literary culture from the culture which preceded it in ancient Israel.

In all this the Bible itself played more than one role. Early Jews elevated the Bible to the status of literary and liturgical paradigm, and it was precisely this status which sometimes rendered the actual form of biblical literature unacceptable. For how was one to deal with biblical texts which seemed to violate the very aesthetic and behavioral norms which had been derived from the Bible? The answer for many early Jews was to rewrite biblical history in the form that it was supposed to have. We have seen that Jews in the Second Temple and rabbinic periods often ascribed songs of praise to biblical heroes who sing no song within the biblical text itself. Several sources speak of a song of Abraham, for example, which they ascribe to the patriarch after his return from battle in Genesis 14. I have argued that they do so because Abraham's actual behavior in Genesis 14—he invokes God in an oath—violated biblically derived notions of how Jews and their ancestors should and should not behave in relation to God. Abraham's song—along with other songs imputed to biblical heroes by early Jews—can thus be understood as a rectification of biblical narrative, seeking to harmonize the Bible with what was expected of it by canon-conscious Jews.

Chapter 5 demonstrated that these canon-conscious expectations literally reshaped biblical narrative itself. Scholars have long believed that several of the songs within biblical narrative represent secondary interpolations, but the motivation for this kind of interpolation had never really been explained. Why impose a song upon a preexisting narrative that seems perfectly comprehensible without a song? Our study has shown that many of these songs represent scripturalizing revisions aimed at reforming biblical narrative in light of its elevation to scriptural status. With episodes such as Exodus 14-15 and Deuteronomy 31-32 standing somewhere in the background, early Jewish readers detected lacunae in many of the Bible's miracle stories, dissonant silences where they expected songs of praise. In many cases their attempts to fill in these lacunae are reflected only in paraphrases and interpretations preserved in postbiblical literature, but in some cases early scribes evidently rewrote the biblical text itself— "postscripted" it—to overcome the difference between biblical narrative as it was and as it was expected to be in the wake of its scripturalization. The interpolations and revisions of these scribes may make certain biblical episodes appear less coherent in our eyes, but they made them more coherent in the eyes of early Jews, bringing the behavior of biblical heroes such as Daniel's three friends, King David, and King Hezekiah into line with the pattern of sacred history perceived within the Pentateuch.

Perhaps the reader will recognize something paradoxical about our conclusion that the elevation of biblical literature to scriptural status played a role in its compositional evolution. Scripturalization is usually associated with the fixing of the canon and the stabilization of the biblical text. The perception of biblical literature as eternally authoritative is thus thought to have *retarded* its literary growth. But what we have seen in this study is that the scripturalization of biblical narrative actually *propelled* its compositional development, albeit in a direction that ultimately led to canonization. Scripturalization had this effect because it transformed the context in which biblical narrative was read. While a modern biblical scholar draws a line between texts such as Daniel 3 and Exodus 14-15, treating them as two distinct narratives composed at different times and by different hands, early canon-conscious readers drew a very different line, connecting these texts together as two instances of a larger pattern in the history of Israel's relationship with God. Early Jews traced this line through disparate biblical texts, drawing them together into a unity, and they etched this line into their own world as well by inscribing the patterns of the biblical past into their liturgical practices and other modes of behavior. All this had obvious consequences for the literary and liturgical behavior in early Judaism, as authors and liturgists imposed biblical form onto their creations. The effect that this redrawing of the Bible's literary borders had on the formation of the Bible itself is less obvious. It is detectable, however, as we have learned through our discovery that songs were recontextualized within biblical episodes so as to recontextualize those episodes within a larger body of scripture.

What we have discovered, then, is that the songs within biblical narrative reflect two distinct literary cultures. The first of them was shared by ancient Israel with the peoples surrounding it in the ancient Near East; the second, specific to Israel, arose in the wake of the scripturalization of the Pentateuch and other biblical compositions. It is not always easy to determine which of the two cultures lies behind the insertion of an individual song, for the cultures themselves can be difficult to tell apart. The culture of canon-consciousness is defined in part by its need to emulate the culture which preceded it, and the earlier culture never completely gave way to its successor. A narrative such as *Tobit*, for example, clearly exhibits the characteristics of canon-conscious literary culture, emulating biblical form, alluding to biblical content, and invoking biblical heroes as behavioral models, but it also participates in ancient Near Eastern literary culture, drawing its situations and even some of its characters from the story of Ahiqar. The two cultures are even more thoroughly fused in some biblical compositions which originated in one culture and were subsequently revised in the other. What has become clear through our investigation, however, is that the two cultures can be distinguished from one another and that both are reflected in biblical narrative. We could not fully account for the insertion of songs in biblical narrative by viewing the Bible within the context of ancient Near Eastern literary practice, but neither could we grasp the role of the scripturalizing imagination in reformulating this practice without considering what it had inherited from the ancient Near Eastern culture that preceded it in Israel. To understand why songs appear in biblical narrative is to recognize the distinct contributions of both cultures to the shaping of the Bible.

In this light it should be clear that I regard the songs in biblical narrative as a synechdoche for the Bible as a whole. One major conclusion of this study is that the insertion of songs in biblical narrative is a literary practice with a history that spans the entire length of the Bible's compositional development. By understanding how this practice changed over time—or, rather, how it was reinterpreted—we discover something of how biblical literature evolved from a species of ancient Near Eastern literature into sacred scripture. We recognize in particular that one of the most significant forces propelling the Bible's literary evolution was precisely the perception that it constituted scripture, that the Pentateuch and other texts were exemplary in their form, inexhaustible in their interconnectivity, and timeless in their relevance. The emergence of this perception obviously played a catalytic role in the Bible's reception history. What I have tried to demonstrate is that it played a catalytic role in the Bible's literary development as well, leading Jews to re-create it in its own image as scripture. This study began with the question: why do songs appear in biblical narrative? For many of the songs examined, the answer we found is that they are there because they were expected to be there. Simple as this conclusion seems, within it lies a lesson essential for understanding both the form and the formation of scripture.

APPENDIX A

The Narrative Role of David's Lament

A central claim of this study is that the insertion of songs within biblical narrative originated not as a single literary convention but as several unrelated scribal practices associated with different kinds of literature. My goal in this appendix is to provide additional support for this proposal by looking at one of the poems embedded within biblical narrative which is not identified as a song: the lament of David in 2 Samuel 1. Using the same comparative method employed in chapters 2 and 3, I will show that the position and role of David's lament within its present narrative setting reflects the structure of a "lament type-scene," a conventionally structured plot pattern shared by biblical narrative with narratives from Late Bronze Age Ugarit, located in present-day Syria. This thesis will shed light on how the lament functions both in its immediate setting and as part of the larger narrative of Samuel. In so doing, it will also provide additional evidence that the insertion of poetic material within biblical narrative reflects not one but several distinct literary practices shared by Israel with other ancient Near Eastern cultures.

As has been the rule in this study, our analysis focuses on the narrative surrounding the lament and what it reveals about the lament's narrative role. Like the songs in biblical narrative, the lament appears to have existed as an independent composition prior to its incorporation within the narrative of 2 Samuel.[1] Garbled though it is, the verse which introduces the lament in 2 Sam 1:18 indicates that the lament's contents have been quoted from the "Book of Yashar"—a poetic composition of some sort, perhaps a collection of poetry or an extended narrative poem, that no longer survives.[2] If, as this verse suggests, the lament existed as an independent composition before it was placed in 2 Samuel 1, we cannot look to its contents to shed light on why it was recontextualized within a prose setting. Rather, we must focus on how the incorporating narrative exploits the lament's contents to serve its own literary purposes.

This is not easy to do. The narrative which introduces David's lament provides little *explicit* information pertaining to the insertion of the lament. Prior to 2 Sam 1:17 the narrative makes no explicit reference to the lament, and even the little information provided in verses 17-18, that David uttered the lament and had it taught to the "sons of Judah," is uncertain in its meaning and may have been subject to scribal interpolation or textual corruption at some point in the narrative's transmission history.[3] To be sure, such difficulties have not prevented scholars from offering explanations for the insertion of the lament in the narrative. Some have maintained that the lament was included in the narrative as testimony that David was unwavering in his allegiance to the House of Saul—even after its fall had cleared the way for his own rise to the throne.[4] Others, interpreting verse 18 to mean that David commanded the lament to be taught *to the sons of Judah in particular*, have concluded that the lament's presentation was calculated to reconcile David's Judahite followers with the House of Saul and its followers.[5] However plausible, these readings are difficult to confirm or expand upon working only with the explicit testimony of the lament's narrative setting.

That said, 2 Samuel does provide us with at least one clue regarding the lament's role within it. To appreciate this clue we must invoke the concept of the type-scene, which I mentioned briefly when discussing the narrative role of the Prayer of Hannah in 1 Samuel 2 (see chapter 5). A type-scene is a scene constructed from a stock set of motifs, presented in a conventionally predetermined manner and used repeatedly by authors within a particular literary community to describe common plot developments (betrothals, battles, deaths, etc.).[6] One can identify a type-scene only when its basic structure surfaces more than once, appearing repeatedly either within a single work or in works by different authors within a single literary community. Of course, individual authors often modify this basic structure to suit their own literary objectives—expanding, contracting, even subverting individual motifs—but the structure itself, that is, the sequence and manner in which the motifs are presented, is fixed by the literary tradition to which the author is heir.

The conventional structure of 2 Samuel 1 emerges when one considers it alongside other scenes of mourning within biblical narrative. Let us briefly recall the contents of 2 Samuel 1. The narrative begins when an Amalekite servant arrives at David's camp with news of Saul's death (2 Sam 1:1-2). In response to David's request for details, the servant recounts the army's defeat, the flight of the people, and the demise of Jonathan and Saul. He then claims to have assisted Saul in taking his own life (2 Sam 1:3-10).[7] Upon hearing this report, David and his men tear their clothes, weep, and fast until evening, during which time David orders the execution of the Amalekite for his role in Saul's death (2 Sam 1:11-16). It is at this point in the narrative that the lament itself is presented (2 Sam 1:17-27). The plot of this scene consists of three basic elements. The scene begins by describing the arrival of a messenger who reports that someone has died;[8] then, after citing the contents of the messenger's report, the narrative describes the listener's response, presenting it as a catalogue of conventional acts of grief—the rending of clothes, weeping, fasting, etc;[9] the episode then culminates with the presentation of the mourner's verbal response to the news, which, like the messenger's report, is cited verbatim. My evidence that the selection and presentation of these motifs is conventional is that the same plot structure appears in several biblical episodes both within and outside of 1-2 Samuel. These episodes do not merely depict the same sequence of events; they represent these events in the same way and in the same sequence, beginning with the messenger's report, depicting the mourner's behavioral response in the form of a catalogue, and ending with the citation of the mourner's verbal response.

Consider briefly what the narrative in 2 Samuel 1 shares in common with two other episodes, 2 Samuel 18 and Job 1. In 2 Samuel 18 the army commander Joab dispatches two messengers to David to announce the news of Absalom's death: first a Cushite messenger and then the ambitious young Ahimaaz, who petitions Joab for permission to carry tidings of Absalom's death to the king. A race ensues between these messengers, presented in the narrative from the vantage point of David's watchman, with Ahimaaz outstripping his Cushite opponent. For all the young soldier's efforts, however, he is unable (or perhaps suddenly unwilling) to provide David with details about his son's fate. The Cushite then arrives to inform David that Absalom is dead, and the king responds by weeping, mourning, withdrawing to a private room, and expressing his grief in a desperate stutter: "O my son Absalom, my son, my son Absalom! Would that I had died instead of you, O Absalom, my son, my son!" The scene in Job 1:13-21 has a similar structure: the arrival and report of the messenger (Job 1:13-19), the catalogue of mournful acts (Job 1:20), and the citation of Job's verbal response (Job 1:21). This time the news is brought not by two but by four messengers, and Job's response is much more resigned than David's grieving stammer; but the structure of this episode—that is, the selection and sequence of motifs within it—is strikingly similar to that in 2 Samuel 18. It is my argument that all these episodes reflect the same type-scene, what I call the lament type-scene. While it is true that the authors of these episodes have introduced modifications into this type-scene—some of which we will discuss here—the similarities among them clearly indicate that they are working from the same literary blueprint.

Additional support for this interpretation of the evidence appears in 2 Samuel 12, which also reflects the conventional structure of the lament type-scene. This story, which describes David's response to the death of the baby son begotten from his affair with Bath-Sheba, actually confirms the existence of the type-scene by parodying it, evoking all the expected elements of this scene—the messenger's report, the catalogue of mournful gestures, the verbal expression of grief—only to invert them in some way. Thus after the narrative notes the baby's death in verse 18, it shifts its focus to David's servants who must report the death to the king, setting the stage for the requisite messenger scene. As the scene develops, however, David's servants prove reluctant to play the role of messenger, for they "feared to tell him that the child was dead," saying to themselves: "Behold, while the child was yet alive we spoke to him, and he did not listen to us; how then can we say to him the child is dead? He may do some harm to himself." A similar twist occurs as the narrative proceeds to the next motif that is characteristic of the lament type-scene, the catalogue of mournful gestures. The servants' justification for their reluctance to tell David of the death—"He may do some harm to himself"—actually prepares the reader for this motif, generating the expectation that the king's physical response to the news will be extremely emotional and even self-destructive. Again, however, 2 Samuel 12 evokes the type-scene only to invert it: "Then David arose from the earth, and washed and anointed himself, and changed his clothes; and went into the house of the Lord; he then went into his own house; and when they asked, they set food before him and he ate" (vs. 20). Though presented in the conventionally predetermined form of a catalogue, David's actions sharply violate what is expected at this point in the narrative sequence. And indeed, so that the reader does not miss the point, the text itself articulates the expectations frustrated by David's actions, formulating them as a question posed by the servants: "What is this thing that you have done? You fasted and wept for the child while it was alive; but when the child died, you arose and ate food?" (12:21).[10] Even if one were not cognizant of how this episode inverts the lament type-scene, the servant's question confirms the unconventionality of David's behavior, making clear that it violates a behavioral if not a literary norm.[11] Finally, the narrative turns its attention to David's verbal response—the last of three structural elements characteristic of the lament type scene—and once again the narrative transgresses convention. In contrast to what the king says in response to Absalom's death, for example, where he expresses the wish to replace Absalom in death, the king in this context explicitly rejects the customary clichés: "Can I bring him back again? I shall go to him, but he will not return to me." Whereas the norm calls for the protagonist to speak with pathos and yearning, 2 Samuel 12 ends with David responding to the news of the son's death with apathetic resignation. 2 Samuel 12 turns out to be an inversion of the lament type-scene, one that evokes this scene's conventionality in order to suggest that there was something unconventional in the behavior of David at this time.

We will have more to say about 2 Samuel 12, but first we must turn to one final piece of evidence from the ancient city of Ugarit. Since Ugaritic was first deciphered, it has been clear that the literature written in this language exhibits poetic devices, plot structures, and other literary forms which also surface in biblical literature, and the most plausible explanation for these similarities is that Ugaritic literature and biblical literature originated in related cultures. It is thus significant that Ugaritic narrative features lament scenes with a basic structure virtually identical to that reflected in 2 Samuel 1, 12, and 18-19 and Job 1. The best Ugaritic example is KTU 1.5:VI 2-25, a passage from the so-called Baal cycle. Like many biblical scenes of mourning, the scene in KTU 1.5:VI 2-25 begins by reporting the arrival of messengers who tell El of the death of Baal:[12] "We found Baal fallen to the ground. Mightiest Baal is dead, the prince lord of earth has perished!" Hearing this news, El then performs a series of mourning gestures, presented in the form of a catalogue:

> Then El the kind, the compassionate descends from the throne and sits on the footstool, from his footstool (he descends and) sits upon the ground. He strews stalks of mourning on his head, the dust in which he wallows on his pate. His clothing he tears, down to the loincloth, his skin he bruises with a rock by pounding, with a razor he cuts his beard and whiskers. He rakes his upper arms, he plows his breast like a garden, like a valley he rakes his chest . . .[13]

The episode then concludes with El's verbal response, placed at the end of the scene and cited verbatim by the narrative: "He raises his voice and shouts: 'Baal is dead! What will happen to the people of Dagon's son: what will happen to the masses? I am descending to the underworld, after Baal!'"[14] This passage clearly exhibits the three requisite elements of the lament type-scene, suggesting its existence in Ugaritic literary culture. As a matter of fact, scholars of Ugaritic literature have recognized that this episode shares its tripartite structure with a second scene from the so-called *Epic of Aqhat* (KTU 1.19.II 27-49).[15] This episode also features a scene which begins with the arrival of young servants who tell of Aqhat's death— "They came on, they lifted up their voices (and cried): 'Hear O Danel (man of Rapiu), the hero Aqhat is dead.'" The episode then proceeds to the familiar catalogue (partially preserved) of Danel's physical responses to the news—trembling feet, a face pouring sweat, the loss of muscular control.[16] Finally, the scene concludes with Danel's verbal response—"he cried out . . ."—which has been all but lost except for one word.[17] To explain the similarities between KTU 1.5.VI 2-25 and KTU 1.19.II 27-49, Ugaritologists have suggested that these scenes adhere to the same conventional plot structure—an explanation remarkably similar to that offered here to account for the structural similarities between 2 Samuel 1 and other scenes of mourning in biblical literature. Indeed, the similarity is so pronounced that it suggests that the lament type-scene was inherited by Israelite scribes from earlier Syro-Palestinian literary culture.[18]

Returning now to the central question of this study—why David's Lament in 1 Sam 1:17-27 was placed in its present narrative setting—our reconstruction of the lament type-scene takes us one step toward an answer. Having identified the narrative's conventional structure, we can now recognize how the insertion of the lament satisfies the third structural requirement of the lament type-scene, the citation of the mourner's verbal response. Such a conclusion does not mean that the lament was composed by the author of the incorporating narrative—as we have seen, it probably predates the narrative—but it does suggest that the incorporation of the lament within the narrative was shaped by a conventional literary logic which also governs the description of the messenger's report in 2 Sam 1:1-10 and the catalogue of mournful gestures in 2 Sam 1:11-12.

There are several questions which this proposal leaves unanswered. The lament type-scene hypothesis does not explain why the author of 2 Samuel 1 appropriated a once-independent poem to serve as David's verbal response when in most other examples of the lament type-scene (including those within 2 Samuel) the mourner's verbal response seems to have been composed by the author of the surrounding narrative. Nor does it explain how the specific contents of David's lament serve its narrative setting. To shed light on these issues we must consider not only how the lament type-scene has shaped the lament's narrative role but also how this type-scene has been adapted by the author of 2 Samuel 1. As it turns out, the adaptation of the lament type-scene in 2 Samuel 1 reflects a larger literary pattern that surfaces throughout the narrative of David's reign in 2 Samuel. If we wish to understand how the author of 2 Samuel 1 has adapted the lament type-scene— including the lament itself—to serve his literary purposes, we must determine how this episode relates to the larger narrative composition within which it appears.

Unfortunately, there is little agreement on what exactly this larger narrative composition is. There is a general consensus that 1 and 2 Samuel are comprised of several distinct compositions that have been combined by a redactor (e.g., the Ark Narrative in 1 Samuel 4-6 and 2 Samuel 6, the History of King David's Rise in 1 Samuel 15-2 Samuel 5, and the Court History in 2 Samuel 9-20, 1 Kings 1-2). While few scholars have challenged this basic source division, scholars differ over precisely where to place the borders between some of these sources. The Court History, for example, is usually thought to begin with 2 Samuel 9, but some recent analyses place its beginning in chapter 6, in chapter 4, even in chapter 2.[19] Scholars also differ in their identifications of redactional material within each of the sources within 1-2 Samuel, and they disagree about the extent to which these sources have been integrated into a single composition.[20] Although no analysis can accommodate the full range of theories seeking to account for the composition of 1-2 Samuel, I believe that the observations offered here will shed some light on its redaction by exposing a line of connection between the episode in 2 Samuel 1 and the Court History.

Let us reconsider the similarity between 2 Samuel 1 and the other scenes of mourning within 2 Samuel. I did not note in our initial analysis of these scenes that many of them share an additional motif not present in manifestations of the lament type-scene external to 2 Samuel, such as Job 1 and the Ugaritic examples. This motif centers on the narrative's report—via the narrator or a figure within the narrative—that David's grief was observed and evaluated by others within the enacted world. In 2 Sam 12, this "public response motif," as I call it, surfaces when David's response to the death of his son is observed by his servants, who are baffled by the king's behavior. It is also present in 2 Sam 19:1-8, where Joab reports to David that his grief is alienating his soldiers, who do not understand why the king mourns for the rebellious Absalom when he should be praising their loyalty and valor. The motif is even present in 2 Samuel 1, which, by reporting that David's men joined him in mourning for Saul and Jonathan, indicates popular sympathy with David's grief. In all three cases, then, the narrative discloses that David's grief has public-relations ramifications, affecting how the king's constituency perceived him. What makes this motif even more significant is that while it does not appear in instances of the lament type-scene outside of 2 Samuel (e.g.,

Job 1, Ugaritic narrative), it is present in at least one mourning scene within 2 Samuel which does not seem to have been shaped by the lament type-scene structure: 2 Sam 3:36. In this episode the narrator reports that David's mourning for Abner was approved by the people: "all the people took notice of it (David's grief), and it pleased them." The distribution of the "public response motif" (present in mourning scenes within 2 Samuel, absent in mourning scenes outside of 2 Samuel) indicates that it was generated not by the generic requirements of the lament type-scene but by a rhetorical agenda specific to 2 Samuel.

What is this agenda? At first glance the answer to this question seems to depend on where one is reading in 2 Samuel. The two mourning scenes at the beginning of 2 Samuel—2 Samuel 1 and 2 Samuel 3—seem designed to convey a similar message. In both scenes the narrative attributes to David a "poetic" lament (2 Sam 1:17-27 and David's elegy for Abner in 2 Sam 3:33-34) and underscores the propriety of the king's grief by reporting that David's expression of it was well-received by those who witnessed it. Such details underscore the propriety of David's grief, perhaps with the goal of exonerating David from any role in the slayings of Saul, Jonathan, and Abner.[21] By contrast, the mourning scenes at the end of 2 Samuel, 2 Samuel 12 and 18-19, leave a very different impression. In these scenes the king's expression of grief is unconventional and elicits bafflement or disapproval from those observing it. Their rhetorical effect is not to clear David of suspicion but to reinforce the impression that David's loss of his sons has contributed to his psychological/political decline.

Since 2 Samuel 1, 3, 12, and 18-19 allegedly stem from different sources (the History of David's Rise versus the Court History), one could argue that the differing portraits of David's grief in these scenes reflect the differing purposes of the original documents from which these scenes stem.[22] The evidence allows for another interpretation, however, for the different impressions of David generated by these episodes can be integrated into a single, evolving portrait of the king's personal and political decline, moving from the king's artful and well-received laments in 2 Samuel 1 and 3, to his unconventional and perplexing response to the death of his baby son in 2 Samuel 12, to his stammering, self-absorbed grief for Absalom in 2 Samuel 18-19. Read in light of one another, the scenes of mourning in 2 Samuel provide the reader with a way to measure David's psychological disposition and public standing at key moments in his reign, depicting a leader who increasingly loses control over his emotions and public image even as the tragedies in his life grow less politically expeditious and more personal. If I am correct in this reading, the author of 2 Samuel has adapted the lament type-scene not only to reinforce David's image after the deaths of his rivals or to reveal the breakdown of his public persona after the deaths of his sons but also to sharpen the contrast between David at the beginning and end of 2 Samuel. Read as part of one narrative sequence, in other words, the scenes of grief in 2 Samuel generate a set of oppositions in David's behavior which complicate our sense of his development.

David's lament, I would suggest further, plays a crucial role in generating these oppositions, working with and against David's later expressions of grief to imply differences in the king's character and stature at the beginning and end of his reign. Meir Sternberg, in his penetrating study *The Poetics of Biblical Narrative,* has argued that in the attempt to shape the reader's evaluation of its contents, biblical narrative often dramatizes or states outright a social, pyschological, or ethical norm in order to make a subsequent infringement of that norm more perceptible.[23] A textbook example can be found in 2 Sam 11:11, where Uriah, the steadfast soldier unwilling to sleep with his wife, Bat-Sheba, while his fellow soldiers remain on the battlefield, exemplifies an ethical norm violated by David. The implicit opposition between Uriah's solidarity with the army and the derelict behavior of David, who has proved willing to sleep with Uriah's wife instead of going into battle in accordance with his duty as king, serves here to underscore the latter's violation of both his military and his moral responsibilities. I would argue that David's lament plays a similar role in relation to the king's later professions of grief. Placed at the beginning of David's reign, the lament establishes a behavioral and literary norm against which later violations can be identified and assessed.

Look at what happens when one reads 2 Sam 12: 22-23 in light of David's lament. The lament, with its touching tribute to the deceased and its profession of personal loss at their deaths, is exemplary as an expression of grief. This conclusion is based not only upon the contents of the lament itself but also upon the impression given by the preceding narrative, which reports that David's followers joined him in his grief and (if we can trust the present form of the text) that the king taught the lament to others. Quite different is the king's response to his baby's death in 2 Samuel 12. There, in stark contrast to the emotional and rhetorical propriety of his lament over Saul and Jonathan, David refuses to offer a lament for his baby son, and indeed, he speaks only to dismiss the behavioral and literary clichés of mourning—"why should I fast? Can I bring him back again?" One does not need to compare this statement with David's lament in order to surmise that it violates cultural and literary norms—the servants' puzzled response in 2 Sam 12:21 ensures that we recognize this. By reading 2 Samuel 12 against the backdrop of 2 Samuel 1, however, we can see that the king's behavior in 2 Samuel 12 also violates a behavioral norm *specific to David.* Having read 2 Samuel 1, after all, we know that David can produce stirring laments even for his political rivals. It is all the more incongruous, therefore, that when his own son dies, the king issues a statement that inverts the conventional content and tone of lamentation. To account for this incongruity would require us to look at the narrative of Samuel in its entirety, a task we cannot undertake in this study. Suffice it to say that there are many ways to reconcile David's differing responses without dissolving the literary unity of 2 Samuel: one can reinterpret David's lament in accordance with the attitude of indifference later expressed in 2 Samuel 12 (perhaps David was only pretending to feel sorrow for Saul and Jonathan); one can supply a psychological motivation to account for David's unconventional behavior in 2 Samuel 12 (perhaps David's grief for his baby was so great that, like Hamlet's grief for his father, it could not be expressed in a publicly acceptable form); or one can postulate a change in David's character resulting from experiences occurring between 2 Samuel 1 and 12 (perhaps David had become so corrupt through his affair with Bat-Sheba and his murder of Uriah that he no longer valued human life). Whatever resolution one prefers, the point is that differences between David's lament in 2 Samuel 1 (the norm) and David's "antilament" in 2 Samuel 12 (the violation of the norm) *serve a literary function,* complicating one's evaluation of David's development.

A similar effect is generated by the juxtaposition of David's lament with his verbal response to the death of Absalom in 2 Sam 18:33 and 19:4. As was true of 2 Samuel 12, one does not need to recall other mourning episodes in 2 Samuel to recognize that there is something excessive, even obsessive, about David's expression of sorrow in 2 Samuel 18-19. Both the form of David's cry (its repetitiveness, its staccato rhythm, its apparent lack of structure) and the setting in which it is spoken (David utters it as he withdraws from public view into a private chamber) bespeak a grief so crushing that it has overwhelmed David's ability to think about anything else, even his standing in the eyes of others. What becomes visible only from the juxtaposition of this episode with David's lament, however, is how far the mighty king has fallen in the time *between* the deaths of Saul and Jonathan and the death of Absalom. David's lament involved a use of language that helped to establish the king's positive public image; David's inarticulate and socially isolating response to the death of Absalom signals the collapse of that image and the political/rhetorical skills which had helped David construct it. It is this difference which I believe the author of 2 Samuel is trying to call to our attention by placing the two similarly patterned mourning scenes at the beginning and end of the narrative. The structural correspondence between these scenes (which they share from the conventional form of the lament type-scene) serves in this context to foreground the differences between David at two defining moments in his life, suggesting in this way the extent to which the personality and public image of the king have declined over the course of his troubled reign.

We see, then, that the narrative role of David's lament thus extends far beyond the immediate episode in which it has been incorporated. Situated at the beginning of David's reign, the lament generates a "first impression" of how the king responds to the death of others that conditions the reader's interpretation of mourning scenes presented later in 2 Samuel (2 Samuel 12, 2 Samuel 18-19). The later scenes now appear as violations of a norm established by David himself in 2 Samuel 1, violations which modern readers can account for by dissolving the narrative's literary unity, as some scholars have done, or, as I prefer, by postulating a development of character not made explicit by the narrative.

If this interpretation of David's lament is valid, it has significant implications for our understanding of the narrative in which it was incorporated. It points to at least one pattern within the fabric of 2 Samuel that weaves the History of David's Rise and the Court History together into a single, evolving portait of King David, a discovery that directly challenges the view of those who argue that these two sections of Samuel represent two distinct narrative sources. Beyond this implication and what it says about the compositional history of Samuel lies another of greater relevance for the present study. The narrative role of David's lament confirms something we learned from the Song of the Sea and the Song of Moses. Our analyses of these songs indicated that their narrative roles reflect not a single literary device designed to express the author's emotions or to relieve the reader's tedium but several different conventions governing the composition of different kinds of literature. We were able to reconstruct these conventions because the insertions of the Song of the Sea and the Song of Moses resemble literary behaviors found elsewhere in Egyptian and Aramaic literature composed at around the same time as Exodus 14-15 and Deuteronomy 31-32. What we have learned about the insertion of David's lament within 2 Samuel fits in with this general picture. Its narrative role reflects yet another scribal convention shared by Israel with a neighboring ancient Near Eastern culture—this time the lament type-scene, which surfaces repeatedly in both biblical and Ugaritic narrative. This is a crucial point for understanding the Bible's mixing of poetry and prose because it suggests that to treat this phenomenon as if it *originated* as a single literary device is to underestimate the multifariousness of ancient Israel's scribal practice and its varied relations to literary behavior in other ancient Near Eastern literary cultures.

APPENDIX B

The Songs of Israel and the
Song of the Angels

Emerging canon-consciousness was not the only religious development which affected the way the songs in biblical narrative were perceived in the Second Temple and post–Second Temple periods. One development worthy of note was the growing belief that humans could participate in the praise sung to God by the angels and other heavenly beings. The notion that heavenly beings sing praise to God is attested in preexilic biblical sources (e.g., Isa 6:1-3) and has antecedents in the ancient Near East.[1] It is only in the Second Temple period, however, that one begins to find descriptions of human beings learning or participating in the praise of heavenly beings.[2] Note the following examples culled from apocalyptic literature, Jewish mystical literature, and Qumran liturgical poetry.

- *The Ascension of Isaiah* viii 17 (R. Charles, *The Ascension of Isaiah* [London: Adam and Charles Black, 1900], p. 57): "And (power) was given to me also, and I also praised along with them *(et glorificavi ego)* and that angel also, and our praise was like theirs."
- *The Apocalypse of Abraham,* p. 58): "'Only worship, Abraham, and recite the song which I have taught you.' . . . And I worshipped, and recited the song which he had taught me."
- *The Apocalypse of Zephaniah* 8:2-4 (O. Wintermute, "The Apocalypse of Zephaniah: A New Translation and Introduction," in Charlesworth, *Old Testament Pseudepigrapha,* pp. 497-516): "I saw all those angels praying. I, myself, prayed together with them."
- *T. Job* 48:3: "She uttered in an angelic voice and offered a hymn to God according to the hymnody of the angels."
- *Hekhalot Rabbati* 24: 1 (A. Jellinek, *Bet Ha-Midrash,* vol. 3 [Jerusalem: Wahrmann, 1967], p. 100): "When he stands before the throne of glory, he begins to recite the hymn which the throne of glory sings every day."
- *3 Enoch* 1:11-13 (H. Odeberg, *3 Enoch* [New York: Ktav, 1973]: "When I opened my mouth and sang a song of praise before the Holy One blessed be He, the holy creatures below and above the throne of glory responded, saying, 'Holy, Holy, Holy' and 'Blessed is the glory of the Lord in his dwelling place.'"
- *The Songs of the Sabbath Sacrifice* 4Q400 2:1-7 (C. Newsom, *The Songs of the Sabbath Sacrifice: A Critical Edition* [Atlanta: Scholars Press, 1985], pp. 110-11): "to praise your glory wondrously with the *elim* of knowledge and the praiseworthiness of your royal power together with the holiest of the h[oly ones]."

- Rev. 14:3: "No one could learn that song except the hundred and forty-four thousand who had been redeemed from the earth."
- The Qedushah (as, for example, preserved in the fourth-century C.E. *Apostolic Constitutions*):[3] "Israel, thy congregation on earth, emulating the heavenly powers, sings with a full heart . . ."

Some of these passages show that biblical figures such as Abraham and Job's daughters were sometimes thought to have learned or participated in the angelic song. The belief that humans could participate in angelic singing thus had an impact on the way in which biblical narrative was perceived and rewritten in the Second Temple period. Beyond this, there are indications in Second Temple and rabbinic sources that some of the songs in biblical narrative were themselves thought to have been recited among, or in communion with, the angels. Thus in a paraphrase of Deuteronomy 32 (*De Virtutibus* 72–75), Philo reports that Moses sang the song "taking his place among the heavenly choir-masters." (This reading may reflect an interpretation of the song's opening line: "Give ear, O heavens, and I will speak . . .") Rabbinic literature also attests to this belief in relation to the Song of the Sea, though it introduces an interesting twist by suggesting that its performance postponed the Song of the Angels (see *Midr. Tehillim*, Psalm 106, p. 454; B. Tanh. *bašallah* 13).[4] Rabbinic literature also includes traditions in which Jacob (when wrestling the angel), Moses (in Deuteronomy 32), and Joshua (in Josh 10:12) either silenced heavenly beings by singing their song or offered to sing in their stead.[5] These traditions, which reflect an idea frequently attested in rabbinical sources that God prefers Israel's praise over that of the angels,[6] may represent a kind of polemic against apocalyptic circles that actively sought to participate in the angelic song. In any event, the idea that humans could join in (or rival) the Angelic Song clearly colored how the songs in biblical narrative were understood by early Jewish readers.

The point of connection between the Angelic Song and the songs in biblical narrative seems to have been the association of each with the liturgy. In at least some branches of early Judaism, worshipers identified their own praise with that sung by the angels. The precise origins of this association are unclear, but it had certainly crystallized by the end of the Second Temple period, when it left an imprint on the *Songs of the Sabbath Sacrifice*, a collection of hymns found at Qumran and Masada which were evidently recited to achieve or express communion with the angels in their heavenly praise.[7] A similar idea surfaces in post–Second Temple Jewish and Christian liturgical rites, which called for worshipers to recite Isa 6:3 (the trisagion) and other verses in emulation of angelic praise (this practice is known as the Qedushah in rabbinic Judaism). It was perhaps this association of the Angelic Song with contemporary liturgical praise that eventually triggered the association of the Angelic Song with the songs in biblical narrative, which were also identified with contemporary liturgical praise, as we have seen. Some early Jews and Christians, especially those who produced apocalyptic literature, believed that just as they themselves recited songs in communion with the angels' song, so too were the songs of their biblical ancestors sung along with the angels. Others, most notably the rabbis, believed that the songs sung in the biblical past, like the songs of Israel's present, took the place of the angels' song.

NOTES

1. Moving between Prose and Poetry

1. See Josephus, *Jewish Antiquites,* Book 2, 16:4; Book 4, 8:44; Book 7, 12:3. In the first passage Josephus claims that the Song of the Sea in Exodus 15 was composed in hexameter verses; in the second he makes the same claim for the Song of Moses in Deuteronomy 32; and in the third he claims that David wrote his songs and hymns in trimeter and pentemeter verses. As James Kugel has argued, such claims probably reflect Josephus's attempt to reconcile biblical literature with the Greek literary categories familar to his audience. See Kugel, *The Idea of Biblical Poetry* (New Haven: Yale University Press, 1981), pp. 127-29, 140-42.

2. Modern translations and critical editions of the Hebrew text often print the Bible as if there were a clear distinction within it between prose and poetic passages. The distinction is marked typographically by the use of a special spacing (sometimes called stichography), italics, or both. See, for example, the various translations of Gen 1:27 cited in S. E. Gillingham, *The Poems and Psalms of the Hebrew Bible* (Oxford: Oxford University Press, 1994), p. 20, a passage which is printed as prose by some versions and as poetry by others. It is true that some songs in biblical narrative were written in a special stichography even in ancient times, as attested by the oldest extant biblical manuscripts from Qumran for "poetic" texts such as Deuteronomy 32 and some of the psalms. It is not clear, however, that the original function of stichography was to mark poetry per se. It is not employed for many passages deemed poetic by modern scholarship, while similar spacing techniques are used for texts not regarded as poetic (the list of the Canaanite kings in Josh 12:9, the list of Haman's sons in Esth 9:7-9). All this suggests at the very least that one cannot rely upon stichography in either modern or premodern biblical texts as a marker of poetry. For further discussion of stichography, see M. Breuer, *The Aleppo Codex and the Accepted Text of the Bible* (Jerusalem: Mossad Ha-Rab Kook, 1976), pp. 149-89 (in Hebrew); Kugel, *Idea of Biblical Poetry,* pp. 119-27; E. Tov, *Textual Criticism* (Minneapolis: Fortress, 1992), pp. 212-13.

3. The best of recent studies of biblical poetry stress how difficult it is to pinpoint the criteria distinguising prose from poetry in biblical literature. See M. O'Conner, *Hebrew Verse Structure* (Winona Lake, Ind.: Eisenbrauns, 1980), pp. 29-38, and J. Kugel, *Idea of Biblical Poetry,* pp. 70-76, 287-304. These studies show that there is no single trait that can be relied upon to distinguish biblical prose from poetry—not meter, not rhyme, not even parallelism, since the first two may not exist in biblical Hebrew and the latter also appears frequently in prose. Many still insist that there is a clear line between biblical prose and poetry, but there is no consensus on how to differentiate them formally.

4. See D. Stuart, *Studies in Early Hebrew Meter,* Harvard Semitic Monograph Series 13 (Missoula: Scholars Press/Harvard Semitic Museum, 1976), pp. 20-24; F. M. Cross, "The Epic Traditions of Early Israel: Epic Narrative and the Reconstruction of Early Israelite Traditions," in *The Poet and the Historian,* ed. R. Friedman

(Chico: Scholars Press, 1983), pp. 13-39, esp. 20-23. Believing that the biblical text's original form has been obscured in the process of transmission (oral or written), scholars often propose that prose passages should be reinterpreted as poetry and poetic passages as prose. For studies which reread prose as poetry, see, for example, J. Kselman, "The Recovery of Poetic Fragments from the Pentateuchal Priestly Source," JBL 97 (1978): 161-73; D. L. Christensen, "Narrative Poetics and the Interpretation of the Book of Jonah," in *Directions in Biblical Hebrew Poetry*, ed. E. Follis (Sheffield: JSOT, 1987), pp. 29-48; W. Koopmans, *Joshua 24 as Poetic Narrative* (Sheffield: JSOT, 1990), pp. 165-76. For poetic passages reread as prose, see Gillingham, *Poems and Psalms*, pp. 32-36. Whatever the merits of these individual studies, it is important to note that prose and poetry are also difficult to distinguish in other literatures from the ancient Near East, which have not undergone the long process of transmission to which the Bible was subject. It is likely, for example, that texts uncovered at the ancient Syrian city of Ugarit are more or less in the form in which they were first composed, and yet scholars of Ugaritic literature have failed to reach consensus on how to identify meter in compositions thought to be poetry and some maintain that Ugaritic poetry is not metrical at all. See G. Douglass Young, "Ugaritic Prosody," JNES 9 (1950): 124-33, who, after reviewing the major metrical systems reconstructed for Ugaritic poetry, concludes that meter in Ugaritic is an "illusion . . . created by the accidents of Semitic morphology and parallelism of thought." For a review of the debate surrounding meter in Ugaritic poetry, see W. G. E. Watson, *Classical Hebrew Poetry: A Guide to Its Techniques* (Sheffield: JSOT, 1984), pp. 94-97.

5. For example, see E. Sievers, *Metrische Studien*, vols. 1 and 2 (Leipzig: Teubner, 1901 and 1904), and G. B. Gray, *The Forms of Hebrew Poetry* (reprint; New York: Ktav, 1972), p. 46. Similar claims have been made for other ancient Near Eastern literatures. See M. Lichtheim, "Have the Principles of Ancient Egyptian Metrics Been Discovered?" *Journal of the American Research Center in Egypt* 9 (1971-72): 103-10.

6. By "song" I mean those texts which are explicitly introduced as songs by their narrative settings or are described as songs, hymns, or odes in early postbiblical sources. There are basically two reasons that I rely on native Israelite/Jewish terminology rather than modern form-critical classifications in defining the corpus for study: (1) modern biblical scholars differ sharply in their use of genre labels (note the debate over biblical poetry mentioned above); (2) one of my principle arguments in this study is that the actual form and function of the songs are less important for understanding their narrative roles than are the songs' form and function as perceived by the authors of biblical narrative and early Jewish readers of it.

7. Because the mixing of prose and poetry was once seen as a distinctively "Semitic" trait, its use by Greek and Latin authors (a practice often referred to by the medieval term *prosimetrium*) was thought to reflect an import from the Orient. See R. Hirzel, *Der Dialog—ein literaturhistorischer Versuch*, vols. 1 and 2 (Leipzig: S. Hirzel, 1895), pp. 380-85, and B. Perry, *The Ancient Romances* (Berkeley: University of California Press, 1967), p. 208. Although many of the Greek authors known for their use of prosimetrium—most notably the Hellenistic authors Menippus of Gadera, Meleagros of Gadera, and Lucian of Samosota—were from the Near East, many have questioned the validity of the Orientalizing explanation, arguing that the mixing of prose and poetry in Greek literature represents an internal Greek phenomenon. See O. Immisch, "Über eine volkstümliche Darstellungsform in der antiken Literatur," *Neue Jahrbücher für das klassische Altertum, Geschichte und deutsche Literatur* 47 (1921): 409-21; D. Bartonková, "Prosimetrium,

the Mixed Style, in Ancient Literature," *Eirene* 14 (1983): 66 and nn. 6–11; J. Hall, *Lucian's Satire* (New York: Arno, 1981), pp. 407–13.

8. One of the earliest scholars to claim that the insertion of poetry within biblical prose served an aesthetic function was H. Gunkel, in *The Psalms: A Form Critical Introduction*, trans. T. Horner (Philadelphia: Fortress, 1967), p. 2 n. c, who suggested that the biblical authors mixed prose and poetry to produce "a pleasing effect" (he does not define the nature of this effect). T. Gaster, *Myth, Legend and Cult in the Old Testament* (New York: Harper and Row, 1969), pp. 240–41, described the insertion of poems within biblical prose as a device for relieving tedium, securing audience participation, and marking logical pauses in the narrative. Some recent scholars also maintain that the insertion of songs was motivated by aesthetic-rhetorical considerations but are more likely to describe the practice as an editorial device used to structure large blocks of narrative material into a literary unity or to emphasize the thematic concerns of the incorporating narrative. See H. G. Reventlow, *Gebet im Alten Testament* (Stuttgart: Kohlhammer, 1986), pp. 287–94; S. Balentine, *Prayer in the Hebrew Bible* (Minneapolis: Augsburg Fortress, 1993), pp. 213–24; J. Watts, *Psalm and Story* (Sheffield: JSOT, 1993). The reasons for my dissatisfaction with these explanations will become evident.

9. See the comments of Watts, *Psalm and Story*, 194: "Prose usually eschews direct commentary . . . [its] comments tend to be formulaic and matter-of-fact. Poetry, by contrast, does not narrate sequentially, but offers vivid descriptions of feelings and emphatic statements of ideas"; of J. C. de Moor and W. Watson, *Verse in Ancient Near Eastern Prose* (Kevelaer: Verlag Butzon and Bercker/Neukirchen-Vluyn: Neukirchener Verlag, 1993), pp. xvii–xviii: "prose is composed for purposes which differ from those for which verse [poetry] is intended. Prose provides information, generally accepted as authentic, whereas verse can be fantasy, entertains and is persuasive"; and of Y. Gitay, "W. F. Albright and the Question of Early Hebrew Poetry," in *History and Interpretation*, ed. M. P. Graham et al. (Sheffield: JSOT, 1993), pp. 192–202: " . . . each is a literary vehicle with its own sphere of use. While prose is the objective language of administration, historical accounts, and law, poetry is the subjective medium of wishes, prayers, praises, and hymns" (p. 198). This characterization of prose and poetry can be traced in the history of biblical scholarship at least as far back as Robert Lowth, *Lectures on the Sacred Poetry of the Hebrews*, trans. G. Gregory (London: Chadwick, 1847), pp. 153–62, who in a series of lectures first published in 1753 described poetry as the language of enthusiasm and "mental emotion" and prose as the "language of reason." For further discussion of Lowth's view of prose and poetry, see Kugel, *Idea of Biblical Poetry*, pp. 278–80; S. Prickett, "Poetry and Prophecy: Bishop Lowth and the Hebrew Scriptures in Eighteenth Century England," in *Images of Belief in Literature*, ed. D. Jasper (New York: St Martin's, 1984), pp. 81–103. The idea that poetry aims to rouse the emotions is much older than Lowth, however. See Plato's *Republic*, x. 602–3.

10. See Gaster, *Myth, Legend and Cult*, pp. 240–41.

11. D. Macdonald, *The Hebrew Literary Genius* (Princeton: Princeton University Press, 1933), pp. 21–22.

12. For an English translation of the relevant passage from Moses Ibn Ezra's treatise on poetry, *Kitāb al-Muḥāḍara wal-Mudhākara*, see A. Berlin, *Biblical Poetry through Medieval Jewish Eyes* (Bloomington: Indiana University Press, 1991), pp. 68–69.

13. Gadamer is among the most influential exponents of the notion that one's prejudices and expectations are always involved in one's understanding of an alien text or tradition. See H. Gadamer, *Truth and Method*, trans. G. Barden and J.

Cumming (New York: Continuum, 1986). Gadamer also argues, however, that one's understanding of an alien text or tradition is altered by the encounter with it. This is a position to which I find myself deeply committed in the present study.

14. The view that the Song of the Sea once functioned as a cultic hymn is based on elements within the song that point to a temple setting (especially the song's reference to God's sanctuary in Exod 15:17) and its similarity to psalms within the Psalter, especially the so-called Enthronement Psalms, which were allegedly recited to celebrate God's coronation in the temple. See P. Haupt, "Moses' Song of Triumph," AJSL 20 (1904): 149-72; H. Schmidt, "Das Meerlied Ex:2-19," ZAW 64 (1931): 59-66; J. Pedersen, *Israel: Its Life and Culture*, vols. 3 and 4 (London: Oxford University Press, 1940), pp. 402-15 and 728-37 (Pedersen believed that the entirety of Exodus 1-15 was once recited cultically as part of a Passover festival); G. von Rad, *The Problem of the Hexateuch and Other Essays* (New York: McGraw-Hill, 1966), pp. 10-11; J. Muilenberg, "A Liturgy on the Triumphs of the Lord," in *Studia Biblica et Semitica: Festschrift T. C. Vriezen* (Wageningen: Veenman and Zonen, 1966), pp. 233-51; F. M. Cross, "The Song of the Sea and Canaanite Myth," *God and Christ: Existence and Providence*, JTC 5 (New York: Harper and Row, 1968), pp. 1-25, and *Canaanite Myth and Hebrew Epic: Essays in the History of the Religion of Israel* (Cambridge: Harvard University Press, 1973), pp. 112-44; G. Coats, "The Song of the Sea," CBQ 31 (1969): 1-17. The precise cultic context reconstructed for the song hinges in part upon how one interprets Exod 15:17: "You brought them in and planted them on the mountain of your own possession, the place, O Lord, that you made your abode, the sanctuary, O Lord, that your hands have established." Some scholars believe that this passage refers to the temple in Jerusalem (see Muilenberg, "Liturgy," p. 249), others to a pre-Solomonic temple (see Cross, *Canaanite Myth and Hebrew Epic*, pp. 142-43).

15. For the argument that the language of Exodus 15 and other songs is archaic, see D. Robertson, *Linguistic Evidence in Dating Early Hebrew Poetry* (Missoula: Society of Biblical Literature, 1972). The song cannot have been composed earlier than the twelfth century B.C.E. because of its reference in verse 14 to the Philistines, who first appear in Palestine at around that time. The reader should note that not all scholars accept an early date of composition for many of the songs in biblical narrative. Some have argued that the language of the Song of the Sea, for example, is postexilic. See A. Bender, "Das Lied Exodus 15," ZAW 23 (1903): 1-43; Haupt, "Moses' Song of Triumph," pp. 152-54; S. Mowinckel, "Psalm Criticism between 1900 and 1935 (Ugarit and Psalm Exegesis)," VT 5 (1955): 13-33, esp. p. 27; A. Lauha, "Das Schilfmeermotiv im Alten Testament," in *Congress Vienna Volume*, VTSup 9 (Leiden: Brill, 1963), pp. 32-46; F. Foresti, "Composizione e Redazione Deuteronomistica in Ex 15, 1-18," *Lateranum* 48 (1982): 41-69. In truth, neither side has made a compelling case. Despite Robertson's claims to the contrary, his study shows that with the evidence currently available it is impossible to prove that the language of the songs in biblical narrative is older than that of the surrounding prose. He does establish that many of the songs exhibit archaic forms, but in the end he admits that only one is consistently archaic in its language—the Song of the Sea (see *Linguistic Evidence*, p. 138). The other songs mix archaic linguistic forms with the later forms of standard biblical Hebrew, suggesting that their language may be archaizing rather than genuinely archaic—that is, they may have been written to sound like archaic Hebrew. Still, the arguments of those who see in the song postexilic Hebrew are methodologically flawed and are based on a selective use of the evidence. Many of the alleged Aramaicisms in the Song of the Sea, for example, can be explained in other ways. In the case of the Song of the Sea, several exilic and postexilic texts appear familiar with it, indicating that

it was already in existence by this time; e.g., Neh 9:11, which appears to echo Exod 15:5, and Deuteronomy 2-3, which seems to have been influenced by the song's language (as shown by W. Moran, "The End of the Unholy War and Anti-Exodus," Bib 44 [1963]: 333-42). Another technique for dating the songs is to examine their orthography for signs of archaic spelling practices. Some scholars believe that the more archaic the spelling, the earlier the date of composition. See F. M. Cross and D. N. Freedman, *Studies in Ancient Yahwistic Poetry* (Missoula: Scholars' Press, 1975), and F. Anderson and A. Dean Forbes, *Spelling in the Hebrew Bible* (Rome: Biblical Institute Press, 1981), pp. 63-65. This method is also suspect, however, because it underrates the variability of orthographic practices reflected in the biblical text and because supposedly archaic practices are not restricted to an early period in Israelite history. See T. Butler, "The Song of the Sea: Exodus 15:1-18: A Study in the Exegesis of Hebrew Poetry, " Ph.D. diss., Vanderbilt University, 1971, pp. 213-37, and J. Barr, *Variable Spellings in the Old Testament* (Oxford: Oxford University Press, 1989), pp. 37-39. One final argument appeals to the prosody or meter of the songs. Following their teacher W. F. Albright, F. M. Cross and D. N. Freedman ("The Song of Miriam," JNES 14 [1955]: 237-50) have argued that the Song of the Sea is archaic on the grounds that its meter resembles metrical patterns found in Ugaritic poetry from the Late Bronze Age. Cf. Muilenberg, "Liturgy," who argues that the form of the refrains in Exod 15:5, 11, and 16 resembles the form of refrains used in Ugaritic poetry. Again, however, it is not clear that a particular prosodic pattern can be confined to a particular period in Israelite literary history. Moreover, our understanding of Ugaritic prosody (or of biblical prosody, for that matter) is not as firm as Cross and Freedman allege it to be. In short, while the language, orthography, and prosody of songs such as the Song of the Sea do seem more archaic than the language, orthography, and prosody of the surrounding prose, the evidence is not conclusive. Even if the language and form of the songs are not more archaic than that of the prose, however, there are still grounds for concluding that they were composed independently of the narrative.

16. Read as part of the narrative, verses 16-17 appear to refer to Israel's entrance into the land as a future event. If one reads the song without reference to its narrative setting, these same verses can be construed as referring to an event that has already happened. The prefixed verbal forms in these verses can support either reading: they "look like" they are in the future tense, but such forms can also have a past-tense meaning, as does the prefixed verbal form in Exod 15:1: "sang" = *yāšir*. While on the subject of Exod 15:1, I. Rabinowitz ("*ʾāz* followed by Imperfect Verb-forms in Preterite Contexts: A Redactional Device in Biblical Hebrew," VT 34 [1984]: 53-62) has proposed another argument in support of the claim that the Song of the Sea originated independently of the preceding prose account in Exodus 14. He suggests that the use of the particle *ʾāz* ("then") followed by a prefixed verbal form with a past-tense meaning in verses such as Exod 15:1 is in fact a redactional device used to introduce into texts material from a source other than that from which the immediately foregoing material has been drawn.

17. The most frequently discussed contradiction is the fact that the narrative in Judges 4 mentions only the tribes of Zebulun and Naphtali as participants in the battle, whereas the song in Judges 5 mentions the participation of six tribes: Ephraim, Benjamin, Machir, Zebulun, Issachar, and Naphtali. See J. Soggin, *Judges*, trans. J. Bowden (London: Scholars Press, 1981), pp. 100-101. Baruch Halpern has proposed an explanation for these differences that works only if the two songs were composed independently of one another. He argues that many of the contradictions between chapters 4 and 5 are the result of the author of Judges 4

having mis- or overinterpreted the contents of the song. See B. Halpern, *The First Historians* (San Francisco: Harper and Row, 1988), pp. 78-82. Of course, some scholars deny that there really are contradictions between the prose and the song. See A. Malamat, "Israel in the Period of the Judges," in *World History of the Jewish People,* First Series, vol. 3, ed. B. Mazar (Jerusalem, 1971), pp. 137-40, who argues that song and prose refer to two different stages in the battle. For further discussion of this issue, see chap. 2.

18. For further discussion of the relation between 2 Samuel 22 and Psalm 18, see chap. 5.

19. For discussion of this case, see chaps. 4 and 5.

20. See also LXX 3 Kgs 8:53 (= MT 1 Kgs 8:12), which attributes Solomon's poetic statement about the temple to a "Book of Song." (The title "Book of Song" may reflect an accidental transposition of the letters *y* and *š* in the word *Yāšār,* producing *šyr* ("song") instead of *yšr.*) Based in part on such references, some scholars have concluded that the songs and other poetic "fragments" within biblical narrative were drawn from an antecedent poetic anthology or epic of some sort. See S. Mowinckel, "Hat es ein israelitisches Nationalepos gegeben?" ZAW 12 (1935): 130-53; W. Albright, *Yahweh and the Gods of Canaan* (Garden City: Doubleday, 1968), pp. 34-35; U. Cassuto, "The Israelite Epic," *Biblical and Oriental Studies,* vol. 2 (Jerusalem: Magnes, 1973), pp. 69-109; Cross "The Epic Traditions of Early Israel," 13-39. This theory was once quite influential, but many scholars now reject it. See C. Conroy, "Hebrew Epic: Historical Notes and Critical Reflections," Bib 61 (1980): 1-30, and S. Talmon, "Did There Exist a Biblical National Epic?" in *Proceedings of the Seventh World Congress of Jewish Studies* (Jerusalem: Perry Foundation for Biblical Research, World Union of Jewish Studies, 1981), pp. 41-61.

21. See N. Sarna, "The Psalm Superscriptions and the Guilds," in *Studies in Jewish Religion and Intellectual History Presented to A. Altman,* ed. S. Stein and R. Loewe (Tuscaloosa: University of Alabama Press, 1979), pp. 281-300; J. Kugel, "Topics in the History of the Spirituality of the Psalms," in *Jewish Spirituality,* vol. 1, ed. A. Green (New York: Crossroad, 1987), pp. 113-44.

22. My discussion of the comparative method draws on the insights of several studies: M. Bloch, "Two Strategies of Comparison," in *Comparative Perspectives: Theories and Methods,* ed. A Etzioni and F. Dublow (Boston: Little, Brown, 1970); S. Talmon, "The 'Comparative Method' in Biblical Interpretation—Principles and Problems," in *Essential Papers on Israel and the Ancient Near East,* ed. F. Greenspahn (New York: New York University Press, 1991), pp. 381-419 (reprint of article first published in VTSup 29 [1977], pp. 320-56); W. Hallo, "Biblical History in Its Near Eastern Setting: The Contextual Approach," in *Scripture in Context I,* ed. W. Hallo et al. (Pittsburgh: Pickwick, 1980), pp. 1-26; J. Z. Smith, "In Comparison a Magic Dwells," *Imagining Religion* (Chicago: University of Chicago Press, 1982), pp. 19-35; M. Malul, *The Comparative Method in Ancient Near Eastern and Biblical Legal Studies* (Neukirchen-Vluyn: Verlag Butzen and Bercker, 1990).

23. Compare J. Z. Smith, *Drudgery Divine* (Chicago: University of Chicago Press, 1990), pp. 47-48 and n. 15.

24. Both analogies are mentioned in Watts, *Psalm and Story,* pp. 187 and 215-16. For the role of verse in Icelandic saga, see H. O'Donoghue, *The Geneses of a Saga Narrative* (Oxford: Clarendon Press, 1991).

25. See A. Ladd, "Lyric Insertion in Thirteenth-Century French Narrative," Ph.D. diss., Yale University, 1973; J. Cerquiglini, "Pour une typologie de l'insertion," *Perspectives Médiévales* (1977): 9-14; J. Taylor, "The Lyric Insertion: Towards a Functional Model," in *Courtly Literature,* ed. K. Busby and E. Kooper (Amsterdam: J. Benjamins, 1990), pp. 539-48; S. Huot, *From Song to Book: The Poetics of Writing in*

Old French Lyric and Lyrical Narrative Poetry (Ithaca: Cornell University Press, 1987); M. Boulton, *The Song in the Story: Lyric Insertions in French Narrative Fiction, 1200–1400* (Philadelphia: University of Pennsylvania Press, 1993).

26. J. Z. Smith, *To Take Place: Toward Theory in Ritual* (Chicago: University of Chicago Press, 1987), pp. 13-14.

27. P. Zumthor, *Langue et techniques poétiques à l'époque romane* (Paris: Klincksieck, 1963), pp. 110, 177; Ladd, *Lyric Insertion,* p. 11.

28. Among the many scholars who have compared Deuteronomy with the form of vassal treaties, see D. J. McCarthy, *Treaty and Covenant: A Study in Form in the Ancient Oriental Documents and in the Old Testament* (Rome: Pontifical Biblical Institute, 1963); M. G. Kline, *Treaty of the Great King: The Covenant Structure of Deuteronomy* (Grand Rapids: Eerdmans, 1963); W. Moran, "The Ancient Near Eastern Background of the Love of God in Deuteronomy," CBQ 24 (1963): 77-87; D. Hillers, "A Note on Some Treaty Terminology in the Old Testament," BASOR 176 (1964): 46-47; R. Frankena, "The Vassal Treaties of Esarhaddon and the Dating of Deuteronomy," OTS 14 (1965): 122-54; K. Baltzer, *The Covenant Formulary* (Philadelphia: Fortress, 1971), pp. 31-38; M. Weinfeld, *Deuteronomy and the Deuteronomistic School* (Oxford: Clarendon Press, 1972).

29. See D. McCarthy, *Old Testament Covenant: A Survey of Current Opinions* (Richmond, Va.: John Knox, 1972), pp. 15-19; E. W. Nicholson, *God and His People: Covenant and Theology in the Old Testament* (Oxford: Clarendon Press, 1986), pp. 70-82.

30. Watts, *Psalm and Story,* 206-20. The mixing of prose and poetry in ancient Near Eastern literature has only recently elicited the sustained attention of scholars. See de Moor and Watson, *Verse in Ancient Near Eastern Prose.* The studies included in de Moor and Watson's volume disagree sharply over how to define prose and poetry and how to assess their interaction, suggesting that there is much work left to be done on this subject.

31. For other attempts to explain the mixture of song and story in biblical narrative in light of ancient Near Eastern literary practice, see N. Sarna, *Exploring Exodus* (New York: Schocken, 1986), p. 114, and K. Taylor, "Heads! Tails! Or the Whole Coin! Contexual Method and Intertextual Analysis: Judges 4 and 5," in *Scripture in Context IV,* ed. K. Younger et al. (Lewiston: Mellen, 1991), pp 109-46. Despite Sarna's and Taylor's claims to the contrary, the ancient Near Eastern analogies they propose are actually not relevant for understanding the *mixing* of song and story in biblical narrative. The examples they cite involve two parallel accounts of military campaigns, one in prose, the other in poetry; e.g., the two separate accounts of Ramesses II's battle against the Hittites at Kadesh, a prose account known as the "Bulletin" and a poetic account known as the "Poem." The composition of corresponding prosaic and poetic accounts, both Sarna and Taylor argue, is comparable to the collocation of poetic and prosaic accounts in biblical texts such as Judges 4-5 and Exodus 14-15. There is, however, a crucial difference, for the prose and poetic accounts of Ramesses II's battle or of any of the other analogies cited by Sarna and Taylor are not combined into a single account, as are the prose narratives and songs in Judges 4-5 and Exodus 14-15. Thus while Sarna and Taylor may have found analogies that shed light on why ancient Israelite authors composed both prose and poetic accounts of battles, their analogues do not illuminate how or why the authors of biblical narrative *integrated* song and story.

32. See Frankena, "Vassal-Treaties," and Weinfeld, *Deuteronomy and the Deuteronomistic School.*

33. Cf. Smith, *To Take Place,* 14.

34. Moran, "Ancient Near Eastern Background."

35. M. Weinfeld, *Deuteronomy 1–11*, AB (New York: Doubleday, 1991), p. 15.

36. See Frankena, "Vassal-Treaties."

37. This claim is common in handbooks and introductions to the Hebrew Bible. For recent examples, see N. Gottwald, *The Hebrew Bible: A Socio-Literary Introduction* (Philadelphia: Fortress, 1987), p. 103, and J. Sanders, *From Sacred Story to Sacred Text* (Philadelphia: Fortress, 1987), pp. 26–29.

38. This claim is also common in handbooks and commentaries. See R. Pfeiffer, *Introduction to the Old Testament* (New York: Harper, 1941), pp. 51–52, and M. Weinfeld, *Deuteronomy 1–11*, p. 84.

39. For the idea of the "heavenly book" or heavenly tablets in the ancient Near East, see L. Koep, *Das himmlische Buch in Antike und Christentum: Eine religionsgeschichtliche Untersuchung zur altchristlichen Bildersprache* (Bonn: Peter Hanstein, 1952); G. Widengren, *The Ascension of the Apostle and the Holy Book* (Uppsala: Uppsala Universitets Årsskrift; A. B. Lundequistska/Leipzig: Otto Harrassowitz, 1950); S. Paul, "Heavenly Tablets and the Book of Life," JANES 5 (1973): 345–53; W. Graham, *Beyond the Written Word* (Cambridge: Cambridge University Press, 1987), pp. 50–51. Several recent studies have discerned evidence of canonizing behavior in Mesopotamia. See F. Rochberg-Halton, "Canonicity in Cuneiform Texts," JCS 36 (1984): 127–44; S. Lieberman, "Canonical and Official Cuneiform Texts: Towards an Understanding of Assurbanipal's Personal Tablet Collection," in *Lingering over Words*, ed. T. Abush et al. (Atlanta: Scholars Press, 1990), pp. 305–36; W. Hallo, "The Concept of Canonicity in Cuneiform and Biblical Literature: A Comparative Appraisal," in *Scripture in Context IV*, pp. 1–19. By "canonization," most of these studies mean textual stabilization and standardization, not the acceptance of a text as binding for religious belief and practice.

40. See the studies cited in chap. 4, n. 9.

41. B. Childs, "The Exegetical Significance of Canon for the Old Testament," in *Congress Volume Göttingen 1977* (VTSup 29 [1977], pp. 68–80, esp. pp. 70–71. For the historical setting of Deutero-Isaiah, see R. Clifford, "Second Isaiah," *Anchor Bible Dictionary*, vol. 3, ed. D. N. Freedman (New York: Doubleday, 1992), pp. 490–501.

2. A Chorus of Approving Voices

1. Scholars differ in their reconstructions of the sources within Exodus 14 and their relation to one another. See S. R. Driver, *An Introduction to the Old Testament* (reprint; Gloucester: Peter Smith, 1972), pp. 29–30 (I will follow Driver's source division); B. Childs, *Exodus: A Commentary* (London: SCM Press, 1974), pp. 220–21; P. Weimar, *Die Meerwundererzählung. Eine redaktionskritische Analyse von Ex 13, 17–14, 31* (Wiesbaden: Harrassowitz, 1985); M. Vervenne, *Het Zeeverhaal (Exodus 13,17–14,31). Een literaire studie* (Leuven, 1986), and "The 'P' Tradition in the Pentateuch: Document and/or Redaction? The Sea Narrative (Ex 13,17–14,31) as a Test Case," in *Pentateuchal and Deuteronomistic Studies*, ed. C. Brekelmans and J. Lust (Leuven, 1990), pp. 67–90; J. Van Seters, *The Life of Moses: The Yahwist as Historian in Exodus-Numbers* (Louisville: Westminster/John Knox, 1994), pp. 128–49. Weimar's study provides an example of how complex the source-critical study of Exodus has become; Weimar sees no less than eight levels in the literary-redaction history of the Sea Narrative. Such results are so complex that recent scholars are again treating Exodus 14 as a unity. See J. Ska, *Le Passage der la mer. Etude de la construction du style et de la symbolique d'Ex 14,1–31* (Rome: Pontifical Biblical Institute 1986). The differing approaches of these analyses reflect a much larger debate about

the nature, date, even the existence of the literary sources within the Pentateuch. No single study can resolve this debate—and I will not even try—but my argument here can be adapted to accommodate various conceptions of Exodus 14 and its compositional development.

2. For the presence of E in Exodus 14, see Childs, *Exodus*, p. 220. For possible deuteronomistic additions, see D. Fuss, *Die Deuteronomistische Pentateuchredaktion in Exodus 3–17* (Berlin: de Gruyter, 1972), pp. 297–327, and M. Brenner, *The Song of the Sea: Ex 15:1–21* (Berlin: de Gruyter, 1991), pp. 11, 46–53.

3. See H. Gressman, *Die Anfänge Israels* (Göttingen: Vandenhoeck and Ruprecht, 1914), p. 58. Those scholars who believe that the Song of Miriam is older than the Song of the Sea cite three arguments to support their claim. First, they claim (falsely) that the shorter version of a text must preserve the more original form. See M. Noth, *Exodus*, trans. J. Bowden, OTL (Philadelphia: Westminster, 1962), p. 121. Second, if the Song of the Sea were the older of the two, there is no apparent reason for why someone would supplement it with the much shorter Song of Miriam. Third, biblical narrative contains several descriptions of women singing victory songs after a battle. See 1 Sam 18:7. For further discussion of the relation of the two songs, see R. Burns, *Has the Lord Indeed Spoken Only through Moses? A Study of the Biblical Portrait of Miriam* (Atlanta: Scholars Press), pp. 14–16, and J. Janzen, "Song of Moses, Song of Miriam: Who Is Seconding Whom?" CBQ 54 (1992): 211–20.

4. See F. M. Cross and D. N. Freedman, "The Song of Miriam," JNES 14 (1954): 237–50, esp. pp. 238–39. Cross and Freedman claim that Exod 15:21 is simply the incipit of the Song of the Sea and that the reader is supposed to understand that Miriam recited all of the song in Exod 15:1–18. For evidence that a single song can be transmitted in distinct narrative sources, see the brief song sung by the women to David and Saul as they return from battle, which appears in three different literary contexts (1 Sam 18:7, 21:12, 29:5).

5. Many early Jewish interpreters believed that the song was sung in antiphony. See L. Ginzberg, *The Legends of the Jews*, 15th ed., trans. H. Szold (Philadelphia: Jewish Publication Society, 1988), vol. 6, p. 12 n. 63, and J. Goldin, *The Song at the Sea* (New Haven: Yale University Press, 1971), pp. 77–79. Although, as we will see in chap. 4, this tradition probably represents a response to interpretive difficulties within the biblical text, it is not impossible that the author of Exodus 15:1–21 intended to suggest that the song was sung antiphonally, for the verb ʿānâ (answer) used to introduce the women's song in Exod 15:20 may mean here "to answer responsively in song." See U. Cassuto, *A Commentary on the Book of Exodus* (Jerusalem: Magnes, 1967) p. 182; Watts, *Psalm and Story*, p. 42 n. 2.

6. For the text of the Piye Stela (along with extensive commentary), see N. Grimal, *La Stèle triomphale de Pi(ânkh)y au Musée du Caire* (Cairo: L'Institut Français d'Archéologie Orientale, 1981). For an English translation of the stela, see M. Lichtheim, *Ancient Egyptian Literature: A Book of Readings*, vol. 3 (Berkeley: University of California Press, 1980), pp. 66–84. All citations of the inscription are drawn from Lichtheim's translation, and all references utilize her lineation.

7. See Grimal, *La Stèle triomphale*, pp. 283–94. For example, the Piye Stela seems to have drawn directly on an earlier daybook account, a genre of battle literature characterized by the use of spare infinitival forms to communicate action. On this point, see also A. Spalinger, *Aspects of the Military Documents of the Ancient Egyptians* (New Haven: Yale University Press, 1982), pp. 185–90.

8. Watts, *Psalm and Story*, pp. 213–14.

9. Lines 60–61. J. Breasted (*Ancient Records of Egypt*, vol. 4 [Chicago: University of Chicago Press, 1906-7], p. 429) translates the phrase rendered here as "shouted

and sang" as "acclaimed and rejoiced." Both translations presuppose the Egyptian words *ḥnw nhm* (which Grimal translates as "chant d'allegresse"), precisely the terminology used to introduce the "song of jubilation" in the second passage extracted in the text. See Grimal, *La Stèle triomphale*, pp. 68, 72 n. 178, and 327.

10. Lines 153–59. The phrase "song of jubilation" is again a translation of *ḥnw nhm.* See Grimal, *La Stèle triomphale*, p. 180 n. 536.

11. The word *zimrāt* (= song) in Exod 15:2a is translated by some scholars as "defense" or "protection." See Cross and Freedman, "Song of Miriam," p. 243. S. Loewenstamm, ("The Lord Is My Strength and My Glory," VT 29 [1969]: 464–70) argues, however, that this word in fact denotes "the glory given to God (in song)." The meaning of the term remains in dispute. See S. Parker's rejoinder to Loewenstamm's argument, "Exodus 15:2 Again," VT 31 (1971): 373–79.

12. The meaning of "to them" here is unclear. The form in Hebrew is masculine plural, suggesting that it refers to the male Israelites. However, some scholars believe that it refers to the women accompanying Miriam, since occasionally in biblical Hebrew a female substantive is referred to by what appears to be a masculine pronoun. See Burns, *Has the Lord Indeed Spoken*, pp. 12–14.

13. The content of Miriam's song is almost identical to the first line of the Song of the Sea with one slight variant which does not substantially alter the song's meaning: instead of the cohortative form ("I will sing") attested in Exod 15:1b, the Song of Miriam attests a masculine plural imperative ("Sing!"). LXX levels out the difference by replacing both forms with a plural cohortative "Let us sing." The phrase "I will sing to the Lord" in Exod 15:1 has reminded many scholars of the opening line of the Ugaritic epithalamium to Nikkal and Yarikh which begins with the word *'ašr* ("I will sing") and is addressed to a king (a similar formula also appears in Akkadian hymns). See Cassuto, *Exodus*, p. 174, and Watts, *Psalm and Story*, p. 210. As we will see, the song shares several other elements in common with Ugaritic literature.

14. It is appropriate to refer to Piye as a divine warrior because the Piye inscription gives clear indications that like most Egyptian kings, he was regarded as a divine being. He is said to have been "born of god" (line 80), and he is given a variety of divine titles and epithets: "beloved of Amun," "living likeness of Atum," "Horus mighty king," etc. Piye is also given divine titles and epithets ("son of Isis," "son of Bastet," various Horus names like "Strong Bull appearing in Thebes," "Bull of his Two Lands") in other inscriptional texts from his reign. See K. Kitchen, *The Third Intermediate Period in Egypt*, 2d ed. (Warminster: Aris and Phillips, 1986), p. 369. As for God's status as a warrior in ancient Israel, see G. von Rad, *Holy War in Ancient Israel*, trans. M. Dawn (Grand Rapids: Eerdmans, 1991); F. M. Cross, "The Divine Warrior in Israel's Early Cult," in *Biblical Motifs*, ed. A. Altman (Cambridge: Harvard University Press, 1966); P. Miller, *The Divine Warrior in Ancient Israel* (Cambridge: Harvard University Press, 1975), esp. pp. 113–17, where he discusses Exodus 15; M. Weinfeld, "They Fought from Heaven—Divine Intervention in War in Ancient Israel and in the Ancient Near East," in *History, Historiography and Interpretation*, ed. H. Tadmor and M. Weinfeld (Jerusalem: Magnes, 1984), pp. 121–47.

15. The songs in Exodus 15 are usually classified as victory songs. See Cross and Freedman, "The Song of Miriam," p. 237; Cassuto, *Exodus*, p. 173; A. Hauser, "Two Songs of Victory: A Comparison of Exodus 15 and Judges 5," in E. Follis, ed., *Directions in Biblical Hebrew Poetry* (Sheffield: JSOT, 1987), pp. 265–84; Brenner, *Song of the Sea*, 36–39. Some scholars do not accept this classification, opting for terms such as "litany," "liturgy," "coronation hymn," and "song of thanksgiving."

See Muilenberg, "A Liturgy on the Triumphs of Yahweh," p. 236, and Childs, *Exodus*, pp. 243–44. Even these scholars acknowledge, however, that the song has features of a victory song or was intended to celebrate a victory. Thus, C. Westermann, *The Praise of God in the Psalms*, trans. K. Crim (Richmond, Va.: John Knox, 1961), p. 90, recognizes that motifs of a victory song are present in Exodus 15, although he maintains that it is not a victory song "because no battle took place." Similarly, Mowinckel, *The Psalms in Israel's Worship*, vol. 2, p. 247, regards Exod 15:1–18 as a hymn of enthronement, but he associates the Song of Miriam (which repeats Exod 15:1) with songs sung "when the warriors come home with victory."

16. Cf. Child's description of the Song of the Sea (*Exodus*, p. 249): "The poem praises God as the sole agent of salvation. Israel did not cooperate or even play a minor role. . . . Yahweh alone effected the miracle of the sea."

17. The appearance of this phrase in the Song of the Sea is one reason that Exodus 15 has been associated with the so-called enthronement festival, a hypothetical festival which celebrates God's "coronation" as Israel's divine king. See Mowinckel, *The Psalms in Israel's Worship*, vol. 1, p. 126; E. Lipínski, "Yāhweh mālāk," Bib 44 (1963): 405–60. That we are dealing here with some sort of formula is further supported by Ugaritic narrative, which seems to feature a similar expression: KTU 1.2. IV. 32: *bꜤlm yml [k]* = "May Baal rule."

18. See F. M. Cross, "The Song of the Sea and Canaanite Myth," *God and Christ: Existence and Providence*, JTC 5 (New York: Harper and Row, 1968), pp. 1–25, and *Canaanite Myth and Hebrew Epic: Essays in the History of the Religion of Israel* (Cambridge: Harvard University Press, 1973), pp. 122–44; P. Craigie, "The Poetry of Ugarit and Israel," *Tyndale Bulletin* 22 (1971): 3–31, esp. pp. 19–26; C. Kloos, *Yahweh's Combat with the Sea* (Amsterdam: Oorshot/Leiden: Brill, 1986), pp. 139–57.

19. See Weimar, *Meerwundererzählung*, p. 81.

20. Examples that follow in the text are drawn mainly from L. Hay, "What Really Happened at the Sea of Reeds," JBL 83 (1964): 397–403. See also F. Stolz, *Jahwes und Israels Kriege* (Zürich: Theologischer Verlag, 1972), pp. 94–97; H. Schmidt, *Der sogenannte Jahwist: Beobachtungen und Fragen zur Pentateuchforschung* (Zürich: Theologischer Verlag, 1976), pp. 54–66; P. Weimar, "Die Jahwe Kriegserzählungen in Exodus 14, Joshua 10, Richter 4 und 1 Samuel 7," Bib 57 (1976): 38–73, and *Meerwunderzählung*, pp. 68–85.

21. B. Margalit ("The Day the Sun Did Not Stand Still: A New Look at Joshua X:8–19," VT 42 [1992]: 466–491, esp. pp. 474–76) observed that the verbal sequence "discomfit" followed by "flee" attested in Exod 14:25–26 reflects the "litmus test criterion" for identifying the "holy war" literary pattern in biblical narrative. Cf. Josh 10:10–11 and Judg 4:15.

22. See Weinfeld, "They Fought from Heaven," pp. 131–36 and 43–45. The translation is from B. Cummings, *Egyptian Historical Records of the Later Eighteenth Dynasty* (Warminster: Aris and Phillips, 1982), p. 4.

23. The song is difficult to assign to either J or P because it shares vocabulary with both. For this reason, some scholars believe that the song was added only after the pentateuchal sources were combined (see Watts, *Psalm and Story*, p. 58). However, the fact that the song contains features distributed among J and P does not necessarily indicate that it was added to the narrative after J and P were combined. J, P, and the song may reflect a common tradition (see Childs, *Exodus*, p. 245), or the song may presuppose one source and be presupposed by the other. The latter scenario is supported by B. Halpern (*The First Historians* [San Francisco: Harper and Row, 1988], pp. 77–78), who has argued that P's claim that the Israelites crossed the sea is based on a misreading of Exod 15:16—"till your people cross

over"—which originally referred to Israel's crossing over the Jordan. Cf. Cross, *Canaanite Myth and Hebrew Epic*, pp. 123-44. If Halpern is right, the song shares vocabulary with P because it is presupposed by it.

24. For a detailed comparison of *Amenemope* and Proverbs, see G. Bryce, *A Legacy of Wisdom: The Egyptian Contribution to the Wisdom of Israel* (Lewisburg: Bucknell University Press, 1979).

25. See R. Giveon, *The Impact of Egypt on Canaan* (Göttingen: Vandenhoeck and Ruprecht, 1978); J. Weinstein, "The Egyptian Empire in Palestine: A Reassessment," BASOR 241 (1981): 1-28; D. Redford, *Egypt, Canaan and Israel in Ancient Times* (Princeton: Princton University Press, 1992), pp. 125-280. For a New Kingdom military inscription found in Palestine, see W. Albright, "The Smaller Beth Shean Stela of Sethos I," BASOR 125 (1952): 24-32.

26. See A. Rainey, ed., *Egypt, Israel, Sinai—Archaeological and Historical Relationships in the Biblical Period* (Tel Aviv: Tel Aviv University, 1987); K. Kitchen, "Egypt and Israel during the First Millennium B.C.," *Congress Volume Jerusalem 1986*, ed. J. Emerton (VTSup 42; Leiden: Brill, 1988), pp. 107-23; and Redford, *Egypt, Canaan and Israel*, pp. 283-394. Redford reminds us (pp. 366, 393) that cultural contact between Israel and Egypt may have been mediated through third parties (e.g., the Phoenicians).

27. See J. Yoyotte, "Plaidoyer pour l'authenticité du scarabée historique de Shabako," Bib 37 (1956): 457-76, and "Sur le scarabée historique de Shabako. note additionnelle," Bib 39 (1958): 206-10. The scarab is in the Royal Ontario Museum (catalogue number 910.28.1).

28. Cf. T. G. H. James, "Egypt: The Twenty-Fifth and Twenty-Sixth Dynasties," in *Cambridge Ancient History*, vol. 3, ed. J. Boardman et al. (Cambridge: Cambridge University Press, 1991), pp. 689-90. For the identification of the sand-dwellers in the inscription as Asian seminomads, see Kitchen, *Third Intermediate Period*, 1st ed. (1973), p. 379.

29. Redford, *Egypt, Canaan and Israel*, p. 393.

30. Consider what has become of the thesis of A. Herman and S. Hermann that certain biblical episodes (e.g., 2 Samuel 7) reflect the influence of an Egyptian genre of military literature known as the *Königsnovelle*. Although this thesis was once widely accepted and is consistent with known cultural contacts between Egypt and Israel, it is now widely regarded as questionable—in part because the genre of *Königsnovelle* itself is often said to represent an oversimplification of the literary evidence, lumping together texts connected by only superficial similarities. For the views of Herman and Hermann, see A. Herman, *Die ägyptische Königsnovelle* (Glückstadt: Augustin, 1938), and S. Hermann, "Die Königsnovelle in Ägypten und in Israel," in *Wissenschaftliche Zeitschrift der Karl-Marx Universität* (Leipzig: Gesellschafts und Sprachwissenschaftliche Reihe 3/1, 1953-5), pp. 51-62, and "2 Samuel VII in the Light of the Egyptian Königsnovelle—Reconsidered," in *Pharaonic Egypt, the Bible, and Christianity*, ed. S. Israelite-Groll (Jerusalem: Magnes, 1985), pp. 129-37. For criticism of the comparison, see Redford, *Israel, Canaan and Israel*, pp. 374-77, and J. Van Seters, *In Search of History* (New Haven: Yale University Press, 1983), pp. 160-64.

31. See Spalinger, *Aspects of the Military Documents*.

32. Spalinger, *Aspects of the Military Documents*, pp. 93-94. The word *nhm* denotes "shouting" and is often used to indicate a "shout for joy," "rejoicing," or "acclamation," often in a military context. It can also be used with a negative connotation and can even denote "thunder." See R. Faulkner, "Notes on the Admonition of an Egyptian Sage," JEA 50 (1964): 24-36, esp. p. 35.

33. The translation is from Breasted, *Ancient Egyptian Records*, vol. 2, pp. 48-50.

For the original text, see K. Sethe, *Urkunden der 18. Dynastie: Historisch-biographische Urkunden Hefte 1–16* (Leipzig, 1908–9 and 1927–30), nos. 137–41.9. For philological and literary analysis, see D. Lorton, "The Assuan/Philae Inscription of Thutmosis II," in *Studies in Egyptology Presented to Miriam Lichtheim*, ed. S. Israelit-Groll (Jerusalem: Magnes, 1990), pp. 668–79.

34. The first scene reports the populace's acclamation without citing the contents of its praise: "Lo, the whole world rejoiced to heaven; the towns and the districts acclaimed these wonders which had happened. . . ." The translation is from Breasted, *Ancient Egyptian Records*, vol. 3, pp. 240–52. The original text appears in K. Kitchen, *Ramesside Inscriptions: Historical and Biographical*, vol. 4 (Oxford: Blackwell, 1968–78), nos. 7.14–12.6. For further discussion of this passage, see Spalinger, *Aspects of the Military Documents*, pp. 91–92.

35. Spalinger, *Aspects of the Military Documents*, pp. 94–95.

36. Spalinger, *Aspects of the Military Documents*, pp. 20–21. As Spalinger notes (p. 120), Egyptian scribes apparently developed another genre, the "scribal war-diary," to describe campaigns in which the king directly participated.

37. For the use of the daybook account within the Piye inscription, see n. 7, this chapter. For the use of wisdom citations in the inscription, see H. Brunner, "Zitate aus Lebenslehren," in *Studien zu altägyptischen Lebenslehren*, ed. E. Hornung and O. Keel (Freiburg/Göttingen: Vandenhoeck and Ruprecht, 1979), pp. 105–71, esp. pp. 144–49. For the use of the *iw.tw* report, see Spalinger, *Aspects of the Egyptian Military Documents*, pp. 15–16.

38. The songs in the Piye inscription represent only two of many speeches within the narrative which acknowledge Piye as ruler. Other speeches are attributed to King Namart and to the ruler of Hnes Peftuaubast, the occupants of Per-Sekhem-kheperre, the occupants of Itj-tawy, the priests of the Temple of Re at Heliopolis, Prince Pediese, Piye's arch-foe Tefnakht, and Piye himself (Piye is responsible for thirteen of a total of thirty-six speeches). See Grimal, *La Stèle triomphal*, pp. 261–65. For an important analysis of one of Piye's speeches, see A. Gardiner, "Piankhi's Instructions to His Army," JEA 21 (1935): 219–31.

39. See W. Y. Adams, *Nubia, Corridor to Africa* (London: Penguin, 1977), p. 267, and James, "Egypt," p. 681. For discussion of the pyramidal structure of Piye's tomb, see Adams, *Nubia*, p. 278. Another example of archaizing behavior in the time of Piye's successors is Shabako's commissioning of a copy of an Old Kingdom theology and cosmogony of the god Ptah; see Kitchen, *Third Intermediate Period*, 2d ed., p. 381.

40. For an account of Piye's reign and campaign, see Grimal, *La Stèle triomphal*, pp. 209–54; Adams, *Nubia*, pp. 261–63; James, "Egypt," pp. 682–89; Kitchen, *Third Intermediate Period*, 2d ed., pp. 363–72; A. Spalinger, "The Military Background of the Campaign of Piye (Piankhy)," SAK (1979): 273–301.

41. Israel's complaint in this passage resembles later complaints that it makes in the wilderness—one characteristic that links J's account of the Red Sea incident to later wilderness traditions in the Pentateuch. See Childs, *Exodus*, p. 223, and G. Coats, "The Traditio-historical Study of the Red Sea Tradition," VT 20 (1970): 406–18. For further discussion of the "murmuring" motif in Exodus 14, see M. Vervenne, "The Protest Motif in the Sea Narrative (Ex 14:11–12): Form and Structure of a Pentateuchal Pattern," *Ephemerides Theologicae Lovaniensis* 63 (1987): 251–71.

42. See P. Trible, "Bringing Miriam out of the Shadows," *BibRev* 5 (1989): 14–25, 34. A recently published Dead Sea Scroll fragment, 4Q 365, partially preserves an expanded version of Miriam's song which differs substantially from the song in Exod 15:1–18. On paleographical grounds, the fragment is dated to about 75–50 B.C.E. It is described in S. White, "4Q 364 and 365: A Preliminary Report,"

in *The Madrid Qumran Congress*, ed. J. Trebolle Barrera and L. Vegas Montaner (Leiden: Brill, 1992), pp. 217–28, esp. pp. 222–24; and it is published in E. Ulrich et al., *Qumran Cave 4 Vol. 7: Genesis to Numbers*, DJDXII (Oxford: Clarendon Press, 1994), pp. 117–19 and plates 18 and 19. As we will see in chap. 4, it was not uncommon in the Second Temple period to rewrite and even expand songs in biblical narrative. Consider, for instance, the expanded version of Deborah's Song in Pseudo-Philo's *Biblical Antiquities* (32:1–18). The expanded form of Miriam's song in 4Q 365 seems also to exemplify this literary trend.

43. See E. Poetig, "The Victory Song Tradition of the Women of Israel," Ph.D. diss., Union Theological Seminary, 1985.

44. See P. Craigie, "An Egyptian Expression in the Song of the Sea," VT 20 (1970): 83–86 and J. Hoffmeier, "Some Egyptian Motifs Related to Warfare and Enemies and Their Old Testament Counterparts," in J. Hoffmeier and E. Meltzer, eds., *Egyptological Miscellanies: A Tribute to Professor Ronald J. Williams, Ancient World* 6 (1983): 53–70.

45. Hoffmeier, "Some Egyptian Motifs," pp. 53–70. For further discussion of this motif in Egyptian battle accounts, see E. Hall, *The Pharaoh Smites His Enemies* (Munich: Deutscher Kunstverlag, 1986). Cf. K. Younger, *Ancient Conquest Accounts* (Sheffield: JSOT, 1990), pp. 192–93.

46. Craigie, "An Egyptian Expression," p. 86. Note that pictorial representations of battles on ivories from Late Bronze Age Syria-Palestine combine Egyptianizing details with native Syro-Palestinian motifs. See H. Kantor, "Syro-Palestinian Ivories," JNES 15 (1956): 153–74, esp. pp. 166–69. The appearance of Egyptianizing elements in the Song of the Sea's depiction of the battle at the Red Sea is thus not altogether unique in the history of Syro-Palestinian battle accounts (broadly defined to include visual battle scenes).

47. The close correspondence suggests that the two poems were constructed from a common pool of formulaic expressions. See M. Coogan, "A Structural Analysis of the Song of Deborah," CBQ 40 (1978): 132–66, esp. pp. 162–65. For detailed studies of the song's content and structure, see A. Globe, "The Literary Structure and Unity of the Song of Deborah," JBL 93 (1974): 493–512; G. Gerleman, "The Song of Deborah in the Light of Stylistics," VT 1 (1951): 168–80; P. Ackroyd, "The Composition of the Song of Deborah," VT 2 (1952): 160–62; C. Rabin, "Judges V.2 and the Ideology of Deborah's War," JJS 6 (1955): 125–32; J. Blenkinsopp, "Ballad Style and Psalm Style in the Psalm of Deborah: A Discussion," Bib 42 (1961): 61–76; H. Müller, "Aufbau des Deboraliedes," VT 16 (1966): 446–59; P. Craigie, "The Song of Deborah and the Epic of Tukulti Ninurta," JBL 88 (1969): 253–65; Watts, *Psalm and Story*, pp. 82–98. For studies earlier than 1900, see the bibliography in G. Moore, *Judges*, ICC (New York: Scribner, 1895), p. 127, and C. Burney, *The Book of Judges* (New York: Scribner, 1895), pp. 94–96.

48. Cf. the use of the same verb *wayyāhom* in Exod 14:24: "The Lord threw the Egyptian army into a panic."

49. This passage resembles theophany scenes found in Ps 68:7–8 and Deut 33:2–3 in which God is represented as a storm god marching into Canaan from the south. See E. Lipínski, "Judges 5, 4–5 et Psaume 68:1–11," Bib 48 (1967): 185–206; Cross, *Canaanite Myth and Hebrew Epic*, pp. 91–111; Blenkinsopp, "Ballad Style and Psalm Style," pp. 67–68; Coogan, "A Structural and Literary Analysis," pp. 161–62. The epithet "The One of Sinai" in verse 5, a phrase which also surfaces in Ps 68:9, has attracted much comment from biblical scholars, in part because of its syntactical awkwardness. It has been explained as a divine appellation (see W. Albright, "The Song of Deborah in the Light of Archaeology," BASOR 62 [1936]: 26–31, esp. p.

30) and as a later scribal annotation (M. Fishbane, *Biblical Interpretation in Ancient Israel* [Oxford: Clarendon Press, 1985], p. 55).

50. This list differs in several respects from the lists of tribes catalogued in Genesis 49 and Deuteronomy 33. The identity of Meroz in verse 23 is uncertain (for the theory that it was a Canaanite town that formed an alliance with the Israelites, see A. Alt, "Meros," ZAW 58 [1940–41]: 244–47); the song apparently uses the name Gilead to refer to Gad (17), and the tribes of Judah, Simeon, and Levi are not mentioned at all.

51. Cf. the observation of B. Margalit ("The Day the Sun Did Not Stand Still," 484) that in Judges 4–5 God's role "is that of an auxilary who extends assistance to the (human) heroes."

52. The tribes of Israel are referred to as "the people of the Lord" two times in the song (vss. 11 and 13).

53. See W. Moran, "The Ancient Near Eastern Background of the Love of God in Deuteronomy," CBQ 25 (1963): 77–87. Note also the expression "the people offered themselves willingly" in Judg 5:2. Rabin ("Judges V. 2 and the Ideology of Deborah's War," 130) has suggested that this word should be understood as "go to war *in answer to a call*"—another indication that Israel functions in the song as God's ally in battle.

54. Cf. M. Sternberg, *The Poetics of Biblical Narrative* (Bloomington: Indiana University Press, 1987), pp 276–77.

55. Robertson's study (*Linguistic Evidence*, 138) identified within Judges 5 a few forms typical of standard biblical Hebrew (i.e., Hebrew typical of the eighth century B.C.E.) alongside more archaic forms, raising the possibility that the song's language may be archaizing rather than archaic. See chap. 1, n. 15. Still, the song is often described as the oldest document in the Hebrew Bible, so old in fact that it is often used to reconstruct the earliest stages of ancient Israelite history. See Albright, "The Song of Deborah"; A. Mayes, "The Historical Context of the Battle against Sisera," VT 19 (1969): 353–60; L. Stager, "Archaeology, Ecology and Social History: Background Themes and the Song of Deborah," in *Congress Volume Jerusalem 1986*, VTSup 42, ed. J. Emerton (Leiden: Brill, 1988), pp. 221–34. A few scholars have questioned the historical reliability of Judges 5. See Ackroyd, "The Composition of the Song of Deborah," and J. Soggin, *Judges: A Commentary*, trans. J. Bowden (London: SCM, 1981), p. 99. Some have even suggested that like Exodus 15, the song was originally performed in a cultic setting, and they interpret the actions described within it as ritual gestures. See A. Weiser, "Das Deboralied: Eine gattungs- und traditionsgeschichtliche Studie," ZAW 71 (1959): 67–97, and J. Gray, "A Cantata of the Autumn Festival: Psalm LXVIII," JSS 22 (1977): 2–26. Whatever the original context of the song in Judges 5, it is puzzling that it is so often treated by modern scholars as a reliable historical document, while the Song of the Sea is viewed as a cultic song of little use for reconstructing history. See the comments of D. N. Freedman, *Pottery, Poetry and Prophecy* (Winona Lake, Ind.: Eisenbrauns, 1980), p. 132. As he points out, "no adequate reasons have ever been adduced for the reversal in method and treatment of essentially equivalent phenomena."

56. Some scholars, noting that "sang" in Judg 5:1 is a singular feminine verb (*wattāšar*), have concluded that "And Barak the son of Abinoam" is a secondary addition. A singular verb can be used with multiple objects in biblical Hebrew, however, as is the case in Exod 15:1. There are thus no linguistic grounds for rejecting the present form of Judg 5:1. I argue later in this chapter that there are no literary grounds either.

57. See Kugel, *Idea of Biblical Poetry*, pp. 1–58.

58. Kugel, *Idea of Biblical Poetry,* pp. 96-134.

59. In this regard one should note the thesis of B. Halpern (*First Historians,* 76-97) that virtually every detail in the prose account of Judges 4 was inferred from a (mis)reading of the song—except for one detail, the name of Deborah's husband. Halpern's arguments are most controversial when he tries to explain details in the prose account that seem to directly contradict the song's account. Thus to explain why the prose version reports that only two tribes participated in the fighting (Zebulun and Naphtali) whereas the song suggests that six showed up for battle, Halpern argues that the author of the prose account understood from the song that the other four tribes (all mentioned in vss. 13-15) were waiting anxiously for the battle's outcome at the gates of their towns but did not actually participate in the fighting. Only verse 18 reports unequivocally that two tribes actually fought, Zebulun and Naphtali. Although I am not always convinced by Halpern's specific arguments (including the one just cited), his larger claim is consistent with what is being argued here.

3. Swan Song

1. Several studies examine the "last-words" literature produced in ancient Israel and the Near East. See J. Munck, "Discours d'adieu dans le Nouveau Testament et dans la litterature biblique," *Aux sources de la tradition chrétienne; Mélanges M Goguel* (Neuchatel: Delachaux & Niestlé, 1950), pp. 155-70; E. Cortés, *Los Discursos de Adiós de Gn a Jn 13–17: Pistas para la historia de un género en la antiqua literatura judía* (Barcelona: Herder, 1976); K. Kitchen, "The Proverbs and Wisdom Books of the Ancient Near East: The Factual History of a Literary Form," *Tyndale Bulletin* 28 (1977): 69-114; E. von Nordheim, *Die Lehre der Alten,* 2 vols. (Leiden: Brill, 1980 and 1985); J. Collins, "Testaments," in *Jewish Writings in the Second Temple Period,* ed. Michael Stone (Assen: Van Gorcum, Philadelphia: Fortress, 1984), pp. 325-55; L. Perdue, "The Death of the Sage and Moral Exhortation: From Ancient Near Eastern Instructions to Graeco-Roman Paraenesis," *Semeia* 50 (1990): 81-109; A. Saldarini, "Last Words and Death-bed Scenes in Rabbinic Literature," *JQR* 68 (1977-1978): 28-45; J. Neusner, "Death Scenes and Farewell Stories: An Aspect of the Master-Disciple Relationship in Mark and in Some Talmudic Passages," *HTR* 79 (1986): 187-97; W. Kurz, "Luke 22:14-38 and Greco-Roman and Biblical Farewell Addresses," *JBL* 104 (1985): 251-68; A. Goshen-Gottstein, "Testaments in Rabbinic Literature: Transformations of a Genre," *JSJ* 25 (1994): 222-51.

2. See the translation of the *Instruction of Ptah-hotep* by J. Wilson in *Ancient Near Eastern Texts,* ed. J. Pritchard, 3d ed. (Princeton: Princeton University Press, 1969), pp. 412-14. Wilson's translation is eclectic, drawing on several manuscripts, but it reflects more or less the narrative prologue attested in all the major versions. Cf. Z. Zaba, *Les Maximes de Ptahhotep* (Prague: Académie Tchécoslovaque de Sciences, 1956), which translates the three major manuscripts independently. The composition of *Ptah-hotep* is placed by scholars at various points between the Fifth Dynasty and the Eleventh (the earliest extant manuscript, the Prisse papyrus, is from the Twelfth Dynasty). For a brief review of the debate, see R. Williams, "The Sages of Ancient Egypt in the Light of Recent Scholarship," *JAOS* 101 (1981): 1-19, esp. p. 9.

3. See Weinfeld, *Deuteronomy and the Deuteronomistic School,* pp. 10-14.

4. An early date for the composition of Deuteronomy 32 was championed by two highly influential scholars: W. F. Albright ("Some Remarks on the Song of Moses in Deuteronomy 32," *VT* 9 [1959]: 339-46), who placed the song in the seventh century but soon reassigned it to the eleventh century, and O. Eissfeldt

(*Das Lied Moses Deut 32:1-43 und das Lehrgedicht Asaphs Psalm 78 samt einer Analyse der Umgebung des Moses-Liedes* [Berlin: Akademie Verlag, 1958], pp. 17-25). There is reason not to date the song too early, however. Robertson (*Linguistic Evidence*, 154) identified several archaic forms within the song, but he was unable to conclude that the song itself is archaic, since it also exhibits characteristics of Hebrew from a later period. Still others have placed it in the exilic or postexilic periods. See G. Von Rad, *Deuteronomy*, OTL (Philadelphia: Westminster, London: SCM, 1966), p. 200; A. D. H. Mayes, *Deuteronomy* (London: Marshall, Morgan and Scott, 1981), p. 382; and J. Tigay, *The JPS Torah Commentary: Deuteronomy* (Philadelphia: Jewish Publication Society, 1996), pp. 293-316, 502-18. For still other conjectures about the song's age, see Watts, *Psalm and Story*, p. 77 n. 1. I see no evidence that compels the conclusion that the language of the song is older than the prose (though it may be archaizing), but neither do I see signs that it is exilic or postexilic. For the present, therefore, I remain agnostic regarding the date of the song's composition. For other studies of the song's contents and provenance not otherwise mentioned in these notes, see A. Kamphausen, *Das Lied Moses* (Leipzig: Brockhaus, 1862); K. Budde, *Das Lied Moses erläutert und übersetz* (Tübingen: J. C. B. Mohr, 1920); E. Baumann, "Das Lied Mose's (Dt 32,1-43) auf seine gedankliche Geschlossenheit untersucht," VT 6 (1956): 414-24; W. Moran, "Some Remarks on the Song of Moses," Bib 43 (1963): 317-27; U. Cassuto, "The Song of Moses (Deuteronomy chapter xxxii 1-43)," *Biblical and Oriental Studies*, vol. 1 (Jerusalem: Magnes, 1973), pp. 41-46; J. Luyten, "Primeval and Eschatological Overtones in the Song of Moses (DT 32,1-43)," in *Das Deuteronomium. Entstehung, Gestalt und Botshaft*, ed. N. Lohfink (Leuven: University Press, 1985), pp. 341-47. For additional bibliography, see O. Eissfeldt, *The Old Testament: An Introduction* (New York: Harper and Row, 1965), p. 227 n. 14; C. J. Labuschagne, "The Song of Moses: Its Framework and Structure," in *De Fructu Oris Sui: Essays in Honour of Adrianus van Selms*, ed. I. Eybers et al. (Leiden: Brill, 1971), pp. 85-98, esp. p. 92 n. 1; J. Wiebe, "The Form, Setting and Meaning of the Song of Moses," *Studia Biblica et Theologica* 17 (1989): 119-63.

5. G. E. Wright, "The Law-suit of God: A Form-Critical Study of Deuteronomy 32," in *Israel's Prophetic Heritage*, ed. B. Anderson and W. Harrelson (New York: Harper, 1962), pp. 26-67; J. Harvey, "Le 'Rib Pattern' prophetique sur la rupture de l'alliance," Bib 43 (1962): 172-96; Wiebe, "Form, Setting and Meaning."

6. The translation is from H. Tredennick and H. Tarrant, *Plato: The Last Days of Socrates* (London: Penguin, 1993 [originally published in 1954]), pp. 144-45.

7. For the connection between last words and prophecy in ancient Egyptian literature, see L. Foti, "The History of the Prophecies of Noferti: Relationship between the Egyptian Wisdom and Prophecy Literatures," *Studia Aegyptica* 2 (1976): 3-15. For this idea in Jewish sources, see A. Kolenkow, "The Genre Testament and Forecasts of the Future in the Hellenistic Jewish Milieu," JSJ 6 (1975): 57-71.

8. For a translation of the *Testament of Moses* (also known as the *Assumption of Moses*), see J. Priest, "The Testament of Moses: A New Translation and Introduction," in *The Old Testament Pseudepigrapha*, vol. 1, ed. J. Charlesworth (Garden City: Doubleday, 1983), pp. 919-34.

9. For one reflection of this tradition, see a midrash from *Bereshit Rabbati* translated by H. Attridge in "The Ascension of Moses and the Heavenly Jerusalem," in *Studies on the Testament of Moses*, ed. G. W. E. Nickelsburg (Cambridge, Mass.: SBL, 1973), p. 1225.

10. For the didactic/wisdom elements in the song, see S. R. Driver, *Deuteronomy*, ICC (New York: Scribner, 1916), p. 345; Von Rad, *Deuteronomy*, pp. 196, 200; J. Boston, "The Wisdom Influence upon the Song of Moses," JBL 87 (1968): 198-202.

11. Xenophon, *Cyropaedia,* trans. W. Miller (Cambridge: Harvard University Press, 1968), VIII.vii.1–24. It has been suggested that Xenophon's account of Cyrus's death may reflect a Persian/Iranian storytelling tradition in which a dying king communicates a political testament to his successors. See H. Sancisi-Weerdenburg, "The Death of Cyrus: Xenophon's Cyropaedia as a Source for Iranian History," *Acta Iranica* 25 (1985): 459–71, and A. Christensen, *The Epics of the Kings in Ancient Iranian Traditions,* trans. F. Vajifder (Bombay: K. R. Cama, 1991), pp. 67–75. If such a tradition existed in ancient Persia, it was not unique to that culture. Texts like the *Instruction of Merikare* indicate that final testaments were attributed to royal figures in Egypt, while the various last words attributed to David suggest that the royal instruction tradition was known in ancient Israel as well. See L. Perdue, "The Testament of David and Egyptian Royal Instructions," in *Scripture in Context II,* ed. W. Hallo et al. (Winona Lake, Ind.: Eisenbrauns, 1983), pp. 79–96.

12. See P. Miller, "'Moses My Servant': The Deuteronomic Portrait of Moses," Int 41 (1987): 245–55, esp. pp. 246–48. Deuteronomy's representation of Moses as a teacher is consistent with its overall didactic character. See J. Malfroy, "Sagesse et loi dans le Deuteronome études," VT 15 (1965): 49–65, and Weinfeld, *Deuteronomy and the Deuteronomistic School,* pp. 244–81, 298–306.

13. Some scholars attribute the seemingly incongruous association of these two terms to a textual accident. See A. Rofé, "The Question of the Composition of Deuteronomy 31 in Light of a Conjecture about a Confusion in the Columns of the Biblical Text," *Shnaton* 3 (1978–79): 49–76. Others believe that the association of the two terms in Deuteronomy 31 arose through a complex redactional process in which one tradition was imposed upon or woven into the other. See O. Eissfeldt, "Die Umrahmung des Moseliedes Dtn 32, 1–43 und des Mosegesetzes Dtn 1–30 in Dtn 31,9–32:47," in *Kleine Schriften,* vol. 3, ed. R. Sellheim and F. Maass (Tübingen: J. C. B. Mohr, 1966), pp. 322–34; N. Lohfink, "Der Bundesschluss im Land Moab-Redaktiongeschichtliches zu Deut. 28,69–32,47," BZ 6 (1962): 32–56, and "Zur Fabel in Dtn 31–32," in *Konsequente Traditionsgeschichte: festschrift Klaus Baltzer,* ed. R. Bartelmus et al. (Göttingen: Vandenhoeck und Ruprecht, 1993), pp. 255–79; S. Carrillo Alday, "Contexto redaccional del Cántico de Moisés (Dt 31,1–32, 47)," *EstBib* 26 (1967): 383–93; Labuschagne, "The Song of Moses," 85–98. The attempt to reconstruct the literary development of Deuteronomy is further complicated by a number of complex textual variants among the versions. For example, a statement corresponding to MT Deut 32:22 is repeated in the Septuagint just before Deut 32:44 (the verse immediately following the song), while the phrase "this song" in MT Deut 32:44 seems to correspond to "this instruction" in the equivalent section of LXX Deut 32:44. For discussion of these and other textual variants, see L. Laberge, "Le Texte de Deutéronome 31 (Dt 31,1–29; 32, 44–47," in *Pentateuchal and Deuteronomistic Studies,* ed. C. Brekelmans and J. Lust (Leuven: Leuven University, 1990), pp. 143–60.

14. Von Rad, *Deuteronomy,* p. 201.

15. See B. Lindars, "Torah in Deuteronomy," in *Words and Meanings,* ed. P Ackroyd (Cambridge: Cambridge University Press, 1968), pp. 117–36, esp. pp. 129–30.

16. See Williams, "Sages of Ancient Egypt," p. 7.

17. For recent discussions of the origins and literary history of *Ahiqar,* see M. Küchler, *Frühjüdische Weisheitstraditionen: Zum Fortgang weisheitlichen Denkens im Bereich des frühjüdischen Jahweglaubens* (Freiburg; Universitätsverlag, 1979), pp. 319–79, and J. Lindenberger, *The Aramaic Proverbs of Ahiqar* (Baltimore: Johns Hopkins University Press, 1983), pp. 3–34. Both works contain references to earlier studies.

It is not known whether the sage Ahiqar was a real person. Scholars frequently cite as evidence for the sage's historicity a Seleucid period tablet (published by J. van Dijk in *H. J. Lenzen, XVIII vorlaüfiger Bericht über die* . . . *Ausgrabungen in Uruk-Warka* [Berlin: Deutsche Orient Gesellschaft Abhandlungen, 1962], pp. 44–52) which mentions Ahiqar as the Aramean name for Aba-enlil-dari, the chief sage at the time of Esarhaddon. As F. de Blois ("The Admonitions of Adurbad and Their Relationship to the Ahiqar Legend," JRAS [1984]: 41–53, esp. p. 51 n. 12) cautions, however, the tablet is much later than the Elephantine version of the *Words of Ahiqar* and proves only that the figure of Ahiqar was known in Seleucid Babylonia, not that he ever actually existed.

18. There is some controversy over the exact relation of the proverbs to the narrative section of *Ahiqar*. Although Lindenberger (*Aramaic Proverbs*, p. 18) has concluded that the Elephantine version of *Ahiqar* "does not integrate the narrative and sayings at all," a number of factors suggest otherwise. First, in all the later versions of *Ahiqar* and compositions thought to be influenced by *Ahiqar*, the proverbs are presented as part of the story, although admittedly there is variation with regard to their precise position within the narrative. Many later versions actually present two proverb collections, one near the beginning of the narrative, one near the end. Second, while there is reason to believe that the proverbs were composed independently of the narrative, a few proverbs seem to allude to the contents of the story, as A. Cowley (*Aramaic Papyri of the Fifth Century B.C.* [reprint; Osnabrück: Otto Zeller, 1967], p. 210) has recognized. Indeed, Lindenberger himself suggests (*Aramaic Proverbs*, 136–37) that these proverbs may have been added to the collection to tie the narrative and the proverbs more closely together. Finally, B. Porten (*Textbook of Aramaic Documents from Ancient Egypt*, vol. 3 [Winona Lake, Ind.: Eisenbrauns, 1993], text C 1.1) has recently restored the original order of the Elephantine version's fourteen preserved columns based on traces of an underlying customs account erased to make room for *Ahiqar*. Porten's restoration suggests that the proverbs were connected to the story and that the narrative bridge—apparently on the outside of the scroll and thus most susceptible to damage—was simply lost. (I thank Professor Linderberger for calling my attention to Porten's work.) Together, these considerations indicate that the proverbs in the Elephantine version were to be read within the context of the narrative as the words uttered by Ahiqar after he foiled Nadan's plot against him.

19. Elephantine MS *Ahiqar* column 1 lines 6–9 (Cowley, *Aramaic Papyri*, pp. 212, 220).

20. Elephantine MS *Ahiqar* column 2 lines 23–25 (Cowley, *Aramaic Papyri*, pp. 212, 220–21).

21. For the Syriac version of Ahiqar I refer to F. C. Conybeare, J. R. Harris, and A. S. Lewis, *The Story of Ahiqar from the Aramaic, Syriac, Arabic, Armenian, Ethiopic, Old Turkish, Greek and Slavonic Versions* (London: C. J. Clay, 1898), especially MS Syriac 2 (Cambridge MS. add. 2020). Chapter and verse citations are according to the English translation in R. Charles, *The Apocrypha and Pseudepigrapha of the Old Testament in English*, vol. 2 (Oxford: Clarendon Press, 1913), pp. 715–84. The passage here comes from MS Syriac 2 *Ahiqar* 1:8–9 (Charles, *Apocrypha and Pseudepigrapha*, p. 726).

22. MS Syriac 2 *Ahiqar* 3.1–2 (Charles, *Apocrypha and Pseudepigrapha*, p. 740).

23. See, for example, Deut 4:1–25.

24. It is true that testamentary literature from the Jewish Hellenistic period and following, such as the *Testaments of the Twelve Patriarchs*, often contains forecasts of future acts of sin and disobedience by Israel—the first part of the "sin-exile-and-return" pattern identified by M. de Jonge, *The Testaments of the Twelve Patriarchs:*

A Study of Their Text, Composition and Origin (Assen: Van Gorcum, 1953), pp. 83–86. See T. *Issachar* 6; T. *Levi* 10:14–15, 16; T. *Judah* 23; T. *Dan* 5:4, 8–9, etc. This motif resembles the description of Israel's future treachery in Deut 31:16–18, but it appears in a literature created under the direct influence of deuteronomic theology and literary form, including the Song of Moses. Therefore it would seem that the frequent appearance of this motif in the *Testaments of the Twelve Patriarchs* and other early Jewish and Christian testaments reveals more about the literary influence of Deuteronomy and deuteronomic theology on later Jewish and Christian literature than it does about the appearance or role of this motif in Deuteronomy 31 itself.

    25. MS Syriac 2 *Ahiqar* 3.3–7 (Charles, *Apocrypha and Pseudepigrapha*, pp. 741–42).

    26. See M. Lichtheim, *Late Egyptian Wisdom in the International Context: A Study of Demotic Intructions* (Göttingen: Vandenhoeck and Ruprecht, 1983), p. 21. Note also that Demotic fragments from Roman Egypt partially preserve an episode involving Ahiqar that is different from anything in the Elephantine version. The fragments are published in K.-Th. Zauzich, "Demotische Fragmente zum Ahiqar-Roman," in *Folia Rara, Festschrift W. Voigt*, ed. H. Franke et al. (Wiesbaden: Verzeichnis der Orientalishen Handschriften in Deutschland Supplementband 19, 1976), pp. 80–85. Lindenberger (*Aramaic Proverbs*, pp. 310–12) provides an English translation.

    27. Lindenberger (*Aramaic Proverbs*, pp. 5, 29 n. 6) has established, for example, that one of the Armenian recensions of *Ahiqar* preserves authentic ancient Near Eastern names of gods.

    28. MS Syriac 2 *Ahiqar* 7.26 (Charles, *Apocrypha and Pseudepigrapha*).

    29. The translation is that of Lichtheim, *Late Egyptian Wisdom*, pp. 13–92. For an alternative translation, see S. Glanville, *Catalogue of Demotic Papyri in the British Museum, Vol. II: The Instructions of Onchsheshonqy* (London: Trustees of the British Museum, 1955).

    30. Lichtheim, *Late Egyptian Literature*, pp. 13–22.

    31. For further discussion of the Greek reflexes of *Ahiqar*, see Conybeare, *Story of Ahiqar*, pp. xxxix–xlv; Küchler, *Weisheitstraditionen*, pp. 338–47; Lindenberger, *Aramaic Proverbs*, pp. 4–5; H. Wilsdorf, "Der Weise Achikaros bei Democrit und Theophrast. Eine Kommunikationsfrage," *Philologus* 135 (1991): 191–206; and N. Holzberg, ed., *Der Äsop-Roman: Motivgeschichte und Erzahlstruktur* (Tübingen: Gunter Narr, 1992), which includes a bibliography on the relation of *Ahiqar* to *Aesop* (pp. 177–78). Especially interesting is a passage from Strabo's *Geography* (16.2.39) which mentions both Moses and Ahiqar in a list of prophets thought worthy to be king because they had issued divine ordinances.

    32. For the influence of *Ahiqar* on the figure of Luqman, a sage mentioned in the Qur'an, see Conybeare, *Story of Ahiqar*, pp. lxxii–lxxxi, and the article "Luqman" in C. Bosworth et al., *Encyclopedia of Islam, New Edition*, vol. 5 (Leiden: Brill, 1986), pp. 811–13. For the influence of *Ahiqar* on Indian literary tradition, see A. Krappe, "Is the Story of Ahiqar the Wise of Indian Origin?" JAOS 61 (1941): 280–84. For the influence of Ahiqar on Persian literature, see de Blois, "Admonitions of Adurbad," pp. 41–53.

    33. For the use of *Ahiqar* in *Tobit*, see Conybeare, *Story of Ahiqar*, pp. xiii, xlviii–liv; H. Cazelles, "Zur Funktion der Achikar Notizen im Buch Tobias," BZ 20 (1976): 232–37; Küchler, *Weisheitstraditionen*, 364–79; J. Greenfield, "Ahiqar in the Book of Tobit," in *De la Torah au Meesie. Études d'exégèse et d'herméneutique bibliques offertes à Henri Cazelles*, ed. J. Doré et al. (Paris: Desclée, 1981), pp. 329–36; I. Nowell, "The Book of Tobit: Narrative Technique and Theology," Ph.D. diss., Catholic University of America, 1983, pp. 60–68.

34. See Conybeare, *Story of Ahiqar,* pp. lv–lxii; S. Talmon, "Wisdom in the Book of Esther," VT 13 (1963): 419–55, esp. pp. 438–43; S. Niditch and R. Doran, "The Success Story of the Wise Courtier: A Formal Approach," JBL 96 (1977): 179–93; J. T. Milik, "Les Modèles araméens du livre d'Esther dans la grotte 4 de Qumran," RQ 15 (1992): 321–406, esp. pp. 384–87.

35. While the copy of *Ahiqar* found at Elephantine is dated on paleographical and archeological grounds to the late fifth century B.C.E., many believe that the composition itself originated in the sixth or possibly the seventh century B.C.E., with the proverbs section perhaps originating earlier than the accompanying narrative. Among the arguments for this position: the composition lacks clear Persian loanwords, which one would expect in a document composed in the fifth century B.C.E., and it draws on motifs found in earlier Babylonian literature, as observed by E. Reiner ("The Etiological Myth of the Seven Sages," Or 30 [1960]: 1–11). For further discussion, see Lindenberger, *Aramaic Proverbs,* pp. 19–20. Although there is debate over the date and provenance of Deuteronomy as well, many scholars place its composition in the seventh or sixth century B.C.E., with the song perhaps originating earlier than the accompanying narrative. For a review of the evidence placing Deuteronomy's composition in the seventh century, see Weinfeld, *Deuteronomy 1–11,* pp. 16–17. For attempts to date Deuteronomy 32, see n. 4, this chapter.

36. It is not clear why in Deut 32:44 the narrative reports that Moses and Joshua recited the song together. Perhaps it is because the narrative's author wished to make clear that Joshua was not the intended recipient of the song's teaching. Or perhaps the author's inclusion of Joshua was triggered by the original command to write down the song in verse 19 which uses a plural verb.

37. In the Syriac version of *Ahiqar,* for example, the sage prays to God and learns from a divine voice that Nadan will be his heir.

38. See J. W. McKay, "Man's Love for God in Deuteronomy and the Father/Teacher-Son/Pupil Relationship," VT 22 (1972): 426–35. The representation of the deity as a teacher is found in both biblical and extrabiblical wisdom literature. For examples, see N. Shupak, "The 'Sitz im Leben' of the Book of Proverbs in the Light of a Comparison of Biblical and Egyptian Wisdom Literature," RB 94 (1987): 98–119 esp. pp. 115–16.

39. Elephantine MS *Ahiqar* column 9 lines 139–40 (Cowley, *Aramaic Papyri,* pp. 217, 224).

40. Lindenberger (*Aramaic Proverbs,* p. 137) cites several Imperial Aramaic texts in which the root *ṣdq* appears as a legal formula referring to winning a lawsuit. He also notes (p. 138) that the idiom "false witness" corresponds exactly to the biblical Hebrew expression "false witness" (Exod 23:1, Deut 19:16, Ps 35:11). Ahiqar's call for someone to vindicate him against the accusations of a "false witness" reminds one of the description of the Song of Moses as a "witness for God against Israel" in Deut 31:19.

41. See Cowley, *Aramaic Papyri,* pp. 218, 225.

42. The generic quality of the proverbs is one sign leading scholars to believe that they were composed independently of the Ahiqar story. See Lindenberger, *Aramaic Proverbs,* pp. 17–19. Another is that the proverbs and the narrative appear to have been written in two different dialects of Aramaic. See J. Greenfield, "The Dialects of Early Aramaic," JNES 37 (1978): 93–99.

43. Wright, "Lawsuit," pp. 54–55.

44. Boston, "Wisdom Influence," pp. 198–202.

45. Deut 32:20 even bears a lexical resemblance to the proverbs of Ahiqar. As J. Greenfield pointed out ("The Background and Parallel to a Proverb of Ahiqar,"

in *Hommages à André Dupont-Sommer*, eds. A. Caquot and M. Philonenko [Paris: Adrien-Maisonneuve, 1971], pp. 49-59, esp. pp. 51-52), the noun *tahpūkōt* (perverse) in the phrase "they are a perverse generation" is consistently used in biblical Hebrew to describe a person who does not keep his word. In this connection, Greenfield compares the usage of this noun in Deut 32:20 with the etymologically related *'pk'* used by Elephantine Ahiqar in his proverbs: "May El twist the mouth of the treacherous (*'pk'*)" (column x. line 156).

46. One such element is the song's conclusion in verse 43: "For he will avenge the blood of his children and take vengeance on his adversaries; he will repay those who hate him, and cleanse the land for his people." This verse, which is textually corrupt and appears in an expanded form in a Qumran fragment of Deuteronomy 32, seems to imply that God will seek vengeance not against Israel but against those who afflict Israel. It also seems to look forward to Israel's eventual deliverance. This ending does not accord with what the narrative says about the song's function as a punitive witness against Israel. Puzzled by this, S. R. Driver (*A Critical and Exegetical Commentary on Deuteronomy*, ICC [Edinburgh: T. and T. Clark, 1902], p. 344) could only conclude that the verse refers to an "eleventh hour act of grace at the moment when annihilation seemed imminent." Another explanation was provided by E. Baumann ("Das Lied Mose's auf seine gedankliche Geschlossenheit untersucht," VT 6 [1956]: 414-24), who proposed that the verse represents a later addition designed to soften the song's bite. For further discussion of verse 43 as reflected in LXX, MT, and Qumran material, see P. Skehan, "A Fragment of the Song of Moses," BASOR 136 (1954): 12-15; P. Bogaert, "Les Trois rédactions conservées et la forme originale de l'envoi du Cantique de Moïse (Dt 32,43)," in *Das Deuteronomium: Entstehung, Gestalt und Botschaft*, ed. N. Lohfink (Leuven: University Press, 1985), pp. 329-40; J. Weaver, *Notes on the Greek Text of Deuteronomy* (Atlanta: Scholars Press, 1995), pp. 533-35. Whatever this verse says about the song's original message or compositional history, it does not appear to have played any role in the interpretation of the song reflected in the preceding narrative. Deuteronomy 31 echoes the song at several points: e.g., 31:17 "I . . . will hide my face from them" = 32:20 "I will hide my face from them"; 31:28 "call heaven and earth to witness against them" = 32:1 "Give ear, O heavens, and I will speak; let the earth hear the words of my mouth." Note that these echoes refer only to the accusatory strain within the song and that nowhere does Deuteronomy 31 anticipate the song's hopeful conclusion. I thus find myself in agreement with Von Rad, who concluded that the narrative of Deuteronomy 31 represents a misinterpretation of the song. See Von Rad, *Deuteronomy*, pp. 190-91. For other echoes of Deuteronomy 32 in Deuteronomy 31, see Watts, *Psalm and Story*, pp. 67-68.

47. For example, the phrase "to turn to other gods" in Deut 31:18 and 20 contrasts with the language that Deuteronomy normally uses to describe apostasy: "to go after other gods." Also, the use of the phrase "to prostitute themselves to the foreign gods" to describe apostasy occurs in Deut 31:16 but nowhere else in Deuteronomy. See Weinfeld, *Deuteronomy and the Deuteronomistic School*, p. 83 n. 2. For other terms and motifs unique to Deuteronomy 31-32, see S. R. Driver, *Deuteronomy*, ICC (Edinburgh: T. and T. Clark, 1895), pp. 337-38.

48. For the first view, see Eissfeldt, *Das Lied Moses*, p. 50, who believed that parts of Deuteronomy 31 and the song were present in E prior to its incorporation within Deuteronomy (Deuteronomy and E share vocabulary). See also the scholars cited in Driver, *Deuteronomy*, pp. 346-47. For the latter view, see Mayes, *Deuteronomy*, pp. 47, 376, 380, 397, who describes Deuteronomy 31-34 as a late addition to the book, consisting of a mixture of deuteronomistic and postdeuteronomistic material.

49. The teachability of virtue was a much-discussed topic among Greek intellectuals as early as the sixth century. See W. K. C. Guthrie, *The Sophists* (Cambridge: Cambridge University Press, 1971), pp. 250-60.

50. Elephantine MS *Ahiqar* column 6 line 81.

51. The term *type-scene* was introduced to biblical studies by R. Alter in *The Art of Biblical Narrative* (New York: Basic Books, 1981), pp. 47-62. Cf. D. Gunn, "Narrative Patterns and Oral Traditions in Judges and Samuel," VT 24 (1974): 286-317. For further discussion of the similarities between Ugaritic and biblical narrative, see S. Parker, *The Pre-Biblical Narrative Tradition* (Atlanta: Scholars Press, 1989), pp. 225-32.

52. See K. Budde, *Die Bücher Samuel*, KHAT 8 (Tübingen: Mohr, 1902), p. 214; H. Hertzberg, *1 and 2 Samuel*, trans. J. Bowden, OTL (Philadelphia: Westminster, 1964), p. 399; P. McCarter, *II Samuel*, AB (Garden City: Doubleday, 1984), pp. 18-19; R. A. Carlson, *David, the Chosen King* (Stockholm: Almqvist and Wiksell, 1964), pp. 246-47; Watts, *Psalm and Story*, pp. 106-7, 116.

53. Carlson, *David, the Chosen King*, pp. 228-59, attributes the insertion of both songs to the "D school."

54. McCarter, *II Samuel*, pp. 18-19.

4. Sing to the Lord a New Song

1. See E. Tov, "The Literary History of the Book of Jeremiah," in *Empirical Models for Biblical Criticism*, ed. J. Tigay (Philadelphia: University of Pennsylvania Press, 1985), pp. 211-37. For further discussion of the use of textual evidence to reconstruct the literary development of the Bible, see S. Talmon, "The Textual Study of the Bible—a New Outlook," in *Qumran and the History of the Biblical Text*, ed. F. M. Cross and S. Talmon (Cambridge: Harvard University Press, 1975), pp. 321-400; E. Tov, *Textual Criticism of the Hebrew Bible* (Minneapolis: Fortress, 1992), pp. 314-49; E. Ulrich, "The Canonical Process, Textual Criticism and Latter Stages in the Composition of the Bible," in *Sha'arei Talmon*, ed. M. Fishbane and E. Tov (Winona Lake, Ind.: Eisenbrauns, 1992), pp. 267-91.

2. For summaries of the arguments in favor of secondary interpolation, see G. Landes, "The Kerygma of the Book of Jonah: The Contextual Interpretation of Jonah," Int 21 (1967): 3-31; J. Ackerman, "Satire and Symbolism in the Song of Jonah," in *Traditions in Transformation*, ed. B. Halpern and J. Levenson (Winona Lake, Ind.: Eisenbrauns, 1981), pp. 213-46; Watts, *Psalm and Story*, p. 141.

3. See Landes, "The Kerygma of the Book of Jonah"; J. Magonet, *Form and Meaning: Studies in the Literary Techniques of the Book of Jonah* (Frankfurt am Main: Lang, 1976), pp. 61-62; Ackerman, "Satire and Symbolism in the Song of Jonah"; J. Holbert, "Deliverance Belongs to the Lord: Satire in the Book of Jonah," JSOT 21 (1981): 59-81; K. Craig, *A Poetics of Jonah* (Columbia: University of South Carolina Press, 1993), pp. 83-123. For further discussion of Jonah's prayer, see chap. 5.

4. Several studies have sought to reconstruct the motives for and the history of the canonization of the Hebrew Bible in early Judaism. Recent studies include J. Sanders, *Torah and Canon* (Philadelphia: Fortress, 1972); J. Blenkinsopp, *Prophecy and Canon: A Contribution to the Study of Jewish Origins* (Notre Dame: Notre Dame University Press, 1977); S. Leiman, *The Canonization of Hebrew Scripture: The Talmudic and Midrashic Evidence* (Hamden, Conn.: Archon, 1976); B. Childs, *Introduction to the Old Testament as Scripture* (Philadelphia: Fortress, 1979), pp. 46-68; J. Barr, *Holy Scripture: Canon, Authority, Criticism* (Philadelphia: Westminster, 1983); S. Amsler et al., *Le Canon de l'Ancien Testament, sa formation et son histoire* (Geneva: Labor et

Fides, 1985); G. Bruns, "Canon and Power in the Hebrew Scriptures," *Critical Inquiry* 10 (1984): 462-80; R. Beckwith, *The Old Testament Canon of the New Testament Church* (Grand Rapids: Eerdmans, 1985); D. N. Freedman, "The Formation of the Canon of the Old Testament: The Selection and Identification of the Torah as the Supreme Authority of the Post-exilic Community," in *Religion and Law,* ed. E. Firmage et al. (Winona Lake, Ind.: Eisenbrauns, 1990), pp. 315-31; R. Vasholz, *The Old Testament Canon in the Old Testament Church* (Lewiston: Mellen, 1990). For additional bibliography, see Childs, *Introduction to the Old Testament as Scripture,* pp. 46-49. Most of these studies rely on evidence from biblical and early Jewish literature, but in recent years scholars have begun to approach canonization and scripture from a comparative perspective. See J. Leopoldt and S. Morenz, *Heilige Schriften: Betrachtungen zur Religionsgeschichte der antiken Mittelmeerwelt* (Leipzig: Otto Harrossowitz, 1953); F. Bruce and E. Rupp, *Holy Book and Holy Tradition* (Grand Rapids: Eerdmans, 1968); W. O'Flaherty, ed., *The Critical Study of Sacred Texts* (Berkeley: Graduate Theological Union, 1979); F. Denny and R. Taylor, eds., *The Holy Book in Comparative Perspective* (Columbia: University of South Carolina Press, 1985); J. Z. Smith, "Sacred Persistence: Toward a Redescription of Canon," *Imagining Religion* (Chicago: University of Chicago Press, 1982), pp. 36-52; W. Graham, *Beyond the Written Word: Oral Aspects of Scripture in the History of Religion* (Cambridge: Cambridge University Press, 1987); M. Levering, ed., *Rethinking Scripture: Essays from a Comparative Perspective* (Albany: State University of New York Press, 1989); W. C. Smith, *What Is Scripture: A Comparative Approach* (Minneapolis: Fortress, 1993).

5. The term *canon-consciousness* was first introduced by I. Seeligmann. See his "Voraussetzungen der Midraschexegese," in *Congress Volume Copenhagen 1953,* VTSup 1 (1953): 150-81. Many recent scholars make a distinction between scripture and canon; the former refers to a body of authoritative and sacred literature (either an authoritative collection of texts or a collection of authoritative texts), the latter to a particular collection of texts assigned scriptural status. See A. C. Sundberg, *The Old Testament of the Early Church* (Cambridge: Harvard University Press, 1964), pp. 107-8; Leiman, *Canonization,* pp. 14-16; Graham, *Beyond the Written Word,* pp. 55-56. It is useful to keep the distinction in mind when thinking about early Judaism. The little surviving evidence suggests that there were many "canons" in early Judaism differing not only in their content but in their status and social function. Some forms of Judaism, such as the form followed by the Pharisees, apparently accepted, alongside the "laws of Moses," extrabiblical traditions transmitted from previous generations (see Josephus's *Antiquities,* Book 13, 10:6). Others venerated esoteric writings not known to Jews outside their group (see *4 Ezra* 14:19-26). Still other groups, such as the Samaritans, consciously accepted only the five books of Moses. Thus when I use the terms *canon* and *canon-consciousness* in reference to early Judaism, the reader should understand that I do not refer to any particular canon but rather to the more general belief found throughout early Judaism that a given body of texts is of sacred and authoritative status.

6. For recent English-language studies of early Jewish biblical interpretation, see G. Vermes, *Scripture and Tradition* (Leiden: Brill, 1961), and "Bible and Midrash: Early Old Testament Exegesis," in *Cambridge History of the Bible* (Cambridge: Cambridge University Press, 1970), pp. 199-231; F. Bruce, *Biblical Exegesis in the Qumran Texts* (Grand Rapids: Eerdmans, 1959); M. P. Horgan, *Pesharim: Qumran Interpretation of Biblical Books* (Washington, D.C.: Catholic Biblical Association of America, 1979); D. Patte, *Early Jewish Hermeneutic in Palestine* (Missoula: Scholars Press, 1975); G. Brooke, *Exegesis at Qumran: 4Q Florilegium in Its Jewish Context* (Sheffield: JSOT, 1985); J. Kugel and R. Greer, *Early Biblical Interpretation* (Philadelphia: Westminster, 1986); J. Mulder, ed., *Miqra: Text, Translation, Reading, and Interpretation of the Hebrew*

Bible in Ancient Judaism and Early Christianity (Assen/Philadelphia: Van Gorcum/Fortress, 1988).

7. For the early history of the liturgical reading of biblical literature (which is difficult to reconstruct prior to the rabbinic period), see I. Elbogen, *Jewish Liturgy: A Comprehensive History* (Philadelphia: Jewish Publication Society/New York: Jewish Theological Seminary, 1993), pp. 129–56; C. Perrot, "The Reading of the Bible in the Ancient Synagogue," in *Miqra*, pp. 149–59; S. Reif, *Judaism and Hebrew Prayer: New Perspectives on Jewish Liturgical History* (Cambridge: Cambridge University Press, 1993), pp. 22–87. For the use of biblical citations and motifs in Second Temple liturgical poetry found at Qumran, see B. Nitzan, *Qumran Prayer and Religious Poetry* (Leiden: Brill, 1994), pp. 11–13, 26–27.

8. See S. Honigman, "The Birth of the Diaspora: The Emergence of a Jewish Self-definition in Ptolemaic Egypt in the Light of Onomastics," in *Diasporas in Antiquity*, ed. S. Cohen and E. Frerichs (Atlanta: Scholars Press, 1993), pp. 93–127.

9. Seeligman, "Voraussetzungen der Midraschexegese"; B. Childs, "The Exegetical Significance of Canon for the Old Testament," in *Congress Volume Göttingen 1977*, VTSup 29 (1977): 66–80, and *Introduction to the Old Testament as Scripture*, pp. 46–106; G. Sheppard, *Wisdom as a Hermeneutical Construct: A Study in the Sapientializing of the Old Testament* (Berlin: de Gruyter, 1980), and "Canonization: Hearing the Voice of the Same God through Historically Dissimiliar Traditions," Int 36 (1982): 21–33; M. Fishbane, *Biblical Interpretation in Ancient Israel* (New York: Oxford University Press, 1985).

10. Childs, "Exegetical Significance," pp. 71–72.

11. For this view, see J. Bright, "The Date of the Prose Sermons of Jeremiah," JBL 70 (1951):15–35. For additional discussion of the Deuteronomic language in Jeremiah, see L. Stulman, *The Prose Sermons of the Book of Jeremiah* (Atlanta: Scholars Press, 1986).

12. See chap. 5.

13. While some scholars identify the "book of Moses" mentioned in Ezra-Nehemiah as the Pentateuch, others believe it consisted only of P, or of Deuteronomy (D), or of some unknown group of laws. See C. Houtman, "Ezra and the Law," OTS 21 (1981): 91–115; R. Klein, "Ezra-Nehemiah, Books of," in *The Anchor Bible Dictionary*, vol. 2 (New York: Doubleday, 1992), pp. 737–38. Whatever the identity of this book, the author of Ezra-Nehemiah was evidently familiar with both D and P, since he alludes to material from both sources.

14. For Deuteronomy's use and interpretation of earlier scriptural texts (e.g., the Covenant Code in Exodus 20–23), see B. Levinson's forthcoming study, *Deuteronomy and the Hermeneutics of Legal Innovation* (Oxford University Press).

15. Philo, "De Vita Mosis," in *Philo*, vol. 6 Loeb Classical Library, trans. F. Colson (Cambridge: Harvard University Press, 1935), pp. 358–59.

16. See D. Dimant, "The Use and Interpretation of Miqra in the Apocrypha and Pseudepigrapha," in *Mikra*, pp. 379–419; A. Chester, "Citing the Old Testament," in *It Is Written: Scripture, Citing Scripture, Essays in Honor of B. Lindars*, ed. D. Carson and H. G. M. Williamson (Cambridge: Cambridge University Press, 1988), pp. 141–69. For a survey of early Jewish narratives, see G. Nickelsburg, "Stories of Biblical and Early Post-Biblical Times" and "The Bible Rewritten and Expanded," in *Jewish Writings of the Second Temple Period*, ed. M. Stone (Assen/Philadelphia: Van Gorcum/Fortress, 1984), pp. 33–156; L. Wills, *The Jewish Novel in the Ancient World* (Ithaca: Cornell University Press, 1995).

17. See S. Holm-Nielsen, "The Importance of Late Jewish Psalmody for the Understanding of Old Testament Psalmodic Tradition," ST 14 (1960): 1–53, esp. pp. 14–23, and *Hodayot: Psalms from Qumran* (Aarhus: Universitetsforlaget I. Aarhus,

1960), pp. 300-15; E. Schuller, *Non-Canonical Psalms from Qumran* (Atlanta: Scholars Press, 1986), pp. 32-38. For a review of early Jewish hymnody, see J. Charlesworth, "A Prolegomenon to the New Study of the Jewish Background of the Hymns and Prayers in the New Testament," *JJS* 33 (1982): 265-85, and D. Flusser, "Psalms, Hymns and Prayers," in *Jewish Writings of the Second Temple Period,* pp. 551-77. In the context of early Judaism and Christianity, by the way, genre labels like "psalm," "hymn," and "ode" developed different nuances—the Greek term translated "psalm," for example, was reserved by some authors for songs written by David, while "ode" (or its Latin equivalent, "canticle") was often used in reference to the songs of Moses and other figures within biblical narrative. All these terms came to signify different kinds of religious songs dedicated to God, however. See A. Bastiaensen, "Psalmi, Hymni and Cantica in Early Jewish-Christian Tradition," *Studia Patristica* 21 (1989): 15-26. As I have done in chapters 2 and 3, I will continue to use native generic labels when referring to the songs of early Judaism in chapters 4 and 5, but the reader should note that for many songs the sources use more than one label to refer to the song or use no label at all. In such cases I will employ the native label that seems most appropriate given the songs generic characteristics, language of composition, and reception-history.

18. For the use of biblical elements in apocalyptic literature, see L. Hartman, *Prophecy Interpreted: The Formation of Some Jewish Apocalyptic Texts and of the Eschatological Discourse, Mark 13 par.* (Lund: Gleerup, 1966), and *Asking for Meaning: A Study of 1 Enoch 1-5* (Lund: Gleerup, 1979); I. Gruenwald, *Apocalyptic and Merkavah Mysticism* (Leiden: Brill, 1980), pp. 19-25; M. Knibb, "Apocalyptic and Wisdom in 4 Ezra," *JSJ* 13 (1982): 56-74; G. Beale, *The Use of Daniel in Jewish Apocalyptic Literature and in the Revelation of John* (New York: University Press of America, 1984); David Halperin, *The Faces of the Chariot* (Tübingen: J. C. B. Mohr, 1988); C. Rowland, "Apocalyptic Literature," in *It Is Written,* pp. 170-89; J. Vanderkam, "Biblical Interpretation in *1 Enoch* and *Jubilees,*" in *The Pseudepigrapha and Early Biblical Interpretation,* ed. J. Charlesworth and C. Evans (Sheffield: JSOT, 1993), pp. 96-125.

19. See chap. 3, n. 24.

20. Scholars are divided concerning the date of *Judith*'s composition, but it is rarely placed later than the end of the second century B.C.E. For a Persian dating, see A. Dubarle, *Judith: Formes et sens des diverses traditions,* vol. 1 (Rome: Institut Biblique Pontifical, 1966), pp. 131-33. For a Maccabean dating, see S. Zeitlin and M. Eslin, *The Book of Judith* (Leiden: Brill, 1972), pp. 26-31.

21. See P. Skehan, "The Hand of Judith," *CBQ* 25 (1963): 94-110; Dubarle, *Judith,* 142-43; T. Craven, *Artistry and Faith in the Book of Judith* (Chico: Scholars' Press, 1983), pp. 111-12. Exodus 15 is cited elsewhere in *Judith.* See the citation of Exod 15:3 in Judith's prayer in Jdt 9:7.

22. My understanding of the workings of literary allusion is based on the study of Z. Ben-Porat, "The Poetics of Literary Allusion," *PTL: A Journal for Descriptive Poetics and Theory of Literature* 1 (1976): 105-28.

23. In some Latin versions of Luke, the Magnificat is attributed to Elizabeth, the mother of John the Baptist. For a review of the debate surrounding the attribution of the Magnificat (most recent scholars seem to prefer Mary), see S. Benko, "The Magnificat: A History of the Controversy," *JBL* 86 (1967): 263-75; R. Brown, *The Birth of the Messiah* (Garden City: Doubleday, 1977), pp. 334-36; J. Fitzmyer, *The Gospel according to Luke (I-IX)* (Garden City: Doubleday, 1981), pp. 365-66; S. Farris, *The Hymns of Luke's Infancy Narratives* (Sheffield: JSOT, 1985), pp. 108-13. See the latter work for discussion of the other poetic passages in Luke, including the "Benedictus" (Luke 1:68-79), the "Nunc Dimittis" (Luke 2:29-32), and the "Gloria in excelsus" (Luke 2:14).

24. The "reversal of fortune" motif appears in a number of biblical and Second Temple period hymns. See E. Hamel, "Le Magnificat et le renversement des situations. Réflexion théologico-biblique," *Greg* 60 (1979): 55–84.

25. P. Winter ("Magnificat and Benedictus," BJRL 37 [1954]: 328–43) argues that the Magnificat was adapted from a Maccabean Hebrew psalm, in contrast to an earlier school of thought which maintained that Luke himself composed the song. See A. Harnack, "Das Magnificat der Elisabeth (Luk 1.46–55) nebst einigen Bemerkungen zu Luk 1 und 2," *Sitzungberichte der Königlichen Preussischen Akademie der Wissenschaften zu Berlin* 27 (1900): 538–66.

26. P. Haupt, "The Prototype of the Magnificat," ZDMG 58 (1904): 617–32; A. Plummer, *A Critical and Exegetical Commentary on the Gospel according to St. Luke,* ICC (Edinburgh: T. and T. Clark, reprint 1981), pp. 30–31; P. Bogaert, "Pour une phénoménologie de l'appropriation la priére. La Cantique d'Anne dans le Ier livre Samuel, dans les Antiquités Bibliques et dans le Nouveau Testament," in *L'Expérience de la priére dans les grandes religions,* ed. H. Limet and J. Ries (Louvain-la-Neuve: Centre d'Histoire des Religions, 1980), pp. 245–59, esp. pp. 256–58; R. Brown, *The Birth of the Messiah,* p. 357; Fitzmyer, *The Gospel according to Luke,* p. 369; Farris, *The Hymns of Luke's Infancy Narratives,* pp. 25 and 116. Farris cautions that the similarity between the Magnificat and Hannah's Prayer "can be over-emphasized," but he seems to be speaking only of the content of the two hymns, not of their contextualization within a narrative setting. For a list of parallels between the Magnificat and various scriptural texts (including but not limited to 1 Samuel 2), see Plummer, *The Gospel according to St. Luke,* pp. 30–31.

27. S. Weitzman, "Allusion, Artifice and Exile in the Hymn of Tobit," JBL 115 (1996): 49–61. Unless stated otherwise, my interpretation of *Tobit* is based on the "longer" Greek version preserved in Codex Siniaticus published in R. Hanhart, *Tobit,* in *Septuaginta: Vetus Testamentum Graecum,* 8/5 (Göttingen: Vandenhoeck and Ruprecht, 1983). This version is almost universally given priority over the "shorter" version of *Tobit* in Codex Vaticanus and Codex Alexandrinus. See J. D. Thomas, "The Greek Text of Tobit," JBL 91 (1972): 463–71, and I. Nowell, *The Book of Tobit: Narrative Technique and Theology* (Washington, D.C.: Catholic University of America Press, 1983), pp. 26–28. I have also consulted the Hebrew and Aramaic fragments of *Tobit* found at Qumran, which Professor J. Fitzmyer has kindly shared with me (they are tentatively scheduled to be published in DJD 13). At least two of the five fragmentary manuscripts of Tobit found at Qumran preserve portions of Tobit 12–13: 4Q Tob^a (12:18–13:6; 13:6–12, 13:12–14:3) and 4Q Tob^e (12:20–13:4; 13:13–14; 13:18–14:2). The former manuscript is in Aramaic, the latter in Hebrew. It is not yet clear which represents the language of composition, but Aramaic seems more likely. For a preliminary listing of the fragments' contents, see J. Milik, "La Patrie de Tobit," RB 73 (1966): 522 n. 3; and for a preliminary review of lower and higher criticism of *Tobit* in light of the Qumran fragments, see C. Moore, "Scholarly Issues in the Book of Tobit before Qumran and After: An Assessment," JSP 5 (1989): 65–81, and J. Fitzmyer, "The Aramaic and Hebrew Fragments of Tobit from Qumran Cave 4," CBQ 57 (1995): 655–75. Some scholars believe that the hymn represents a secondary interpolation added at some point after the destruction of the Second Temple. See F. Zimmerman, *The Book of Tobit* (New York: Harper, 1958), pp. 24–27. The Qumran fragments, which preserve portions of the hymn, argue against this view, showing that the hymn was part of the narrative at a fairly early stage in its literary transmission. See Moore, "Scholarly Issues," p. 77, and Weitzman, "Hymn of Tobit," p. 55 n. 5.

28. Vaticanus Tob 12:20 reads "write everything which has happened *in a book,*" adding a phrase which brings this verse into even closer alignment with Deut

31:24: "Moses had finished writing the matters of this instruction *in a book.*" Note also the observation of A. Di Lella (*"The Deuteronomic Background of the Farewell Discourse in Tob 14:3-11," CBQ 41 [1979]: 380-89, esp. p. 386) that the phrase "and now" plus the imperative in verses such as Tob 12:20 mimics an expression often used in Deuteronomy (e.g., LXX Deut 31:19).

29. Sinaiticus Tob 13:1 merely reports that Tobit "said" the hymn. Most recent scholars accept the reading of Vaticanus in this case, which seems to agree with 4Q Tob^c.

30. As Di Lella has shown ("Deuteronomic Background"), Tobit's farewell address in Tobit 14 is saturated with deuteronomic language and motifs.

31. As previous readers have noted (e.g., W. Van Unnik, *Das Selbstverständnis der jüdischen Diaspora in der Hellenistich-Römischen Zeit* [Leiden: Brill, 1993], p. 113), Tob 13:2 seems to represent a conflation of Deut 32:39 and 1 Sam 2:6 (Hannah's Prayer). This fusion complicates my claim that Tob 13:2 is specifically intended to evoke Deut 32:39, but in light of all the other parallels between Tobit 12-13 and Deuteronomy 31-32 presented in this study, I maintain that *in its present narrative setting* (as part of Tobit's final hymn) the verse is intended to echo the Song of Moses. In this connection I would also note that previous commentators have recognized parallels between Tob 13:5-6 and Deut 30:1-10 (esp. Tob 13:5 and Deut 30:3), thus reinforcing the connection between these verses and the language of Deuteronomy in particular. See P. Griffin, "Theology and Function of Prayer in the Book of Tobit," Ph.D. diss., Catholic University, 1984, pp. 262-69.

32. The motif of God hiding his face appears frequently in biblical literature (see Deut 31:17-18; Isa 50:6, 54:8, 64:6; Jer 33:5; Ez 39:29; etc.), and it is thus possible that reflected in Tob 13:6 is a literary or liturgical cliché rather than an echo of a specific biblical verse. See the preceding note, however, for why I believe that this explanation is less likely than my claim that Tob 13:6 is specifically intended to evoke Deut 32:20.

33. It is interesting to note that rabbinic tradition asserts that a dying Moses foresaw a glorified Jerusalem, using language that resembles Tobit's vision of a restored Jerusalem. See the midrash cited in chap. 3 n. 9. For the eschatological elements in Deuteronomy 32, see J. Luyten, "Primeval and Eschatological Overtones in the Song of Moses (DT 32, 1-43)," in *Das Deuteronomium: Entstehung, Gestalt und Botshaft,* ed. N. Lohfink (Leuven: Leuven University, 1985), pp. 341-47. As D. Flusser has observed ("Psalm, Hymns and Prayers," pp. 556-58), Tobit's eschatological conclusion is typical of a psalmic genre well attested in the Second Temple period, the "eschatological psalm," which looks forward to Israel's deliverance from its foes, the gathering of the dispersed, and the glorification of Jerusalem. Our analysis suggests why the author of *Tobit* chose to insert this kind of hymn in his narrative—he sought to imitate the prophetic Song of Moses.

34. The Hebrew text was republished in A. Neubauer, *The Book of Tobit: A Chaldee Text* (Oxford: Clarendon Press, 1878), pp. 17-35, and is translated on pp. xliv-lxiii.

35. Some scholars believe that this manuscript represents a Hebrew translation of an Aramaic version close to that later published by A. Neubauer in 1879, with some affinities with the Greek version in Codex Sinaiticus. See Neubauer, *Book of Tobit,* pp. xi-xii, and Zimmerman, *Tobit,* pp. 135-36.

36. Aside from the evidence provided by the hymns of *Judith, Tobit,* and the Magnificat, there are other hints from Second Temple and post-Second Temple period sources that Exodus 15 and other songs in biblical narrative were perceived as exemplary texts. Philo, for example, describes Exodus 15 as "the most sacred of odes" and as a "reminder" of how "to thank and to hymn" God for his bene-

factions (*De Somniis* II 268–69). Also revealing is the fact that Exodus 15 is presented in rabbinic sources as the model for the eschatological song sung by Israel when it is redeemed in the future. See, for instance, *Eccl. Rab.* 1.9: "The rabbis say: in the World to Come the generations will assemble in the presence of the Holy One, blessed be He, and say before Him, 'Lord of the Universe, who shall utter a song before thee first?' He will answer them, 'In the past, none but the generation of Moses uttered a song before Me, and now none but that generation shall utter a song before Me.' What is the proof? As it is said, 'Sing unto the Lord a new song, and His praise from the end of the earth; ye that go down to the Sea.'" A similar tradition also surfaces in Christian tradition. See Rev 15:3, where those who have conquered the beast sing "the Song of Moses and the Song of the Lamb," the former a possible allusion to Exodus 15 or Deuteronomy 32 (Rev 15:3 is thought by some to contain an allusion to Deut 32:4). For further discussion of the hymns in Revelation, see K. Jörns, *Das Hymnischer Evangelium* (Gütersloh: Güttersloher Verlagshaus, 1971). All this indicates that songs such as Exodus 15 were perceived by early canon-conscious readers not only as events in Israel's past but as behavioral models for the present and future as well.

37. Skehan, "Hand of Judith."

38. See E. Burrows, *The Gospel of the Infancy and Other Biblical Essays* (London: Burns, Oates and Washbourne, 1940), pp. 1–41, and Brown, *The Birth of the Messiah*, pp. 451 and 469. Some scholars have also discerned parallels between Luke 1–2 and the stories of Abraham in Genesis. See M. Coleridge, *The Birth of the Lukan Narrative: Narrative as Christology in Luke 1–2* (Sheffield: JSOT, 1993).

39. For *Tobit*'s allusions to Genesis 24 and 29, see I. Abrahams, "Tobit and Genesis," JQR 5 (1895): 348–50; L. Ruppert, "Das Buch Tobias—Ein Modellfall nachgestaltender Erzählung," in *Wort, Lied und Gottespruch: I Beitrage zur Septuaginta*, ed. J. Schriener (Würzburg: Echter Verlag, 1972), pp. 109–19, esp. pp. 113–14; Nowell, *Book of Tobit*, pp. 69–74. For the allusions to the Joseph story, see Ruppert, "Das Buch Tobias," pp. 114–15, and Nowell, *Book of Tobit*, pp. 68–69. For the allusion to Job, see Nowell, *Book of Tobit*, pp. 74–75, and Dimant, "Use and Interpretation of Mikra," pp. 417–19. For the allusions to Deuteronomy, see Di Lella, "Deuteronomic Background."

40. Thus, according to *T. Job* 28:7, Job is said to be the king of Egypt; Aristeas the exegete places him on the border of Idumea and Arabia; and the rabbis place him in Mesopotamia and elsewhere outside Israel, including among the exiles in Babylonia (*Bab. Bat.* 15a).

41. Many scholars have concluded that *Tobit* was written to address the problems of living in exile, which is represented by the story as a "root misfortune" ultimately responsible for all the individual misfortunes that beset Tobit and Sarah. See W. Soll, "Misfortune and Exile in Tobit: The Juncture of a Fairy Tale Source and Deuteronomic Theology," CBQ 51 (1989): 209–31, and A. J. Levine, "Diaspora as Metaphor: Bodies and Boundaries in the Book of Tobit," in *Diaspora Jews and Judaism* (Atlanta: Scholars Press, 1992), pp. 105–17. *Tobit*'s preoccupation with the problem of exile is one of the main reasons that many (though not all) scholars place its composition in the diaspora.

42. For more on the rabbis' efforts to interrelate scriptural verses, see J. Kugel, "Two Introductions to Midrash," *Prooftexts* 3 (1983): 131–55, and *In Potiphar's House* (San Francisco: HarperCollins, 1990), esp. pp. 261–64; D. Boyarin, *Intertextuality and the Reading of Midrash* (Bloomington: Indiana University Press, 1994).

43. For an introduction to early Christian biblical exegesis and its effort to relate the New Testament with the Old, see Kugel and Greer, *Early Biblical Interpretation*, pp. 126–54. For the use of typology in the early Church, see L. Goppelt,

Typos: The Typological Interpretation of the Old Testament in the New, trans. D. Madvig (Grand Rapids: Eerdmans, 1982).

44. See S. Lowy, *The Principles of Samaritan Bible Exegesis* (Leiden: Brill, 1977), pp. 417–38.

45. This kind of behavior is more difficult to find in prerabbinic Jewish sources, but it is attested there as well. As a prerabbinic example of "back-referencing," Kugel (*In Potiphar's House,* p. 269 n. 10) cites the *Testament of Zebulun,* which interprets Amos 2:6 in light of the story of Joseph. Other examples can be cited as well. The figure of Job, for instance, is associated by several Second Temple period sources with persons or events in Genesis. Thus *T. Job* 1:1, the LXX translation of Job (42:17d), and Aristeas the exegete all identify Job with Jobab, an Edomite descendant of Abraham mentioned in Gen 36:33; and *T. Job* (1:6) and Pseudo-Philo (*Bib. Ant.* 8:8) report that Job married Jacob's daughter Dinah.

46. Fishbane, *Biblical Interpretation,* p. 407.

47. For the text of Pseudo-Philo, see D. Harrington and J. Cazeaux, *Les Antiquités Bibliques* (Paris: Les Editions du Cerf, 1976). For a review of recent scholarship, see D. Harrington, "A Decade of Research on Pseudo-Philo's *Biblical Antiquities,*" JSP 2 (1988): 3–12.

48. The name Abino here appears to represent a truncated form of Abinoam. It may have arisen from a misreading of the word Abinoam in Judg 5:1 as Abino + ʿam (the latter word means "people" in Hebrew). See D. Harrington, "Pseudo-Philo's Biblical Aniquities," in *Old Testament Pseudepigrapha,* vol. 2, p. 345 n. a. This may have provided the textual justification for Pseudo-Philo's claim that "the people" joined Deborah and Barak in the performance of the song. As we will see, however, Pseudo-Philo had other reasons for attributing the song to all the people.

49. R. Bauckham, "The Liber Antiquitatem Biblicarum of Pseudo-Philo and the Gospels as 'Midrash,'" in *Gospel Perspectives III: Studies in Midrash and Historiography,* ed. R. France and D. Wenham (Sheffield: JSOT, 1983), pp. 33–76, esp. p. 47.

50. P. Enns, "A Retelling of the Song of the Sea in Wis 10, 20–21" Bib 76 (1995): 1–24.

51. For the Greek text of the *Wisdom of Solomon,* see J. Ziegler, *Sapientia Salomonis,* Septuaginta: Vetus Testamentum Graecum, 12/1 (Göttingen: Vandenhoeck and Ruprecht, 1980). It is not known exactly when the *Wisdom of Solomon* was composed, but a date in the first half of the first century C.E. seems likely. See D. Winston, *The Wisdom of Solomon,* AB (New York: Doubleday, 1979), pp. 20–25.

52. See chap. 2, n. 5.

53. The same motif appears in connection with Pseudo-Philo's description of Hannah's prayer. After describing her song, the narrator reports that the people went down "with one accord" (*unanimiter*) to Shiloh with timbrels, dances, lutes, and harps (*Bib. Ant.* 51:7). Similarly, in *Bib. Ant.* 21:8–9, Israel sings "in one voice" (*unanimiter*) after dedicating an altar in the time of Joshua.

54. The Akedah plays an especially prominent role in the song's catalogue of historical events and is referred to elsewhere by Pseudo-Philo in *Bib. Ant.* 18:5, 23:8, and 40:2–3. For the significance of this event for Pseudo-Philo and other early Jews, see R. Daly, "The Soteriological Significance of the Sacrifice of Isaac," CBQ 39 (1977): 45–75, and P. Davies and B. Chilton, "The Aqedah: A Revised Tradition History," CBQ 40 (1978): 514–46.

55. The song's comparison of the battle against Sisera to earlier biblical events reflects a technique used throughout the *Biblical Antiquities* in which biblical heroes compare their present situation to previous events in biblical history. See O. Eissfeldt,

"Zur Kompositionstechnik des Pseudo-Philonischen *Liber Antiquitatem Biblicarum*," *Kleine Schriften*, vol. 3 (Berlin: Mohr, 1966), pp. 340-53.

56. The historical superscription should be distinguished from the superscription *lǝdāwid* (to David; for David) appearing before many of the psalms in the Psalter. The latter may not have originated as a statement about authorship at all but rather as some sort of literary classification. Eventually, however, it was interpreted as a statement of authorship, as suggested by Greek translations of the Psalter, where this phrase is sometimes translated not as "to David" or "for David" but as "of David." See A. Pietersma, "David in the Greek Psalms," VT 30 (1980): 213-26; J. Kugel, "Topics in the History of the Spirituality of the Psalms," in *Jewish Spirituality*, vol. 1, ed. A. Green (New York: Crossroad, 1987), pp. 113-44, esp. p. 135. Note also that not all the psalms in the Psalter are associated with David. Psalm 90, for example, is imputed to Moses. Non-canonical psalms from Qumran also contain superscriptions imputing the psalms to figures other than David. See E. Schuller, *Non-Canonical Psalms from Qumran* (Atlanta: Scholars Press, 1986), pp. 27-32.

57. For the "cultic interpretation" of the Psalms, see S. Mowinckel, *The Psalms in Israel's Worship*, trans. D. Ap.-Thomas (New York: Abingdon, 1962); E. Gerstenberger, "Psalms," in *Old Testament Form Criticism*, ed. J. Hayes (San Antonio: Trinity University Press, 1974), pp. 179-224; J. H. Eaton, "The Psalms and Israelite Worship," in *Tradition and Interpretation: Essays by Members of the Society for Old Testament Study*, ed. G. Anderson (Oxford: Clarendon Press, 1979), pp. 238-73.

58. See Pietersma, "David in the Greek Psalms"; J. M. Vosta, "Sur les titres des Psaumes dans la Pešitta, surtout d'après la recension orientale," Bib 25 (1944): 210-35; H. D. Preuss, "Die Psalmüberschriften in Targum und Midrasch," ZAW 71 (1951): 44-54; A. Cooper, "The Life and Times of King David according to the Book of Psalms," in *The Poet and the Historian: Essays in Literary and Historical Biblical Criticism*, ed. R. Friedman (Chico: Scholars Press, 1983), pp. 117-32.

59. B. Childs, "Psalm Titles and Midrashic Exegesis," JSS 16 (1971): 137-50; F. Bruce, "The Earliest Old Testament Exegesis," OTS 17 (1972): 40-52; E. Slomovic, "Toward an Understanding of the Formation of Historical Titles in the Book of Psalms," ZAW 91 (1979): 350-80.

60. See Slomovic, "Toward an Understanding," p. 371.

61. This conclusion presupposes that the Psalter had "scriptural" status at the time of the composition of the historical superscriptions. To accept this assumption it is not necessary to assume that the present form of the Psalter in the MT was canonical at this time, only that individual psalms were considered scriptural. J. Sanders has argued that the "canonical" form of the Psalter was not fixed as late as the first century C.E. His evidence for this claim is the so-called Psalms Scroll from Qumran cave 11, which arranges the psalms in an order different from that of the canonical Psalter and includes several compositions not included in the present form of MT. Sanders argues that this scroll was considered "canonical" by the Qumran community, as sacred to it as the MT Psalter was and is to other Jewish communities. See J. Sanders, *The Psalms Scroll from Qumran Cave 11 [11QPsᵃ]*, DJD 4 (Oxford: Oxford University Press, 1965), pp. 11-13, and "The Qumran Psalms Scroll (11QPsᵃ) Reviewed," in *On Language, Culture and Religion: In Honor of Eugene A. Nida* (The Hague: Mouton, 1974), pp. 79-99. If Sanders is right, there may have been several "canonical" Psalters in circulation in the Second Temple period (actually he claims that only the final third of the Psalter, Psalms 101-50, was still fluid at this time; Psalms 1-100 appear to have stabilized already). Others have argued, however, that the Qumran Psalms Scroll simply represents an arrangement of psalms used for liturgical purposes and has no bearing on the

canonical status of the Psalter at this time. See M. Goshen-Gottstein, "The Psalms Scroll [11QPsᵃ]: A Problem of Canon and Text," *Textus* 5 (1966); P. Skehan, "Qumran and Old Testament Criticism," *Qumran: Sa piété, sa théologie et son milieu* (Louvain: Ducolot, 1978), pp. 163–82. Regardless of when the Psalter as a whole was fixed, there is evidence that individual psalms were regarded as sacred texts at least by the second century B.C.E.; see 1 *Macc* 7:16-17, which quotes Ps 79:2-3 as a prophecy fulfilled by the Hasmoneans.

62. The phrase ψαλμον καινον also appears in some manuscripts of Judith at 16:1 (in place of ψαλμον και αινον). See Zeitlin and Enslin, *The Book of Judith*, pp. 168–69. The phrase "new song"—which may originally have had the straightforward meaning of "another song" or "a song composed anew for this occasion"—appears often in post–Second Temple traditions centered on songs, mostly in connection with the song sung at Israel's final redemption (cf. Isa 42:10) or the song sung by the angels (the latter tradition is perhaps based on Ps 96:1: "sing to the Lord a new song, sing to the Lord all the earth!"). For the rabbinic use of this phrase, see K. Grözinger, *Musik und Gesang in der Theologie der frühen jüdischen Literatur* (Tübingen: Mohr, 1982), pp. 76-77, 205-9. See also Rev 4:9, 14:3. For other connections between Judith 16 and the Psalms, see Skehan, "The Hand of Judith," pp. 103-6; Dubarle, *Judith*, p. 158; S. Holm-Nielson, "Religiöse Poesie des Spätjudentums," in W. Hausse, ed., *Aufstieg und Niedergang der Romischen Welt II*, 19.1 (Berlin/New York: de Gruyter, 1979), p. 162; Zeitlin and Enslin, *The Book of Judith*, p. 174.

63. For discussion of Pseudo-Philo's retelling of Hannah's Prayer, see Bogaert, "Pour une phénoménologie de l'appropriation de la prière," pp. 252-56.

64. See H. Schneider, "Die biblischen Oden im christlichen Altertum," Bib 30 (1949): 28-65, 239-72, 433-52, 479-500; E. Werner, *The Sacred Bridge* (London: Dennis Dobson, 1959), pp. 139-42; J. Kugel, "Is There But One Song?" Bib 63 (1982): 329-50. As Kugel points out, a similar tradition is reflected in rabbinic literature, which preserves several lists of ten songs, nine from biblical history and the last from the eschatological future. For further discussion of the "ten song" tradition, see J. Goldin, "This Song," in *Studies in Midrash and Related Literature* (Philadelphia: Jewish Publication Society, 1988), pp. 151-61.

65. S. Talmon may have uncovered another way in which early interpreters connected the Psalms to biblical narrative in his article "Pisqa Be ʾemsaᶜ Pasuq and 11QPsA," *Textus* 5 (1965): 11-21. The pisqāʾ bĕ ʾemsaᶜ pāsûq is a lacuna inserted in the midst of biblical verses. Such lacunae appear to be concentrated in the historiographical narrative of the Bible, particularly those parts of the books of Samuel which narrate the life of David, and they often appear in precisely those historical episodes referred to in the psalm historical superscriptions. With these characteristics in mind, Talmon has suggested that the purpose of the pisqāʾ bĕ ʾemsaᶜ pāsûq is to allude to "literary expansions" of the episode in question— including canonical psalms meant to be read in the context of the episode—or at least to evoke exegetical correlations with such texts. For example, Talmon believes that Psalm 3 was meant to be read within the context of 2 Samuel 16, which allegedly refers to the psalm by means of a pisqāʾ bĕ ʾemsaᶜ pāsûq in 2 Sam 16:13. If Talmon's suggestion is valid, we have in this notation yet another attempt to correlate biblical narrative with other scriptural texts, including canonical psalms. For another view of this notation's function, see D. Weisberg, "'Break in the Middle of a Verse': Some Observations on a Massoretic Feature," in *Pursuing the Text: Studies in Honor of Ben Zion Wacholder*, ed. J. Reeves and J. Kampen (Sheffield, JSOT, 1994), pp. 34-45.

66. Leopoldt and Morenz, *Heilige Schriften,* p. 17. The term *liturgy* is as problematic as the term *canon* and is even more difficult to define. In Second Temple Judaism, there does not appear to have been a fixed liturgy like that developed in later rabbinic Judaism (on this, see L. Hoffman, *The Canonization of the Synagogue Service* [Notre Dame: University of Notre Dame Press, 1979]). One can glean some information about liturgical practice from Qumran literature and other sources, but it is not clear whether this evidence is representative of Judaism as a whole or only of certain forms of Judaism. Nor does it allow one to distinguish clearly between extratemple liturgical practices and those performed in the temple cult. For the purposes of this study, I will use the term *liturgy* quite loosely to refer to the communal worship of God and the forms of discourse used for this purpose. I do not mean to suggest by this that there was a uniform, standardized liturgy in the Second Temple period, only that there existed at this time conventional practices and literary genres used in the public worship of God.

67. See n. 5.

68. See n. 7.

69. See b. *Rosh. Has.* 31a. Note also M. Lehman, "Yom Kippur in Qumran," RQ 3 (1961): 120–21, who argued that Deuteronomy 32 was recited in the Samaritan and Qumran Yom Kippur rituals. For additional information on the liturgical recitation of the Song of the Sea, the Song of the Well, and the Song of Moses in the Second Temple and rabbinic periods, see I. Elbogen, *Jewish Liturgy: A Comprehensive History,* trans. R. Scheindlin from 1913 edition (Philadelphia: Jewish Publication Society, 1993), pp. 98–99; Kugel, "Is There But One Song?" p. 338 n. 21; Hoffman, *The Canonization of the Synagogue Service,* pp. 130–31. To this day, the Song of the Sea is recalled by Jews in a blessing following the Shema in the daily liturgy (the Blessing of Redemption): "the people saw his power, and they extolled and praised his name; they willingly accepted his kingship upon them. Moses and the children of Israel sang to you the song [of the Sea] with great rejoicing." After reciting these words, the worshiper recites three verses from the Song of the Sea: "Who is like You among the gods . . . " (Exod 15:11), "This is my God" (Exod 15:2), and "The Lord shall reign forever and ever" (Exod 15:18).

70. G. Östborn, *Cult and Canon: A Study of the Canonization of the Old Testament* (Uppsala: Lundequistska Bokhandeln, 1950).

71. See Leiman, *Canonization,* p. 141 n. 37.

72. B. *Pes.* 117a. For the origins and development of the Egyptian Hallel, see L. Finkelstein, "The Origin of the Hallel," HUCA 23 (1950–51): 319–37; S. Zeitlin, "The Hallel: A Historical Study of the Canonization of the Hebrew Liturgy," JQR 53 (1962–63): 22–29; E. Goldschmidt, *The Passover Haggadah: Its Sources and History* (Jerusalem: Bialik, 1960), p. 55; L. Hoffman, *The Canonization of the Synagogue Service,* pp. 118–24. The association between the Hallel and Exodus may have been suggested in part by the contents of Hallel itself, which evoke the Exodus and the miracle at the Red Sea. See Ps 114:1, "When Israel went out from Egypt . . . the house of Jacob from a people of strange language, Judah became God's sanctuary, Israel his dominion. The sea looked back and fled. . . . Why is it, O sea, that you flee?" Note also the verbal correspondence between Ps 118:14 and Exod 15:2.

73. See b. *Pes.* 117a, which associates the Hallel with the "Song in the Torah" (= Exodus 15); b. *Meg.* 14a; b. *Arak.* 10a-b.

74. All citations from Philo are according to the text as published in R. Arnaldez, J. Pouilloux, and C. Mondésert, eds., *Les Oeuvres de Philon d'Alexandrie* (Paris: Editions du Cerf, 1961 f.). For additional information on the Therapeutae, see

E. Schürer, *The History of the Jewish People in the Age of Jesus Christ: A New Version Revised and Edited by G. Vermes, P. Millar and M. Black*, vol. 2 (Edinburgh: T. and T. Clark, 1979), pp. 591–97.

75. One wonders whether the custom of the Therapeutae to sing until dawn is also modeled on the Israelites' singing at the Red Sea as it was perceived in the Second Temple period, for Josephus remarks in *Jewish Antiquities* (Book II, 16:4) that after crossing the sea the Israelites stayed up *all night* composing songs to the Lord.

76. For the liturgical connotation of the word *eucharistia* in Philo, see J. Laporte, *Eucharistia in Philo* (New York: Mellen, 1983), pp. 49–97. As Laporte points out (p. 27), the term *eucharistia* is associated at least ten times with the word *hymnos* or its equivalents in Philo. For examples, see *De Ebrietate* 121, and *De Plantatione* 135.

77. Deborah's allusion to a second song sung "in the renewal of creation" seems to presuppose a tradition that in the eschatological age the redeemed will sing a song of praise to the Lord. See 1 *Enoch* 27:3–4; 61:11–12; Rev 5:9, 14:3; *Midr. Tehillim* Ps. 48, p. 276; *Cant. Rab* 1.9; *Eccl. Rab.* 1.9; and the "Hymn of Return" mentioned in the *War Scroll* from Qumran which is sung on the battlefield after the sons of light defeat the kittim. For the latter source, see Y. Yadin, *The Scroll of the War of the Sons of Light against the Sons of Darkness* (Oxford: Oxford University Press, 1962), pp. 324–29.

78. See *Eccl. Rab.* 3.14.

79. The references in Pseudo-Philo's version of Judges 5 to impending nightfall ("Wait, you hours of the day . . . for night will be upon us . . .") gives one cause to wonder whether the song was rewritten in light of some sort of evening prayer (note also that the song repeatedly refers to stars). A similar claim has been made of the Song of Abraham in chap. 17 of the *Apocalypse of Abraham*. R. Rubinkiewics (*L'Apocalypse d'Abraham* [Lublin: Société des Lettres et des Sciences de l'Université Catholique de Lublin, 1987], p. 161) has suggested that the song—with its many references to the appearance of light—may have been drawn from the morning liturgy. To be more specific, perhaps Pseudo-Philo was influenced here by liturgical songs sung on Passover eve, an occasion which the song clearly evokes in the next clause: "It will be like the night when God struck the firstborn of the Egyptians for the sake of his firstborn."

80. There are other signs that Pseudo-Philo has sought to integrate the songs in biblical narrative with the narratives which precede them. In *Bib. Ant* 31:1, for instance, Pseudo-Philo incorporates information from the Song of Deborah (Judges 5:20, which describes how the stars fought in the battle against Sisera) into the prose account of the battle ("I see the stars . . . prepared to fight along with you"). A similar phenomenon is reflected in Pseudo-Philo's paraphrase of the Prayer of Hannah. In *Bib. Ant.* 50:2 Pseudo-Philo incorporates a citation from Hannah's Prayer in 1 Sam 2:3 ("Talk no more so very proudly, let not arrogance come from your mouth") into the preceding prose account of Samuel's birth.

81. See H. Jansen, *Die spätjüdische Psalmendichtung, ihr Entstehungskreis und ihr Sitz im Leben. Eine literaturgeschichtlich-soziologische Untersuchung* (Oslo: Dybwad, 1937), and N. Johnson, *Prayer in the Apocrypha and the Pseudepigrapha: A Study of the Jewish Concept of God* (Philadelphia: Society of Biblical Literature and Exegesis, 1948). For several unsuccessful attempts to reconstruct Second Temple period liturgy from later rabbinic liturgical texts, see the studies cited in Reif, *Judaism and Hebrew Prayer*, p. 343 n. 1.

82. See L. Shiffman, "The Dead Sea Scrolls and the Early History of the Liturgy," in *The Synagogue in Late Antiquity*, ed. L. Levine (Philadelphia: ASOR, 1987), pp. 33–48; J. Maier, "Zu Kult und Liturgie der Qumrangemeinde," *RevQ* 56 (1990):

543-86; M. Weinfeld, "Prayer and Liturgical Practice in the Qumran Sect," in *The Dead Sea Scrolls: Forty Years of Research,* ed. D. Dimant and U. Rappaport (Leiden: Brill, Jerusalem: Magnes, 1992), pp. 241-58; E. Schuller, "Prayer, Hymnic and Liturgical Texts from Qumran," in *The Community of the Renewed Covenant,* ed. E. Ulrich and J. Vanderkam (Notre Dame: University of Notre Dame Press, 1994), pp. 153-71; E. Chazon, "Prayers from Qumran and Their Historical Implications," DSD 1 (1994): 265-84. There remains fragments of several liturgical documents from Qumran yet to be published. For a listing, see E. Tov, "The Unpublished Qumran Texts from Caves 4 and 11," *JJS* 43 (1992): 101-36.

83. The manuscripts of the *Words of the Luminaries* and the *Festival Prayers* from Cave 4 are published in M. Baillet, *Qumran Grotte 4,* DJD VII (Oxford: Clarendon Press, 1982), pp. 137-75 (the *Words of the Luminaries*) and 175-215 (the *Festival Prayers*). The copies of the *Festival Prayers* from Cave 1 (1Q 34 and 1Q 34 bis) were published in D. Barthélemy and J. T. Milik, *Qumran Cave 1,* DJD 1 (Oxford: Clarendon Press, 1955), pp. 136, 152-55. The English translations cited here are from F. G. Martinez and W. G. E. Watson, *The Dead Sea Scrolls Translated* (Leiden: Brill, 1994), pp. 411-18. My understanding of the *Words of the Luminaries* is indebted to Estelle Chazon's 1991 Hebrew University doctoral dissertation, "A Liturgical Document from Qumran and Its Implications: *Words of the Luminaries*" (in Hebrew with English summary).

84. Pseudo-Philo's historical catalogue appears longer than anything preserved in the Qumran material, but this difference can be partly attributed to the fact that the historical prologues of the Qumran prayers are only partially preserved. Even so, some are as long as fifteen lines and several refer to more than one incident from biblical history. See Chazon, "Liturgical Document," pp. 19-20.

85. For parallels to this midrash, see b. *Sanhedrin* 94a and *Lamentations Rabbah,* ed. S. Buber (Wilna: Wittwe and Gebrüder Romm, 1899), p. 32 (proem 30).

86. See b. *Sanh.* 99a. The origins of this tradition are unclear.

87. The rabbis differed in how they interpreted the Song of the Well in Num 21:17-18. Some, like those in the tradition cited here, saw it as a song of praise sung to thank God for the miraculous appearance of the waters. See *Midr. Tehillim,* Psalm 5, p. 50. Others described it as the means Israel used to cause the waters to spring up. See *The Fragment Targums of the Pentateuch,* vol. 1, ed. M. Klein (Rome: Biblical Institute, 1980), p. 101: "They would sing to it and it would spring up." The biblical text itself is unclear as to how the author of the narrative perceived the song's function.

88. For another rabbinic tradition which expresses disappointment with a biblical figure who does not sing to God in response to his miracles, see B. *Tanh.* Bereshit 25: "'He drove out the man' (Gen 3:24). The Holy One Blessed Be He said to him (Adam), 'You ought to have sat and sung songs for my creation of you, and for the things I have done for you, but you did not sing a song,' and I will sing my own song to myself—'Let me sing for my beloved a love song concerning his vineyard (Isa 5:1).'"

89. For the rabbinic tradition ascribing Psalm 92 to Adam, see M. Friedman, *Pesikta Rabbati* (Vienna: J. Kaiser IX, 1880), p. 46, 187b; *Midr. Tehillim,* Psalm 92, p. 404; R. Melamed, *Targum to Canticles* (Philadelphia: Dropsie College, 1921), p. 57; C. Horowitz, *Pirke de Rabbi Eliezer* (Jerusalem: Makor, 1972), p. 69. For still other texts which attribute Psalm 92 or some other psalm to Adam, see b. *Bab. Bat.* 14b; *Cant. Rab.* 4.3; *Midr. Tehillim,* Psalm 5, pp. 51-52, and Psalm 139, p. 528. For further discussion of Adam's song, see Grözinger, *Musik und Gesang,* pp. 162-64.

90. For the Song of Abraham tradition, see S. Weitzman, "The Song of Abraham," HUCA 65 (1994): 21-33.

91. See R. Rubinkiewics, "The Apocalypse of Abraham: A New Translation and Introduction," in *Old Testament Pseudepigrapha*, vol. 1, p. 697: "And he said: 'Only worship, Abraham, and recite the song which I have taught you.' . . . And I recited the song which he had taught me. And he said: 'Recite without ceasing.' And I recited and he himself recited the song. . . ." Abraham then sings a song consisting of an enumeration of divine epithets and praise culminating with a plea from the patriarch that his sacrifice be accepted and that he be granted a revelation of the future.

92. Weitzman, "The Song of Abraham."

93. J. Fitzmyer, *Genesis Apocryphon of Qumran Cave 1* (Rome: Biblical Institute, 1971), pp. 66–67.

94. For the song of Abraham in rabbinic sources, see A. Epstein. "Širat ᵓAbrāhām ᵓAbīnū," *Mimmizrāḥ umimmaᶜārāb*, vol. 1 (1894): 85–89, and Grözinger, *Musik und Gesang*, p. 187. One tradition ascribes a song to Abraham after he defeats the kings in Genesis 14 (*Gen. Rab.* 43.9). Another reports that Abraham offered "praise and thanksgiving" to the Lord after he is shown the ram's horn (i.e., the shofar) on Mount Moriah (see B. *Tanḥ.*, wayērā' 46 p. 115). According to still another midrash, the patriarch sings a song after his escape from the furnace. See S. Schechter, *Agadat Shir Ha-Shirim* (London: Deighton Bell, 1896), p. 29. Saadyia Gaon also referred to a song of Abraham in his version of the "ten song" tradition (see n. 64, this chapter), though his students seem puzzled by the reference ("We have not heard of a song of Abraham"). See A. Harkaby, *Tᵊšūbōt hag-Gᵊ'ōnim* (reprint; New York: Menorah, 1959), no. 66, pp. 30–31. Note, finally, that Abraham is associated in rabbinic sources (b. *Bab. Bat.* 15a) with Ethan the Ezrahite, the composer of Psalm 89. For a Christian reference to a song of Abraham, see C. Turner, "De utilitate hymnorum," *JTS* 24 (1923): 225–52, esp. p. 234, where Bishop Niceta refers to a lost work known as *Inquisitio Abrahae* in which a song is imputed to Abraham.

95. *Gen. Rab.* 43.9 (p. 423) reads: "And the king of Sodom said to Abraham, 'Give me the persons, but take the goods for yourself.' But Abraham said to the king of Sodom, 'I have sworn *(hărimōtí)* to the Lord God Most High' (Gen 14:21). The sages say, 'He composed a song, as it says' (in Exodus 15:2), 'I will exult him *(waᵓărōmĕmenhû)*.' Rabbi Berachiah said in the name of Elazar: 'Moses said, With the same expression that my father used in song *'hărimōtí,'* I will sing a song *''ābî waᵓărōmĕmenhû'.*'"

96. B. *Tanḥ.*, intro., p. 127: "The angel said to Jacob, 'The time has now come for me to sing a song.' . . . He responded, 'I will not let you go until you bless me.' . . . The angel said to him, 'What will become of the song whose time has already arrived?' He said to him, 'Your friends will praise.' He responded, 'But it is my time to praise.' He said, 'You can praise tomorrow if not today.' He said, 'If I come upon my companion, he will say if in your time you did not praise, so you will not praise in a time that does not belong to you' . . . (the angel) told him, 'Wait until (you are) in Bethel, and God will be there, and I will be there too. If the blessings which you took by treachery from your father meet the agreement of God, I will agree too and Esau will no longer be able to complain and murmur, as it says, "In Bethel he will find him and he will speak with us" (Hos 12:5). The verse does not say with you but with us.' . . . He said to him, 'I will not let you go until you bless me.' He said to him, 'Who will sing the song?' He said, 'I will sing in your stead,' as it says, 'He sang for the angel' (Hos 12:5 *wayyāśar 'el-maĺ'āk*)." Although this particular conclusion (where Jacob sings instead of the angel) is unique to this passage, the tradition as a whole (where the angel begs his leave of Jacob in order to sing his song) is quite common in rabbinic sources

and often concludes with the citation of Hos 12:5. See the translations in *Tg. Neofiti* and *Pseudo-Jonathan* of Gen 32:27; *Gen. Rab.* 78.2, p. 918; b. *Hul.* 92a; *Cant. Rab.* 3.6; *Lam. Rab.* 3:23, sec. 8; *Num. Rab.* 3.6; *Pirqe de Rabbi Eliezer,* p. 37; and *Bib. Ant.* 18.6. Note, in particular, *Pirqe de Rabbi Eliezer,* where the verb *wayyāśar* in Hos 12:4 is also interpreted as "to sing" but is applied to the angel who sings from the earth when Jacob refuses to release him. For further discussion of this tradition, see Grözinger, *Musik und Gesang,* pp. 81–84. For other traditions in which a biblical hero sings instead of the angels, see appendix B.

97. See C. Burchard, "Joseph and Aseneth: A New Translation and Introduction," in *Old Testament Pseudepigrapha,* vol. 2, pp. 177–247, esp. pp. 236–38. For an alternative version of the text which does not include this hymn, see M. Philonenko, *Joseph et Aséneth* (Leiden: Brill, 1968). The absence of the hymn in the latter version raises the possibility that it represents a secondary interpolation. Further evidence for this conclusion is the fact that the narrative introduction to the hymn varies from manuscript to manuscript. In MS Greek 966 in the Library of the Academy of the People's Republic of Rumania, for example, Aseneth's hymn is introduced with the statement "after she recognized (the) living God, and was released from the pollution of the idols and had renounced the dead and dumb images of the Egyptian gods, and had obtained what she wanted, giving thanks, she said to the Most High." For further discussion of the textual evidence, see C. Burchard, *Untersuchungen zu Joseph und Aseneth* (Tübingen: Mohr [Paul Siebeck], 1965), pp. 76–90, 106–7. Whether the hymn is secondary or not, it still exemplifies the larger literary/exegetical trend of retroactively imputing songs to biblical figures.

98. See S. Lieberman, ed., *Deuteronomy Rabbah* (Jerusalem: Bamberger and Wahrmann, 1940) 2.20, p. 59. Note also the tradition preserved in *Midr. Tehillim,* Psalm 90, p. 387, which attributes eleven psalms to Moses.

99. See *Tg. Jonathan* 1 Kgs 5:12b; Judg 5:1, 12a; 2 Sam 22:1; Isa 26:19; 30:29a; Zep 3:14; *Tg. Onk.* Exod 15:1; Num 21:17; Deut 31:19, etc.

100. See chapter 2, n. 42.

101. See B. *Tanh.,* 'aḥare 14, p. 68: "For from the rising of the sun to its setting my name is great among the nations" (Mal 1:11). "From the hour that the sun rises until the hour that it sets, the sun does not cease to praise God as it says 'from the rising of the sun . . .' Thus you find that when Joshua arose to fight at Gibeon, what is written there: 'Then spoke Joshua to the Lord in the day when the Lord gave the Amorites over to the men of Israel; and he said in the sight of Israel, "Sun, be still . . ."'" (Josh 10:12). "When Joshua sought to stop the sun, he said, 'Sun, be quiet,' not 'Sun, stand still.' Why did he do this? Because as long as the sun praises, it has the power to move; the moment it falls silent, it stops. Therefore, in order to stop it, Joshua told it to be quiet. The sun said to him, 'You are telling me to be quiet? Is there a young man who can tell an older man to shut up? I was created on the fourth day and you were created on the sixth day and you tell me to shut up?' Joshua replied, 'If a young master has an older servant, does the former not have the right to tell the latter to be quiet? Did not Abraham our father acquire the heavens and all its contents, as it says, "Blessed be Abraham by the Lord most High, possessor of Heaven and earth" (Gen 14:19), and is this not why you bowed before Joseph, as it says, "and behold, the sun and the moon and eleven stars were bowing before me" (Gen 37:9), so be quiet!' The sun responded, 'Are you telling me to be quiet?' Joshua replied, 'Yes.' The sun said, 'But who will say my praise in my stead?' Joshua said 'Be still, and I will say it,' as it says, 'and then (*'āz*) Joshua spoke.' Is the *'āz* not a song as it says, 'and then (*'āz*) Moses sang' (Exod 15:1)." For parallels, see *Tanh.* 'aḥare 9; *Gen. Rab.* 6.9, p. 50; *Midr. Tehillim,* Ps 19, p. 170; the targumic rendering of Josh 10:12; and the medieval

biblical paraphrase *Sefer Ha-Yashar,* ed. Y. Dan (Jerusalem: Bialik Institute, 1986), chap. 21, pp. 337–38.

102. A similar interpretation may lie behind the "Book of Song" mentioned in LXX 3 Kgs 8:53 (= MT 1 Kgs 8:12), which may reflect a metathesized reading of "Book of Yashar." Note also the translation of "Yashar" in the Syriac version of Josh 10:12 as *tešboḥta* (praise). For other aggadic traditions centered on a pun on the Hebrew root for song, see I. Gruenwald, "A Technique of the Midrash: Linkage by Sound Patterns," *Hasifrut* 1 (1968): 726–27 (in Hebrew).

103. C. Newsom, "'The Psalms of Joshua' from Qumran Cave 4," *JJS* 39 (1988): 56–73.

104. b. *Abod. Zar.* 24b; *Gen. Rab.* 54.4, pp. 581–82; *Midrash Samuel* (S. Buber; Cracow: J. Fisher, 1893), 12.3; *Seder Eliyahu Rabbah* (M. Friedman, reprint; Jerusalem: Bamberger and Wahrman, 1960), chap. 12; *Tanh.* wayyakhēl 7; *Eccl. Rab.* 11.58. According to b. *Aboda Zara,* Rabbi Ashi associates Rabbi Nappaḥa's song with another biblical verse, Num 10:35, claiming that the Israelites recited it during the wilderness period "whenever the ark set out."

105. See G. Scholem, "The Merkabah Hymns and the Song of the Kine in a Talmudic Passage," *Jewish Gnosticism, Merkabah Mysticism and Talmudic Tradition* (New York: Jewish Theological Seminary of America, 1960), pp. 20–30. For an alternative assessment of the song, see I. Gruenwald, *Apocalyptic and Merkavah Mysticism,* p. 41 n. 56: "the song of the Kine . . . is in its form and in its style closer to the angelological liturgy of Qumran than . . . to the . . . Hekhalot hymns."

106. Cf. the examples of similar word play cited by Gruenwald, "A Technique of the Midrash," p. 727. In one example, Exodus 15 is placed in the mouth of an ox. For other rabbinic traditions which ascribe divine praise to nonhuman creatures, see M. Bet Ariyeh, "Pereq širāh: An Introduction and Critical Edition," Ph.D. diss., Hebrew University, Jerusalem, 1966, chap. 4 (in Hebrew).

107. For David's growing reputation as a poet in early Judaism, see J. Kugel, "Topics in the History of the Spirituality of the Psalms," in *Jewish Spirituality,* vol. 1, ed. A. Green (New York: Crossroad, 1987), pp. 134–36. The songs of David recorded in biblical narrative will be discussed in chap. 5.

108. For analysis of this song, see J. Strugnell, "More Psalms of David," CBQ 27 (1965): 207–16.

109. See P. Bogaert, "Les Antiquités Bibliques de Pseudo-Philon à lumière des découvertes de Qumrân. Observations sur l' hymnologie et particulièrement sur la chapitre 60," in *Qumran: Sa piété, sa théologie et son milieu,* pp. 313–31.

110. See J. Sanders, *Psalms Scroll,* pp. 134–37.

111. Note also that LXX 3 Kgs 8:53 (= MT 1 Kgs 8:12) reports that Solomon's benediction spoken at the consecration of the temple is preserved in a "Book of Song." See n. 102. For translations of the *Psalms of Solomon* and *Odes of Solomon,* see R. Wright, "Psalms of Solomon: A New Translation and Introduction," in *Old Testament Pseudepigrapha,* vol. 2, pp. 639–70, and J. Charlesworth, "Odes of Solomon: A New Translation and Introduction," in ibid., pp. 725–71.

112. *Aggadat Bereshit,* ed. S. Buber, (Cracow: J. Fischer, 1903), sec. 59, pp. 119–20.

113. R. Kraft with H. Attridge, R. Spittler, and J. Timble, *Testament of Job according to the SV Text* (Missoula: Scholars Press, 1974), pp. 74–75. For the hypothesis that the *Testament of Job* originated among the Therapeutae, see M. Philonenko, *Le Testament de Job: Introduction, traduction et notes, Semitica* 18 (Paris: Adrien-Maisoneuve, 1968), pp. 21–23, and R. Spittler, "The Testament of Job: A New Translation and Introduction," in *Old Testament Peudepigrapha,* vol. 1, pp. 833–34. For analysis of the other poetic passages within the *Testament of Job,* see Flusser, "Psalms, Hymns and Prayers," pp. 563–64.

114. In addition to the songs attributed to David and Solomon, note also two Syriac apocryphal psalms attributed to King Hezekiah. For translations, see "More Psalms of David," *Old Testament Pseudepigrapha*, vol. 2, pp. 620–24. One of the two psalms is said to have been performed when Hezekiah was surrounded by the Assyrians.

115. In this context we cannot enter into the enormous and still unresolved debate over the relation of Philo's biblical exegesis to rabbinic exegesis. Among the many who see a connection, see E. Stein, *Philo und der Midrash* (Giessen, 1931); S. Belkin, *Philo and Oral Law* (Cambridge: Harvard University Press, 1940), esp. p. 10; and N. Cohen, "The Jewish Dimension of Philo's Judaism: An Elucidation of de Spec. Leg. IV 132-150," *JJS* 38 (1987): 165–86. For those who minimize the connection, see I. Heineman, *Philons griechische und Jüdische Bildung* (Breslau: M. and H. Marcus, 1932), and S. Sandmel, *Philo's Place in Judaism* (New York: Ktav, 1971), pp. 3–26.

116. For Philo's attitude toward oaths and vows, see Belkin, *Philo and the Oral Law*, pp. 140–78.

117. For early Jewish attitudes toward oaths and vows, see S. Liebermann, *Greek in Jewish Palestine* (New York: Jewish Theological Seminary, 1942), pp. 115–43, and L. Schiffman, *Sectarian Law in the Dead Sea Scrolls: Courts, Testimony and the Penal Code* (Chico: Scholars Press, 1983), pp. 133–54.

118. Compare *Tg. Onkelos*'s translation of Genesis 14:22, which renders the phrase "I have raised my hand" as "I have raised my hand *in prayer.*" The raising or stretching out of the hands appears to have been construed as a gesture of prayer or blessing even in biblical times. See Pss. 63:5 and 134:2 and Josephus, *Against Apion* 1, 22, which quotes the pagan Agatharchides, who, when mocking the Jewish observance of the Sabbath, remarks that the Jews *spread out their hands in their holy places* and pray until evening. Note also that early Jewish synagogue art sometimes represents figures, including biblical figures, with raised arms—perhaps to indicate that they are praying. For example, in the partially preserved image of Daniel in the lion's den from the Naaran synagogue (sixth century C.E.), he stands with raised arms (see R. Hachili, *Ancient Jewish Art and Archaeology in the Land of Israel* [Leiden: Brill, 1988], pp. 294–95).

119. Rabbi Berachiah's association of the Song of the Sea with Abraham's song in Genesis 14 is based on the verbal similarity between *hărimōtî* ("*I have raised* my hand") in Gen 14:22 and *waʾărōměmenhû* ("I will exult him") in Exodus 15:2.

5. Self-fulfilling Poetry

1. For the evidence bearing on the date of the additions, see C. Moore, *Daniel, Esther and Jeremiah: The Additions*, AB (Garden City: Doubleday, 1977), pp. 44–49, and J. Collins, *Daniel* (Minneapolis: Augsburg Fortress, 1993), p. 207. For a review of the evidence placing the original form of Daniel 3 in the Persian or Greek period, see Collins, *Daniel*, pp. 193–94.

2. Both the Theodotian and the LXX versions of the additions are printed in J. Ziegler, *Susanna, Daniel, Bet et Draco, Septuaginta*, Vetus Testamentum Graecum Auctoritate Societatis Litterarum Gottingensis 16/2 (Göttingen: Vandenhoeck and Ruprecht, 1954). Most scholars agree that the prayer and song were originally composed not in Greek but in a Semitic language, either Aramaic or Hebrew. M. Gaster ("The Unknown Aramaic Original of Theodotian's Additions to the Book of Daniel," PSBA 16 [1894]: 280–317, and 17 [1895]: 75–91) published an Aramaic version of the additions; but whatever the original language of composition, it is unlikely that Gasters text preserves *the* original Aramaic version of Theodotian's additions, as Gaster claimed. See Collins, *Daniel*, pp. 199, 205.

3. Following general practice, I refer to the prayer as the Prayer of Azariah

because it is attributed to Azariah in the Theodotian version. In the LXX, it is attributed to all three martyrs. It is not clear which attribution is more original, but the latter is consistent with the use of the first person plural in the prayer itself.

4. The first verse number indicates the position of the verse if one were to read it as part of the narrative in Daniel 3; the second indicates the position of the verse if one reads the additions as an independent text (i.e., as it appears in NRSV).

5. The tension between the prose inset and the preceding narrative in Dan 3:22 argues against the claim that the prose inset originated as an integral part of the story and somehow fell out of MT. See Moore, *Additions*, pp. 64-65.

6. Compare W. Daubney, *The Three Additions to Daniel* (Cambridge: Deighton Bell, 1906), p. 42; C. Kuhl, *Die drei Männer im Feure*, BZAW 55 (Giessen: Alfred Töppelmann, 1930), pp. 161-64; Moore, *Additions*, pp. 60, 64-65; Collins, *Daniel*, p. 198.

7. Scholars believe that the Prayer of Azariah may have been added after the song and the prose inset were already in place in Daniel 3 because the brief narrative preceding the prayer in vss. 24-25 = 1-2 makes more sense as an introduction to the Song of the Three than it does as an introduction to the prayer: "They walked around in the midst of the flames, *singing hymns to God and blessing the Lord*." This suggests that the prayer was interposed between vss. 24-25 and the song which originally belong together. Also, the prayer's petition for help seems superfluous given that the three friends appear immune to the flames even before its recital. See Moore, *Additions*, p. 65.

8. Other Second Temple period compositions also report the "conversion" of foreign kings once hostile to the Jews. At the end of 3 *Maccabees*, for example, the Hellenistic Egyptian king Ptolemy IV Philopater relents from persecuting the Jews and then praises God (6:22-29). The same is true of Antiochus IV, in 2 *Maccabees*, who is said to have actually become a Jew (9:17).

9. Cf. Moore, *Additions*, p. 26: "Intended or not, the effect of the Prayer of Azariah and the Hymn of the Three Young Men is to shift the spotlight from the pagan king and the story's lavish setting to the faith of three martyrs and the greatness of their God."

10. See b. *Pes* 118a; *Exod. Rab.* 18.5; *Midr. Tehillim*, Psalm 117, p. 480.

11. The root *šyr* was sufficiently familar to early Jewish speakers of Aramaic that it was sometimes left untranslated in Aramaic translations of the Bible. See *Tg. Neofiti* for Gen 31:27.

12. LXX has a different rendering: "Then Hananiah, Azariah and Mishael prayed and sang hymns to the Lord when the king commanded them to be thrown into the furnace." If my analysis is correct, Theodotian's text preserves the more original reading.

13. Since the dousing of the flames is not mentioned in the Semitic version of Daniel in MT, 3 *Maccabees* would appear to preserve the earliest reference to the Greek additions. See Collins, *Daniel*, p. 72.

14. See Moore, *Additions*, p. 26. Whether or not the song was composed for use in a liturgical setting, it was eventually adopted for liturgical use in Christianity and is included in Christian lists of canticles/odes. See Daubney, *Three Additions*, pp. 83-97.

15. The song's reference to the temple represents an anachronism, since at the time of the story (just after the Babylonian exile), the temple was not standing. Some have concluded from this that the song is not referring to the temple in Jerusalem but to the heavenly temple. See Moore, *Additions*, pp. 69-70.

16. See m. *Yoma* 3:8, which reports that the phrase "Blessed be the name of the glory of his kingdom forever" was recited in the temple in response to the pronouncement of God's name by the high priest on the Day of Atonement. The refrain was evidently well known by the end of the Second Temple period. Note that it was added to the version of Psalm 145 in the Psalms Scroll found in Qumran cave 11. See J. Sanders, *The Psalms Scroll from Qumran Cave 11 [11QPs^a]*, DJD 4 (London: Oxford University Press, 1965), pp. 66–67.

17. Some scholars believe that the song was directly influenced by Psalm 136. See Daubney, *Three Additions*, pp. 25–26; Moore, *Additions*, pp. 75–76; Flusser, "Psalms, Prayers and Hymns," p. 554. There are also striking parallels between the song and Psalm 148. It is not clear whether the song was consciously modeled on biblical psalms, but such modeling would be consistent with the canon-conscious identification of the Psalms with the songs sung by biblical heroes.

18. When this line appears within a narrative setting, it is often cited in the context of levitical or cultic singing. See 1 Chr 16:34, 41; 2 Chr 7:3, 6; Ezra 3:11.

19. See n. 14, this chapter.

20. One wonders whether this temporal marker was meant to evoke Exodus 15 and Judges 5, for it fuses the language used to introduce the Song of the Sea (*"Then* Moses sang") and the Song of Deborah and Barak ("Deborah and Barak . . . sang *on that day*").

21. In Chronicles the word "regularly" is used almost exclusively in liturgical contexts to describe the regular daily or weekly performance of the sacrificial service. See J. Kleinig, *The Lord's Song* (Sheffield: JSOT, 1993), p. 53.

22. The Chronicler represents David as having played a central role in establishing cultic practices in the Jerusalem Temple. See 1 Chr 6:31-32 [Heb 6:16-17], 23:4-5, 30-31, 25:1; 2 Chr 8:14, 23:18, 29:25, and 35:15. With this evidence in mind, many scholars argue that 1-2 Chronicles represents a kind of charter for the cult of the Second Temple period, seeking to justify current cultic practices by attributing them to Israel's most illustrious king. See J. Newsome, "Toward a New Understanding of the Chronicler and His Purposes," JBL 94 (1975): 201-17; S. J. de Vries, "Moses and David as Cult Founders in Chronicles," JBL 107 (1988): 619-39; J. Kleinig, "The Divine Institution of the Lord's Song in Chronicles," JSOT 55 (1992): 75-83, and *Lord's Song*; S. Japhet, *The Ideology of the Book of Chronicles and Its Place in Biblical Thought* (Frankfurt am Main: Peter Lang, 1989), pp. 226-32; W. Riley, *King and Cultus in Chronicles: Worship and the Reinterpretation of History* (Sheffield: JSOT, 1993).

23. J. Wellhausen, *Prolegomenon to the History of Ancient Israel* (reprint; Gloucester, Mass.: Peter Smith, 1973). Many scholars now reject Wellhausen's dating of P to the postexilic period. See Y. Kaufman, *The History of the Israelite Religion: From Antiquity to the End of the Second Temple* (Tel Aviv: Dvir, 1937-1948) (in Hebrew); M. Haran, *Temples and Temple Service in Ancient Israel* (Oxford: Clarendon Press, 1978); A. Hurvitz, "The Evidence of Language in Dating the Priestly Code," *Revue Biblique* 81 (1974): 24-56, and *A Linguistic Study of the Relationship between the Priestly Source and the Book of Ezekiel* (Paris: J. Gibalda, 1982).

24. Cf. G. von Rad, *Das Geschichtsbild des chronistischen Werkes* (Stuttgart: Kohlhammer, 1930), pp. 98-115, and P. Hanson, *The People Called: The Growth of Community in the Bible* (San Francisco: Harper and Row, 1986), pp. 302-3.

25. See S. Japhet, "Conquest and Settlement in Chronicles," JBL 98 (1979): 205-18.

26. Japhet, "Conquest and Settlement," pp. 217-18. If the contents of the song reflect the ideology of the Chronicler, it is obviously unlikely that it represents a secondary interpolation, as some scholars have claimed (e.g., W. Rudolph,

Chronikbücher [Tübingen: Mohr, 1955], p. 127). For this and other reasons, most recent commentators believe that the Chronicler constructed the song himself. See J. A. Loader, "Redaction and Function of the Chronistic 'Psalm of David'," in *Studies in the Chronicler,* ed. W. van Wyk (Johannesburg: University of Pretoria, 1976), pp. 67–75; T. C. Butler, "A Forgotten Passage from a Forgotten Era (1 Chr. XVI 8–36)," VT 28 (1978): 142–50; A. E. Hill, "Patchwork Poetry or Reasoned Verse? Connective Structure in 1 Chron. 16," VT 33 (1983): 97–101; Kleinig, *Lord's Song,* pp. 134–48.

27. See E. Slomovic, "Toward an Understanding of the Formation of Historical Titles in the Book of Psalms," ZAW 91 (1979): 350–80; Hill, "Patchwork," p. 99; Kleinig, *Lord's Song,* pp. 134–39.

28. Scholars differ over how to understand the word "invoke" here. One view is that it refers to praise sung during the presentation of the memorial offering in the sacrificial ritual. Cf. Pss 38:1 and 70:1 and Isa 66:3. Another is that it was meant to recall the use of trumpets in Num 10:9-10, which employs the same verb to describe the blowing of trumpets on festival days. For a review of the possibilities, see Kleinig, *Lord's Song,* p. 36.

29. When the Chronicler refers to the "law of Moses" (2 Chr 23:18), the "book of Moses" (2 Chr 25:4), or the "law of Yahweh" (1 Chr 16:40), it is not clear whether he is referring to the Pentateuch as such or to some other sacred corpus. See J. Shaver, *Torah and the Chronicler's History Work* (Atlanta: Scholars Press, 1989). Whatever the identity of this text, the Chronicler obviously has some sacred text in mind; moreover, he exhibits other behaviors characteristic of a scripturalizing imagination, looking to the biblical past as recorded in narratives such as 1-2 Samuel to address the needs of the present, seeking out links between biblical narrative and other sacred texts such as Psalms, and reading the biblical past in light of the liturgical present.

30. The composition of Chronicles is placed at various points between the sixth century B.C.E. and the third century B.C.E. The mention of the Persian kingdom in 2 Chr 36:20 makes 539 the earliest date of composition, while the absence of Greek influence on the book suggests it was composed before the Hellenistic age. For these reasons, many scholars place the date of composition in the fourth century. For further discussion, see H. G. M. Williamson, *1 and 2 Chronicles,* NCB (London: Marshall, Morgan, and Scott, 1982), pp. 15-16, and S. Japhet, *I and II Chronicles* (Louisville: Westminster, 1993), pp. 23-28.

31. See W. Gesenius, *Philologish-kritischer und historischer Commentar über den Prophet Jesaja,* vol. 2 (Leipzig: Vogel, 1821), pp. 932-36. Since Genesius's analysis, most commentators have held the view that the narrative material in Isaiah 36-39 has been borrowed from Kings and incorporated within Isaiah as an historical appendix. Some now disagree, however, arguing that Isaiah 36-39 is original to Isaiah. See A. Jepsen, *Die Quellen des Königbuches* (Halle: M. Niemeyer, 1953), p. 77; K. Smelik, "Distortion of Old Testament Prophecy: The Purpose of Isaiah XXXVI and XXXVII," OTS 24 (1989): 70-93, and "King Hezekiah Advocates True Prophecy," *Converting the Past* (Leiden: Brill, 1992), pp. 93-128; C. Seitz, *Zion's Final Destiny: The Development of the Book of Isaiah* (Minneapolis: Fortress, 1991). For analysis of the textual problems in Isaiah 38 = 2 Kings 20, see K. Fullerton, "The Original Text of 2 K 20:7-11 = Is. 38:7,8,21," JBL 44 (1925): 44-62; H. Orlinsky, "The Kings-Isaiah Recensions of the Hezekiah Story," JQR 30 (1939-40): 33-49; H. Nyberg, "Hiskias Dankleid Jes 38, 9-20," ASTI 9 (1973): 85-97.

32. Among the many scholars who have held this view, see O. Kaiser, *Isaiah 13-39: A Commentary,* trans. R. Wilson, OTL (London; SCM, 1974), pp. 401-4; H. Wilderberger, *Jesaja. III. Jesaja 28-39,* BKAT (Neukirchen-Vuyn: Neukirchener Ver-

lag, 1982), pp. 1455-58; Watts, *Psalm and Story,* p. 126. Although there is no way to date the interpolation itself with any precision, it is worth noting that the book of Isaiah as a whole underwent significant revision in the postexilic period. Chapters 40-66 (Second Isaiah and Third Isaiah) are universally attributed by modern scholars to the postexilic period.

33. The use of the term *miktāb* ("writing") to describe the song, a term which in later dialects of Hebrew came to mean "letter," has been explained in a number of ways. H. Ginsberg ("Psalms and Inscriptions of Petition and Acknowledgement," in *L. Ginzberg Jubilee Volume* [New York: American Academy for Jewish Research, 1945], pp. 159-71, esp. p. 169) reads it as an indication that Hezekiah's psalm was originally published as a votive inscription (a similar term *miktām* is translated as "stela" in the LXX). More recently, W. Hallo ("The Royal Correspondence of Larsa: A Sumerian Prototype for the Prayer of Hezekiah," in *Kramer Anniversary Volume,* ed. B. Eichler [Kevelaer: Butzon and Bercker, 1976], pp. 209-24) has connected the term *miktāb* to an ancient Near Eastern tradition of royal "letter-prayers" addressed by the king to a deity. I find these analogies intriguing, but I would also note that at least two narratives composed in the Second Temple period describe the writing down of a hymn or hymns attributed to righteous Israelites. See *Tobit* 13:1; T. *Job* 51:3. This evidence suggests that the writing down of a hymn of praise may be a motif drawn not from ancient Near Eastern literary practice but from early Jewish literary practice.

34. Cf. Childs, "Psalm Title and Midrashic Exegesis," pp. 141-42, 148.

35. E. Tov, *Textual Criticism of the Hebrew Bible* (Minneapolis: Fortress, 1992), pp. 340-42. See also Y. Zakovitch, "Assimilation in Biblical Narrative," in *Empirical Models for Biblical Criticism,* ed. J. Tigay (Philadelphia: University of Pennsylvania Press, 1985), pp. 175-96, esp. pp. 181-85.

36. See Watts, *Psalm and Story,* p. 127 n. 1.

37. See *Cant. Rab.* 4.19.

38. Second Chr 32:24-25 is often thought to allude to Hezekiah's arrogant display of his wealth to foreign emissaries as described in 2 Ki 20:12-19. See E. Curtis and A. Madsen, *The Book of Chronicles* (Edinburgh: T. and T. Clark, 1910), p. 491. There is no reason to believe that this interpretation is more likely than the reading proposed here, which argues that Hezekiah's failure to "respond for the benefit done to him" refers to his failure to thank God properly after his recovery. Cf. Kleinig (*Lord's Song,* pp. 127-28), who suggests that the verse refers to Hezekiah's failure to make a thanksgiving offering.

39. The first to classify Hezekiah's psalm as a thanksgiving hymn was J. Begrich, *Der Psalm des Hiskia: Ein Beitrag zum Verstadnis von Jesaja 38: 10-20* (Göttingen: Vandenhoeck and Ruprecht, 1926), p. 17. Most commentators accept this classification, though they note that the psalm does exhibit characteristics of other genres as well. Cf. Seitz, *Zion's Final Destiny* (pp. 168-69): "the classification 'thanksgiving' is appropriate so long as the fluidity of the genre is kept in mind."

40. See B. Stade, "Anmerkungen zu 1 Kö 15-21," ZAW 6 (1886): 156-89, esp. p. 185, and B. Duhm, *Das Buch Jesaia,* HKAT (Göttingen: Vandenhoeck and Ruprecht, 1902), p. 247.

41. Hallo, "Royal Correspondence."

42. The debate surrounding the prayer's genre is summarized by G. Landes, "Kerygma of the Book of Jonah: The Contextual Interpretation of the Jonah Psalm," Int 21 (1967): 3-31, esp. pp. 3-5;, and J Ackerman, "Satire and Symbolism in the Song of Jonah," in *Traditions in Transformation: Festschrift for F. M. Cross,* ed. B. Halpern and J. Levinson (Winona Lake, Ind.: Eisenbrauns, 1981), pp. 213-15.

43. Both Landes and Ackerman hold this view, which actually represents a return

to a position held long ago by H. Gunkel. See Gunkel, *Ausgewählte Psalmen,* 3d ed. (Göttingen: Vandenhoeck and Ruprecht, 1911), p. 289.

44. For a brief review of early interpretations of the Prayer of Jonah (many of which see it as a song of thanksgiving), see E. Bickerman, *Four Strange Books of the Bible* (New York: Schocken, 1967), p. 12.

45. See E. Schuller, *Non-Canonical Psalms from Qumran* (Atlanta: Scholars Press, 1986), pp. 26–27. For the semantic range of the word "prayer" in biblical Hebrew, see J. Sawyer, "Types of Prayer in the Old Testament: Some Semantic Observations on Hitpallel, Hithannen, etc.," *Semitics* 7 (1980): 131–39, esp. pp. 133–34.

46. B. Childs, "The Canonical Shape of the Book of Jonah," in *Biblical and Near Eastern Studies: Essays in Honor of William Sanford LaSor* (Grand Rapids: Eerdmans, 1979), pp. 122–28.

47. J. Miles, "Laughing at the Bible: Jonah as Parody," *JQR* 65 (1974–1975): 168–81; Ackerman, "Satire and Symbolism"; Holbert, "Deliverance Belongs to Yahweh," J. Magonet, *Form and Meaning: Studies in the Literary Techniques of the Book of Jonah* (Frankfurt: Lang, 1976), pp. 51–53; M. Orth, "The Effects of Parody in the Book of Jonah," in W. Hallo et al., eds., *The Bible in the Light of Cuneiform Literature* (Lewiston: Mellen, 1990), pp. 257–81; Watts, *Psalm and Story,* p. 144.

48. M. Sternberg, *The Poetics of Biblical Narrative* (Bloomington: Indiana University Press, 1985), pp. 318–20; A. Hauser, "Jonah in Pursuit of the Dove," *JBL* 104 (1985): 21–37.

49. H. Jauss, *Toward an Aesthetic of Reception,* trans. T. Bahti (Minneapolis: University of Minnesota Press, 1982), p. 23.

50. See E. Qimron, "The Language of the Book of Jonah," *BM* 25 (1980): 181–82 (in Hebrew); A. Rofé, *The Prophetical Stories* (Jerusalem: Magnes, 1988), pp. 152–70; J. Sasson, *Jonah,* AB (Garden City: Doubleday, 1990), pp. 20–28.

51. See Magonet, *Form and Meaning,* pp. 44–49, and Ackermann, "Satire and Symbolism," p. 221.

52. Those who have argued that the Prayer of Hannah is a secondary interpolation include O. Thenius, *Die Bücher Samuels,* 2d ed. (Leipzig: Hirzel, 1864), pp. 11–12; H. Smith, *The Books of Samuel,* ICC (New York: Scribner, 1899); K. Budde, *Die Bücher Samuel,* KHAT (Tübingen: Mohr, 1902), pp. 13–14; H. Thackeray, "The Song of Hannah and Other Lessons and Psalms for the Jewish New Year's Day," *JTS* 16 (1914–15): 177–204, esp. pp. 183–84; Hertzberg, *I & II Samuel* (London: Scholars Press, 1964), p. 29. As was true of Jonah's Prayer, I refer to 1 Samuel 2 as a "prayer" because of the way it is introduced in the MT: "Hannah also prayed and said." The versions preserve several different forms of this verse. Codex Vaticanus omits the reference to prayer and reads simply "And she said," a reading which some scholars — T. Lewis, for example ("The Textual History of the Song of Hannah: 1 Samuel 2:1-10," *VT* 44 [1994]: 18–46, esp. p. 25) — prefer over that which is attested in the MT. By contrast, LXX MS v seems expansionistic: "And she prayed this song until the end and said . . . " The phrase "this song" here is probably a secondary expansion, for manuscripts of LXX often add the phrase "this song" in verses introducing songs or songlike compositions in biblical narrative. See LXX Judg 5:1; 2 Ki 22:2; Isa 5:1, 26:1, 38; Hab 3:1. The addition of this phrase seems to reflect the developing tradition of "ode" collections in early Christianity.

53. The textual evidence is discussed by Smith, *The Books of Samuel,* pp. 13–14; E. Tov, "Some Sequence Differences between the MT and LXX and Their Ramifications for the Literary Criticism of the Bible," *JNSL* 13 (1987): 151–160, esp. pp. 157–58; P. K. McCarter, *I Samuel,* AB (Garden City: Doubleday, 1980), pp. 57–58; Watts, *Psalm and Story,* pp. 34–36. For the publication of 4QSam^a, see F.

M. Cross, "A New Qumran Biblical Fragment Related to the Original Hebrew underlying the Septuagint," BASOR 132 (1953): 15-26.

54. S. Walters ("Hannah and Anna: The Greek and Hebrew Texts of 1 Samuel 1," JBL 107 [1988]: 385-412) has argued that the Hebrew and Greek versions of 1 Samuel 2 represent two distinct narratives, with one version deliberately changed in part to exclude women from participation in the cult.

55. For mention of this type-scene and its conventional motifs, see Alter, *Art of Biblical Narrative*, p. 181. Note also the comparison of Judges 13 with 1 Samuel 1 in Y. Zakovitch, *The Life of Samson* (Jerusalem: Magnes, 1982), pp. 21-33 (in Hebrew).

56. Some scholars have argued that the language and text of 1 Samuel 2 are later than Psalm 113 (see D. N. Freedman, "Psalm 113 and the Song of Hannah," *Pottery, Poetry and Prophecy,* pp. 243-61), a thesis which would seem to support my contention that 1 Samuel 2 is citing Psalm 113. However, A. Hurwitz ("Originals and Imitations in Biblical Poetry: A Comparative Examination of 1 Samuel 2:1-10 and Psalm 113:5-9," in *Biblical and Related Studies Presented to Samuel Iwry,* ed. A. Kort and S. Morshauser [Winona Lake, Ind.: Eisenbrauns, 1985]) has demonstrated that the language of Ps 113:5-9 is in fact more recent than that reflected in 1 Samuel 2 by showing that Psalm 113 contains "pseudo-archaisms" from the post-exilic period which imperfectly imitate standard biblical Hebrew. This discovery may at first seem to rule out the possibility that 1 Samuel 2 is citing Psalm 113 (how can an earlier text cite a later text?), but it does not, for 1 Samuel 2 may be citing an archaic version of Psalm 113 in a textual form no longer extant. On its own merits, this suggestion is no more and no less likely than other explanations for the similarity, but the point is that the linguistic/textual relationship between these two texts cannot be used to determine their *literary* relationship, since we know so little about the transmission of the biblical text in the Second Temple period. I wish to thank Professor Hurvitz for discussing this issue with me.

57. *Pesikta Rabbati* (Vienna: J. Kaiser IX, 1880) 43, p. 189b.

58. Cf. L. Feldman, "Prolegomenon," in *The Biblical Antiquities of Philo,* ed. M. James (New York: Ktav, 1971), p. cxxx; and see also L. Ginzberg, *The Legends of the Jews,* vol. 6 (Philadelphia: Jewish Publication Society, 1967), p. 216 n. 9.

59. For a detailed commentary on Pseudo-Philo's version of Hannah's Prayer, see M. Philonenko, "Une Paraphrase du Cantique d' Anne," *Revue d'Histoire et de Philosophie Religieuses* 42 (1963): 157-68.

60. The Song of Hannah has been dated by some scholars to the early monarchic period based on stylistic, orthographic, and linguistic evidence. See W. F. Albright, *Yahweh and the Gods of Canaan* (New York: Doubleday, 1969), pp. 5-10; J. T. Willis, "The Song of Hannah and Psalm 113," CBQ 25 (1973): 139-54; D. N. Freedman, "Divine Names and Titles in Early Hebrew Poetry," in *Magnalia Dei: The Mighty Acts of God: Essays on the Bible and Archaeology in Memory of G. Ernest Wright,* ed. F. M. Cross et al. (Garden City: Doubleday, 1976), pp. 55-107, esp. pp. 55 and 96. For an attempt to date the song to the post-exilic period, see R. Tourney, "Le Cantique d'Anne," in *Mélanges Dominique Barthélemy,* ed. P. Casetti (Göttingen: Vandenhoeck and Ruprecht, 1981), pp. 553-76. The date of the song's composition remains an open question.

61. For the Hallel's origins, see the studies cited in chap. 4, n. 72.

62. The hymn in 2 Samuel 22, which appears to be a doublet of Psalm 18, is almost universally identified as a thanksgiving song or victory ode. See E. Briggs, *A Critical and Exegetical Commentary on the Book of Psalms,* vol. 1 (Edinburgh: T. and T. Clark, 1906), p. 139; A. Weiser, *The Psalms: A Commentary* (London: SCM, 1962),

p. 185; D. Berry, *The Psalms and the Reader: Interpretive Strategies for Psalm 1* (Sheffield: JSOT, 1993), pp. 59–80.

63. Many scholars have noted that these narratives share a number of traits. The first episode in 2 Sam 21:1–14 describes how David lifted a famine from the land by executing seven sons of Saul to expiate for the latter's slaughter of the Gibeonites; the second narrative in 2 Samuel 24 describes how David's census brought a plague upon Israel, which is lifted when David builds an altar to the Lord on the threshing floor of Araunah, the future site of the Jerusalem Temple. Both narratives involve divine anger resulting in catastrophe (famine and pestilence) and an act of expiation by King David, and both bear some connection to a cultic site (Gibeon; the future site of the temple in Jerusalem). For discussion of these parallels and their significance for understanding the literary development of 2 Samuel 21–24, see W. Fuss, "II Samuel 24," ZAW 74 (1962): 145–64.

64. See H. P. Smith, *A Critical and Exegetical Commentary on the Books of Samuel,* ICC (New York: Scribner, 1899), p. xxvii; K. Budde, *Die Bücher Samuel* KHAT 8 (Tübingen: Mohr, 1902), p. 304; P. K. McCarter, *II Samuel,* AB (Garden City: Doubleday, 1984).

65. The verse which introduces the song, 2 Sam 22:1, betrays an awareness that the preceding narrative does not provide clear information about the song's temporal setting, for it tucks this information into its introduction to the song: "And David spoke the words of this song *on the day when the Lord delivered him from the hand of all his enemies and from the hand of Saul.*" An instructive contrast is Deut 31:30, the syntactically similar verse which introduces the Song of Moses. This verse does not contain a bulky temporal clause as does 2 Sam 22:1 because the song's setting and motivation have been described in the preceding narrative in chapter 31.

66. See Budde, *Die Bücher Samuel,* p. 313.

67. The relation of 2 Samuel 22 to Psalm 18 is as difficult to assess as the relationship between Hannah's Prayer and Psalm 113. Some believe that the author of 2 Samuel 22 has simply repeated or adopted Psalm 18. See, for example, R. Carlson, *David, the Chosen King* (Stockholm: Almqvist and Wiksell, 1964), pp. 250–52, who argues that the redactor of 2 Samuel introduced subtle changes into the song so that it would better fit its narrative context in the story of David. Others have argued that the version preserved in 2 Samuel 22 is actually older than the version in Psalm 18. See E. Melamed, "2 Samuel 22–Psalm 18," in *Biblical Studies in Texts, Translations and Commentaries* (Jerusalem: Magnes, 1984), pp. 49–60 (in Hebrew), who claims that Psalm 18 represents a reworking of 2 Samuel 22 done by Levitical singers in the First Temple period. As was true of 1 Samuel 2 = Psalm 113, the orthography and language of 2 Samuel 22 appear older than that of Psalm 18. See F. M. Cross and D. Freedman, "A Royal Song of Thanksgiving: 2 Samuel = Psalm 18," JBL 72 (1953): 15–34, and A. Hurvitz, *The Transition Period in Biblical Hebrew* (Jerusalem: Bialik, 1972), pp. 183–84 (in Hebrew). Cf. 2 Sam 22:46 *mimmisgĕrôtām,* whose *-ām* pronominal ending is characteristic of preexilic Hebrew, to Psalm 18:46 (45) *mimmisgĕrôtēyhem,* whose *-ēyhem* ending is characteristic of postexilic Hebrew. Such evidence seems to rule out the possibility that the author of 2 Samuel 22 is citing Psalm 18. Once again, however, linguistic and orthographic priority do not necessarily imply literary priority, for 2 Samuel 22 might presuppose Psalm 18 in an archaic textual form no longer extant. For a detailed comparison of the two texts, see G. Schuttermeyer, *Psalm 18 und 2 Samuel 22 Studien zu einem Doppeltext* (Munich: Kösel Verlag, 1971).

68. See the studies cited in chap. 3, n. 52.

69. Note, for example, that the rabbis find several parallels between David and Moses. See *Midr. Tehillim*, Psalm 1, p. 3.

70. See McCarter, *I Samuel*, p. 76; B. Childs, *Introduction to the Old Testament as Scripture* (Philadelphia: Fortress, 1979), p. 272; L. Eslinger, *Kingship of God in Crisis* (Sheffield: Almond, 1985), pp. 99–102; R. Polzin, *Samuel and the Deuteronomist* (San Francisco: Harper and Row, 1989), pp. 33–34; Watts, *Psalm and Story*, pp. 26–29; W. Brueggemann, "1 Samuel 1: A Sense of a Beginning," ZAW 102 (1990): 33–48; R. Bailey, "The Redemption of YHWH: A Literary Critical Function of the Songs of Hannah and David," *Biblical Interpretations* 3 (1995): 213–31.

71. For the vocabulary and phraseology shared by 1 Samuel 2 and 2 Samuel 22, see Watts, *Psalm and Story*, pp. 23 n. 3 and 24. Ancient readers apparently perceived a link as well. *Tg. Jonathan*, for example, inserts 1 Sam 2:2a into 2 Sam 22:32.

72. See chap. 4, n. 72.

73. See G. Wilson, *The Editing of the Hebrew Psalter* (Chico: Scholars Press, 1985), pp. 199–200. Early Jewish readers also perceived an analogy between the Psalter and the Pentateuch. See U. Simon, *Four Approaches to the Book of Psalms* (Albany: State University of New York, 1991), pp. 1–57.

74. Thackeray, "Song of Hannah."

75. See also the studies cited in appendix B, n. 3. The earliest references to the recitation of the trisagion appear in apocalyptic sources from the end of the Second Temple period (*1 Enoch* 39:12; Rev 4:8). The practice is not reflected in the liturgical materials within the Dead Sea Scrolls, however (though these texts do refer to angelic praise). It is possible that originally the trisagion was recited only in the temple and was transferred to extratemple ritual after the destruction of the temple in 70 C.E. See J. Maier, "Zu Kult und Liturgie der Qumrangemeinde," *RevQ* 14 (1990): 543–86.

76. See A.L. Warren, "A Trisagion Inserted in the 4Q Sam[a] Version of the Song of Hannah, 1 Sam 2:1–10," JJS 45 (1994): 278–85.

Appendix A. The Narrative Role of David's Lament

1. For studies of the lament as a work of poetry, see S. Gevirtz, *Patterns in the Early Poetry of Israel* (Chicago: University of Chicago Press, 1963); W. Holliday, "Form and Word-Play in David's Lament over Saul and Jonathan," VT 20 (1970): 153–89; W. Shea, "Chiasmus and the Structure of David's Lament," JBL 105 (1986): 13–25; D. N. Freedman, "The Refrain in David's Lament over Saul and Jonathan," *Pottery, Poetry and Prophecy*, pp. 263–74; D. Zapf, "How the Mighty Are Fallen: A Study of 2 Samuel 1:17–27," *Grace Theological Union* 5 (1984): 95–126.

2. For discussion of the Book of Yashar, see chap. 1 n. 20.

3. Second Sam 1:18 reads literally: "And he said to teach the sons of Judah a bow. Behold, it is written in the Book of Yashar." This verse has long perplexed commentators. Perhaps the most puzzling element is the word "bow," which is syntactically awkward and is omitted altogether by certain Greek witnesses. Scholars have offered various explanations for this word, characterizing it as an intrusive secondary gloss, as the lament's title, or as a corrupted part of the lament itself. For a review of the possibilities, see McCarter, *II Samuel*, pp. 66–67.

4. See J. Vanderkam, "Davidic Complicity in the Deaths of Abner and Eshbaal," JBL 94 (1980): 521–39, esp. p. 529.

5. See McCarter, *II Samuel*, p. 77. This interpretation is complicated by the fact that Codex Alexandrinus reads "Israel" instead of "Judah," while the so-called

Lucianic manuscripts read "Israel and Judah." The Greek witnesses to the lament are analyzed in R. Nysse, "An Analysis of the Greek Witnesses to the Text of the Lament of David," in *The Hebrew and Greek Texts of Samuel*, ed. E. Tov (Jerusalem: Academon, 1980), pp. 69–104.

6. Alter, *The Art of Biblical Narrative*, pp. 47–62. An earlier formulation of the same idea is found in D. Gunn, "Narrative Patterns and Oral Traditions in Judges and Samuel," VT 24 (1974): 286–317.

7. The Amalekite's description of Saul's death (where Saul orders the Amalekite to kill him) conflicts with that of the narrator in 1 Samuel 31 (where Saul takes his own life). Scholars still differ over how to explain the contradiction. Some believe it arose inadvertently when independent accounts were integrated into a single narrative (see H. P. Smith, *A Critical and Exegetical Commentary on the Books of Samuel*, ICC [New York: T. and T. Clark, 1899], p. 254); others resolve the contradiction by assuming that the Amalekite is lying to curry favor with David (see McCarter, *II Samuel*, pp. 62–64).

8. Gunn ("Narrative Patterns and Oral Tradition," pp. 290–92) has observed a single conventional structure behind several messenger scenes in biblical narrative, including the messenger scene in 2 Samuel 1. He does not recognize, however, that many of these scenes are themselves part of a larger conventional narrative pattern which includes the mourner's response to the bad news.

9. Biblical literature reflects several conventional techniques for depicting the physical reaction to bad news. For one such technique, see D. Hillers, "A Convention in Hebrew Literature: The Reaction to Bad News," ZAW 77 (1965): 86–90. For further discussion of the conventions of mourning in ancient Israel, see E. Ward, "Mourning Customs in 1,2 Samuel," JJS 23 (1972–1973): 1–27, 145–66.

10. M. Sternberg, (*Poetics of Biblical Narrative*, p. 313) cites the servants' question in 2 Sam 12:21 as an example of the "echoing interrogative," a device used frequently in biblical narrative to signal that a piece of information essential to narrative coherence (in this case the reason for David's bizarre response to the news of his baby's death) has been deliberately withheld by the narrative.

11. While no commentator has noted how 2 Samuel 12 inverts the conventional characteristics of the lament type-scene per se, many have noted the unconventionality of David's behavior in this scene. Thus McCarter (*II Samuel*, p. 301) describes David in 2 Samuel 12 as "curiously indifferent to conventional rules of behavior," while Hertzberg (*I and II Samuel*, p. 316) characterizes the king's actions as "barely comprehensible, indeed shocking to his contemporaries and to posterity."

12. Interestingly, like the messenger scene in 2 Samuel 18, this episode features two messengers. See H. L. Ginsberg, "Baʿal's Two Messengers," BASOR 95 (1944): 25–30. For analysis of the "dueling messengers" scene in 2 Samuel 18, see D. Gunn, "Traditional Composition in the 'Succession Narrative,'" VT 26 (1976): 214–29.

13. The translation of this passage is that of G. Anderson, *A Time to Mourn, a Time to Dance: The Expression of Grief and Joy in Israelite Religion* (University Park: Pennsylvania State University Press, 1991), pp. 60–63. For an alternative translation (by H. L. Ginsberg), see J. Pritchard, *The Ancient Near East*, vol. 1 (Princeton: Princeton University Press, 1958), p. 110. For a detailed analysis of this passage, see M. Dietrich and O. Loretz, "Die Trauer Els und Anat," UF 18 (1986): 101–10.

14. Beyond its structural similarity to biblical scenes of mourning, KTU 1.5.VI 2–25 also employs phraseology reminiscent of phraseology found in various biblical scenes of mourning. Cf. Jacob's verbal response to the news of Joseph's death in Gen 37:34–35: "I shall go down to Sheol to my son, mourning" with El's verbal

response to the death of Baal: "Baal is dead! . . . I am descending to the under-world, after Baal!" ('aθr. b'l. 'ard. b'arṣ).

15. See K. Aitken, "Oral Formulaic Composition and Theme in the Aqhat Narrative," UF 21 (1989): 1-16.

16. My understanding of this passage is based on the reconstruction of B. Margalit, "The Messengers of Woe to Dan'el: A Reconstruction and Interpretation of KTU 1.19.II 27-48," UF 15 (1983): 105-17. Margalit translates the catalogue of Dan'el's distress as follows: "[Dan'el's feet] did shake, [his brow a]bove (began to) sweat, The muscles of his back collap[sed; the corners of his vestment fluttered] in unison with tho[se of his back. He raised his voice] and cried out . . . " Aitken observes a difference between this scene and KTU 1.5.VI 3-25: the former enumerates Danel's physical reactions to the bad news, whereas the latter lists a series of conventional mourning gestures. Despite the difference, what is crucial in my mind is that both narratives employ the form of a catalogue to describe the mourner's response to the bad news.

17. The only word which survives from Dan'el's verbal expression of grief is *mḥṣ* (KTU 1.19.II 49), a word which has been construed as "smitten" or "smiter" based on a Hebrew cognate. See M. Held, "*mḥṣ/mḫš* in Ugaritic and other Semitic Languages (a Study in Comparative Lexicography)," JAOS 79 (1959): 169-76.

18. Cf. S. Parker, *Pre-Biblical Narrative Tradition* (Atlanta: Scholars Press, 1989), p. 124, who briefly notes a correspondence between Ugaritic and Hebrew lament scenes.

19. L. Rost (*Die Uberlieferung von der Thronnachfolge Davids*, in *Beiträge zur Wissenschaft vom Alten und Neuen Testament* 3/6 [Stuttgart: Verlag von Kohlhommer, 1926]) first proposed that the Court History (or the Succession Narrative, as he called it) began in 2 Samuel 9, but more recent scholars have redefined its borders to include material from 2 Samuel 2-4. See, for example, D. Gunn, *The Story of King David* (Sheffield: JSOT, 1978), pp. 65-84, and J. Van Seters, *In Search of History* (New Haven: Yale University Press, 1983), pp. 278-86.

20. For recent reviews of the debate over the compositional history of 1 and 2 Samuel, see Van Seters, *In Search of History*, 249-91; R. Gordon, "In Search of David: The David Tradition in Recent Study," in *Faith, Tradition and History*, ed. A. R. Millard, J. K. Hoffmeier, and D. W. Baker (Winona Lake, Ind.: Eisenbrauns, 1994), pp. 285-98.

21. Several recent studies have detected behind 1-2 Samuel an effort to clear David of complicity in the deaths of his political rivals. See Vanderkam, "Davidic Complicity in the Deaths of Abner and Eshbaal"; P. K. McCarter, "The Apology of David," JBL 99 (1980): 489-504; F. Cryer, "David's Rise to Power and the Death of Abner: An Analysis of 1 Samuel 26:14-16 and Its Redaction-Critical Implications," VT 35 (1985): 385-94.

22. Consider how C. Conroy (*Absalom, Absalom! Narrative and Language in 2 Sam 13-20* [Rome: Biblical Institute Press, 1978], p. 75 n. 134) explains the difference between David's behavior in 2 Samuel 12 and his behavior in 2 Samuel 18-19: "Contrast the David of 2 Samuel 12:19-24 whose attitude to the death of his son is detached and even coldly rational. There he radically contests the meaningfulness of mourning rites, while in 2 Samuel 19 he practices them to blind excess. Admittedly a father's grief for the death of an infant son where the promise of life was scarcely unfolded would certainly have been much less than his grief for a grown son of much promise (cf. 14:25-27), but the David of chapter 12 did not merely show less grief than in the case of Absalom; he explicitly rejects all signs of mourning, and this for reasons that could apply equally well to Absalom's case

(see 12:23). So, while it cannot be concluded that ch. 12 and 19 illustrate contradictory aspects of the undoubtedly complex character of David, the suspicion cannot be brushed aside that the difference in presentation *may be due to two different hands*" (italics added).

23. Sternberg, *Poetics of Biblical Narrative*, pp. 249–58.

Appendix B. The Songs of Israel and the Song of the Angels

1. For the Song of the Angels in biblical, rabbinic, and Christian tradition, see H. Bietenhard, *Die himmlische Welt im Urchristentum und Spätjudentum* (Tübingen: Mohr [Paul Siebeck], 1951), pp. 137–42; M. Weinfeld, "Traces of Kedushah in Yozer and Psukei DeZimrah in the Qumran Literature and in Ben Sira," *Tarbiz* 45 (1976): 15–26 (in Hebrew), and "The Heavenly Praise in Unison," in *Meqor Ḥajjim. Festschrift für Georg Molin zu seinem 75. Geburstag*, ed. I. Seybold (Graz: Akademische Druck und Verlagsanstalt, 1983), pp. 427–37; D. Allison, "The Silence of the Angels: Reflections on the Songs of the Sabbath Sacrifice," RQ 13 (1988): 189–97; M. Mach, *Entwicklungsstadien des jüdischen Engelglaubens in vorrabbinischer Zeit* (Tübingen: Mohr, 1992), pp. 219–28. For ancient Near Eastern antecedents, see M. Weinfeld, "Traces of Kedushah."

2. See Weinfeld, "The Heavenly Praise in Unison," pp. 429–32; C. Newsom, *Songs of the Sabbath Sacrifice: A Critical Edition* (Atlanta: Scholars Press, 1985), pp. 62–72; M. Himmelfarb, "Heavenly Ascent and the Relationship of the Apocalypses and the Hekhalot Literature," HUCA 59 (1988): 73–100, esp. pp. 91–93.

3. For a listing of the various introductions to the Qedushah, see J. Petuchowski, "The Literature of the Synagogue: History, Structure and Contents," in *Approaches to Ancient Judaism*, vol. 4, ed. W. Green (Chico: Scholars Press, 1983), pp. 1–64, esp. pp. 51–53. For discussion of the complex development of the Qedushah, see I. Elbogen, *Jewish Liturgy: A Comprehensive Development*, trans. R. Scheindlin from 1913 ed. (Philadelphia: Jewish Publication Society, 1993), pp. 54–62; E. Werner, "The Doxology in Synagogue and Church, a Liturgico-Musical Study," HUCA 19 (1945–46): 275–351; E. Fleischer, "The Diffusion of the Qedushot of the ʿAmida and the Yozer in the Palestinian Jewish Ritual," *Tarbiz* 38 (1969): 255–84 (in Hebrew); D. Flusser, "Sanktus und Gloria," in *Abraham unter Vater: Festschrift für O. Michel*, ed. O. Betz et al. (Leiden: Brill, 1963), pp. 129–52; M. Weinfeld, "Traces of the Qedushah" (Weinfeld identifies traces of the Qedushah in Second Temple period sources); I. Gruenwald, "Angelic Songs: The Qedushah and the Problem of the Origin of the Hekhalot Literature," *From Apocalypticism to Gnosticism* (Frankfurt am Main: Lang, 1988), pp. 145–73.

4. This tradition should not be confused with the related aggadic tradition discussed by J. Heinemann ("The Work of My Hands Is Being Drowned in the Sea," *Bar Ilan* 7–8 [1970]: 80–84) in which the angels are prevented from singing their song because of God's sorrow for the drowning Egyptians (b. *Meg.* 10b), or according to a parallel Palestinian aggadic tradition (*Exod. Rab.* bəšallaḥ 23.7), because Israel is still in distress.

5. For the story of Jacob's silencing of his angelic wrestling partner, see chap. 4 n. 96. For Moses' silencing of the angels so that he could sing Deuteronomy 32, see L. Finkelstein, ed., *Sifre on Deuteronomy* (reprint; New York: Jewish Theological Seminary, 1969), p. 333. For Joshua's silencing of the sun and moon, see chap. 4 n. 101. For a tradition in which the earth seeks to sing God's praises in the place of a biblical hero (thus reversing the motif shared by the traditions cited here), see b. *Sanh.* 94a, in which the earth offers to sing a song instead of King Hezekiah.

6. See b. *Hag.* 12b; *Gen. Rab.* 65.21 (p. 739); *Midr. Tehillim,* Psalm 104, p. 439. These traditions reflect a theme running throughout rabbinic literature of rivalry or conflict between humans and the angels. See J. P. Schultz, "Angelic Opposition to the Ascension of Moses and the Revelation of the Law," JQR 61 (1970-71): 282-307, and P. Schäfer, *Rivalität zwischen Engeln und Menschen* (Berlin/New York: de Gruyter, 1975).

7. See C. Newsom, *Songs of the Sabbath Sacrifice,* pp. 62-72.

SOURCE INDEX

Daniel (*Gk*)

The following verse numbers for the Greek editions to Daniel indicate the position of the verse when read as part of the narrative in Daniel 3; the verse numbers in parentheses indicate the position of the verse when the additions are read as an independent text (i.e., as it appears in NRSV).

AUTHOR INDEX

STEVEN WEITZMAN is Assistant Professor of Religious
Studies at Indiana University.